Who's Running America?

Who's Running America?
The Bush Restoration

Seventh Edition

Thomas R. Dye
Florida State University

Upper Saddle River, New Jersey 07458

Library of Congress Cataloging-in-Publication Data

Dye, Thomas R.
    Who's running America? : the Bush restoration / Thomas R. Dye.—7th ed.
      p. cm.
    Includes index.
    ISBN 0-13-097462-5 (pbk.)
      1. Elite (Social sciences)—United States.   2. United States—Politics and
government—1993–2001.   3. Power (Social sciences)   4. Leadership.   I. Title: Who is
running America?.   II. Title.

    HN90.E4 D93 2002
    305.5'2'0973—dc21

                                                         2001054896

Senior Acquisitions Editor: Heather Shelstad
Editorial/production supervision and interior design: Mary Araneo
Marketing Manager: Claire Rehwinkel
Marketing Assistant: Jennifer Bryant
Prepress and Manufacturing Buyer: Ben Smith
Cover Art Director: Jayne Conte
Cover Designer: Bruce Kenselaar
Cover photo: Susan Biddle/The White House Photo Office

This book was set in 10/12 New Baskerville by A & A Publishing Services, Inc.,
and was printed and bound by Courier Companies, Inc. The cover was
printed by Phoenix Color Corp.

© 2002, 1995, 1990, 1986, 1983, 1979, 1996 by Pearson
Education, Inc.
Upper Saddle River, New Jersey 07458

Printed in the United States of America

10 9 8 7 6 5 4 3 2 1

ISBN   0-13-097462-5

Pearson Education LTD., London
Pearson Education Australia PTY, Limited, Sydney
Pearson Education Singapore, Pte. Ltd
Pearson Education North Asia Ltd, Hong Kong
Pearson Education Canada, Ltd., Toronto
Pearson Educación de Mexico, S.A. de C.V.
Pearson Education — Japan, Tokyo
Pearson Education Malaysia, Pte. Ltd
Pearson Education, Upper Saddle River, New Jersey

Contents

Preface ix

1   **Elitism in a Democracy**   1

The Inevitability of Elites   2
The Institutional Basis of Power   3
Power as Decision-Making: The Pluralist View   5
Identifying Positions of Power   7
Dimensions of America's Elite   10
Some Questions for Research   11

2   **The Corporate Directors**   13

The Concentration of Economic Power   13
The Globalization of Economic Power   16
Institutionalizing the Global Economy   18
Who Controls Corporate America?   21
The Managers: Climbing the Corporate Ladder   24
The Inheritors: Starting at the Top   26
Paychecks of the Corporate Chiefs   30

Corporate Counterrevolutions   30
The Battle for IBM   31
Hostile Takeovers   33
The Limits of Corporate Power   35
Summary   37

3   The Money Elite   39

The Concentration of Financial Resources   39
The Banking Boardrooms   41
Banking "Reform"   43
The Federal Reserve Board   45
Controlling the Money Supply   46
Alan Greenspan: Ruling over Money   47
The Securities and Exchange Commission   48
The Superrich: Distinguishing Wealth from Power   49
Summary   54

4   The Governing Circles   55

The Concentration of Governmental Power   56
The Fat Cat Contributors   57
The Politicians: Ambition and Office Seeking   58
Bill Clinton: The Political Climber   62
The Bush Family Dynasty   67
Executive Decision-Makers: The Serious People   73
The Bush Restoration   77
The Congressional Establishment   82
Ted Kennedy: The Political Inheritor   84
Hillary Clinton: Power and Ambition   86
The Judges   88
The Military Establishment   93
Summary   95

5   The Media Moguls   97

Agenda-Setting: Deciding What Will Be Decided   97
The Concentration of Media Power   99
Ted Turner: Maverick Media Mogul   103
Katherine Graham: The Most Powerful Woman in America   104
The Celebrity Newsmakers   106

Bad News and Good Profits   107
Liberal Bias in the News   108
Prime Time: Socializing the Masses   110
Summary   112

6 The Civic Establishment   115

The American "Establishment"   115
The "Superlawyers"   117
The "Fixers": Peddling Power for Profit   121
The Foundations   123
The Policy-Planning Organizations   126
The Billion Dollar Universities   131
Summary   133

7 The Structure of Institutional Power   135

Questions in Elite Research   135
Convergence or Specialization at the Top?   136
Sources of Elite Cohesion   137
"Interlockers" and "Specialists"   139
The Rockefellers: End of a Dynasty?   142
Elite Recruitment: Getting to the Top   146
Class: A Touchy Subject   150
African Americans at the Top   152
Women at the Top   154
Elite Factionalism: Cowboys and Yankees   158
The New Tycoons   165
Summary   168

8 How Institutional Elites Make Public Policy   171

Policy as Elite Preference   171
An Oligarchical Model of National Policy-Making   172
The Council on Foreign Relations and the Trilateral
    Commission   175
The Business Roundtable and the Committee on Economic
    Development   180
The Brookings Institution   184
Competition among Elites: AEI and Heritage   187
Liberal and Conservative Factions among Elites   191

The "Vast Right-Wing Conspiracy"   194
The "Proximate Policy-Makers"   200
Summary   201

9   **Institutional Elites in America**   **203**

Institutional Power in America
Hierarchy and Polyarchy among Institutional Elites   204
Summary of Findings   207
 Concentration of Institutional Resources   207
 The Size of the Nation's Elite   207
 Interlocking versus Specialization   208
 Inheritors versus Climbers   208
 Separate Channels of Recruitment   208
 Social Class and Elite Recruitment   209
 Conflict and Consensus among Elites   209
 Factionalism among Elites   210
 An Oligarchic Model of National Policy-Making   211
Power: Insider and Outsider Views   212
Who's Running America?   212

Index   **215**

Preface

Who's Running America? has *not* been supported by any grant or contract from any institution, public or private. It grew out of a graduate seminar "Research on Power and Elites" at Florida State University. Initially, biographical data for over 5,000 members of various institutional elites were collected and coded by students. These computerized biographies constituted the original database for the continuing project *Who's Running America?* The database has been revised periodically, and data on over 7,000 institutional elites have been collected and coded.

Two articles based on this data from the early 1970s were published in social science journals:

> Thomas R. Dye, Eugene R. DeClercq, and John W. Pickering, "Concentration, Specialization, and Interlocking among Institutional Elites," *Social Science Quarterly* (June 1973), pp. 8–28.

> Thomas R. Dye and John W. Pickering, "Governmental and Corporate Elites: Convergence and Specialization," *Journal of Politics* (November 1974), pp. 900–25.

We are indebted to a number of commentators who wrote to us before and after publication of these articles, including scholars G. William Domhoff, Suzanne Keller, John Walton, Robert Lineberry, Harmon Zeigler, and Charles Bonjean.

The First Edition of this book was published in 1976 and described national leadership in the Nixon-Ford years. The First Edition was subtitled *Institutional Leadership in the United States.*

The Second Edition of this volume, *The Carter Years*, reflected changes in national leadership which occurred with the election of Jimmy Carter to the presidency and the advent of a new Democratic administration.

The Third Edition of this book, *The Reagan Years*, involved the collection of an entire new database for national leaders in 1980–81. Special topics were addressed in several articles in professional journals, including:

> Thomas R. Dye, "Oligarchic Tendencies in National Policy-Making: The Role of the Private Policy-Planning Organization," *Journal of Politics*, 40 (May 1978), 309–31.

> Thomas R. Dye and Julie Strickland, "Women at the Top," *Social Science Quarterly*, 63 (March 1982).

The Fourth Edition, *The Conservative Years*, discussed changes in national leadership during the 1980s. Additional research on corporate ownership was examined in professional journals:

> Thomas R. Dye, "Who Owns America?" *Social Science Quarterly*, 64 (December 1983), 862–70.

> Thomas R. Dye, "Strategic Ownership Positions in U.S. Industry and Banking," *American Journal of Economics and Sociology*, 44 (January 1985), 9–22.

The Fifth Edition, *The Bush Era*, updated both corporate and governmental leadership to 1990. Additional detailed analysis of institutional power was published in:

> Thomas R. Dye, "Organizing Power for Policy Planning," in *Power Elites and Organizations*, eds. G. William Domhoff and Thomas R. Dye (Beverly Hills: Sage, 1987).

The Sixth Edition, *The Clinton Years*, chronicled changes in leadership in Washington accompanying the arrival of the first Democratic administration in twelve years. We observed that the "Friends of Bill and Hillary" differed from previous administrations in their lack of experience outside of government. Almost all top Clinton officials were lawyers, lobbyists, politicians, and bureaucrats; very few had any background in business, banking, the media, or the military. An article developed in conjunction with the Sixth Edition appeared as:

> Thomas R. Dye, "The Friends of Bill and Hillary," *P.S. Political Science and Politics*, 26 (December, 1993), 693–95.

The Seventh Edition, *The Bush Restoration,* describes the return of "The Bush Dynasty" to power. It also adds a new chapter on "The Money Elite" that describes the power of the banking and financial community as well as the Federal Reserve Board. Important issues concerning elite interlocking, recruitment, social characteristics, class, and factionalism have been integrated into a single chapter, Chapter 7, "The Structure of Institutional Power."

Our discussion "How Institutional Elites Make Public Policy" (Chapter 8) has been expanded significantly.

Among new discussions in the Seventh Edition are the following: "The Globalization of Economic Power," "Institutionalizing the Global Economy," "Paychecks of the Corporate Chiefs," "The Battle for IBM," "The Federal Reserve Board," "Alan Greenspan: Ruling over Money," "The Bush Family Dynasty," "The Bush Restoration," "Hillary Clinton: Power and Ambition," "The 'Fixers': Peddling Power for Profit," "Liberal and Conservative Factions among Elites," "The 'Vast Right-Wing Conspiracy.'"

Our continuing work on the topic of Chapter 8, "How Institutional Elites Make Public Policy" was expanded into a full-length book:

Thomas R. Dye, *Top Down Policymaking* (New York: Chatham House, 2001).

Also, papers on this topic were delivered at the Seventeenth World Congress of the International Political Science Association, Quebec, 2000, and the American Political Science Association Annual Meeting, Washington, 2000.

The decision to "name names" was carefully considered. We know that occupants of top institutional positions change over time and that some of our information will be out of date by the time of publication. And with thousands of names, some mistakes are inevitable. However, the biographical sketches provide "flesh and bones" to the statistical analysis; they "personalize" the numbers and percentages in our research. The people who run America *are* real people, and we know of no better way to impress this fact upon our readers.

Thomas R. Dye

Who's Running America?

Elitism in a Democracy

Great power in America is concentrated in a handful of people. A few thousand individuals out of 281 million Americans decide about war and peace, wages and prices, consumption and investment, employment and production, law and justice, taxes and benefits, education and learning, health and welfare, advertising and communication, life and leisure. In all societies—primitive and advanced, totalitarian and democratic, capitalist and socialist—only a few people exercise great power. This is true whether or not such power is exercised in the name of "the people."

Who's Running America? is about those at the top of the institutional structure in America—who they are, how much power they wield, how they came to power, and what they do with it. In a modern, complex industrial society, power is concentrated in large institutions: corporations, banks, insurance companies, media empires, the White House, Congress and the Washington bureaucracy, the prestigious law firms and powerful lobbyists, the large investment houses, the foundations, the universities, and the private policy-planning organizations. The people at the top of these institutions—the presidents and principal officers and directors, the senior partners, the governing trustees, the congressional committee chairpersons, the Cabinet and senior presidential advisers, the Supreme Court Justices—are the objects of our study in this book.

We want to ask: Who occupies the top positions of authority in America? How concentrated or dispersed is power in this nation? How do these institu-

1

tional leaders attain their positions? What are their backgrounds, attitudes, and goals? What relationships exist among these people of power? How much cohesion or competition characterizes their relationships? Do they agree or disagree on crucial issues confronting the nation? How do they go about making important decisions or undertaking new programs or policies?

THE INEVITABILITY OF ELITES

The *elite* are the few who have power in society; the *masses* are the many who do not. We shall call our national leaders "elites" because they possess formal authority over large institutions that shape the lives of all Americans.

America is by no means unique in its concentration of great power in the hands of a few. The universality of elites has been a prominent theme in the works of scholars throughout the ages. The Italian sociologist Vilfredo Pareto put it succinctly: "Every people is governed by an elite, by a chosen element of the population."[1]

Traditional social theorizing about elites views them as essential, functional components of social organization. The necessity of elites derives from the general need for *order* in society. Whenever human beings find themselves living together, they establish a set of ordered relationships so that they can know how others around them will behave. Without ordered behavior, the concept of society itself would be impossible. Among these ordered relationships is the expectation that a few people will make decisions on behalf of the group. Even in primitive societies someone has to decide when the hunt will begin, how it will proceed, and what will be done with the catch.

Nearly two centuries ago Alexander Hamilton defended the existence of the elite by writing:

> All communities divide themselves into the few and the many. The first are the rich and well-born, the other the masses of people. The voice of the people has been said to be the voice of God; and however generally this maxim has been quoted and believed, it is not true in fact. The people are turbulent and changing, they seldom judge or determine right.[2]

The Italian political scientist Gaetano Mosca agreed:

> In all societies—from societies that are very underdeveloped and have largely attained the dawnings of civilization, down to the most advanced and powerful societies—two classes of people appear—a class that rules and a class that is ruled. The first class, always the less numerous, performs all of the political functions, monopolizes power, and enjoys the advantages that power brings, whereas the second, the more numerous class, is directed and controlled by the first, in a manner that is now more or less legal, now more or less arbitrary and violent.[3]

[1] Vilfredo Pareto, *Mind and Society* (New York: Harcourt Brace Jovanovich, 1935), p. 246.
[2] Alexander Hamilton, *Records of the Federal Convention* of 1787.
[3] Gaetano Mosca, *The Ruling Class* (New York: McGraw-Hill, 1939), p. 50.

American social scientists have echoed the same theme. Sociologist Robert Lynd writes:

> It is the necessity in each society—if it is to be a society, not a rabble—to order the relations of men and their institutional ways of achieving needed ends. . . . Organized power exists—always and everywhere, in societies large or small, primitive or modern—because it performs the necessary function of establishing and maintaining the version of order by which a given society in a given time and place lives.[4]

[handwritten: elite order]

Political scientists Harold Lasswell and Daniel Lerner are even more explicit:

> The discovery that in all large-scale societies the decisions at any given time are typically in the hands of a small number of people confirms a basic fact: Government is always government by the few, whether in the name of the few, the one, or the many.[5]

Elitism is *not* a result of inadequate education of the masses, or of poverty, or of capitalism, or of any special problem in society. The necessity for leadership in social organizations applies universally. Robert Michels, who as a student was active in socialist politics in Europe in the early 1900s, concluded reluctantly that elitism was *not* a product of capitalism. *All* large organizations—political parties, labor unions, governments—are oligarchies, even radical *socialist* parties. In Michels's words, "He who says organization says oligarchy." Michels explains his famous "iron law of oligarchy" as a characteristic of *any* social system.[6]

Thus, the elitist character of American society is not a product of political conspiracy, capitalist exploitation, or any specific malfunction of democracy. *All* societies are elitist. There cannot be large institutions without great power being concentrated within the hands of the few at the top of these institutions. *[handwritten: Elitism is inevitable — MICHELS]*

THE INSTITUTIONAL BASIS OF POWER

Power is not an attribute of individuals, but of social organizations. Power is the potential for control in society that accompanies certain roles in the social system. This notion reflects Max Weber's classic formulation of the definition of power:

> In general, we understand by "power" the *chance* of a number of men to realize their own will in a communal act even against the resistance of others who are participating in the action.[7]

[handwritten: WEBER power]

---

[4] Robert Lynd, "Power in American Society," in *Problems of Power in American Society*, ed. Arthur Kornhauser (Detroit: Wayne State University Press, 1957), pp. 3–4.

[5] Harold Lasswell and Daniel Lerner, *The Comparative Study of Elites* (Stanford, Calif.: Stanford University Press, 1952), p. 7.

[6] Robert Michels, *Political Parties: A Sociological Study of the Oligarchical Tendencies of Modern Democracy* (1915) (New York: Free Press, 1962), p. 70.

[7] Hans Gerth and C. Wright Mill, eds., *From Max Weber* (New York: Oxford University Press, 1946), p. 180.

"Chance" in this context means the opportunity or capacity for effecting one's will. Viewed in this fashion, power is not so much the *act* of control as the *potential to act*—the social *expectation* that such control is possible and legitimate—that defines power.

Power is simply the capacity or potential of persons in certain roles to make decisions that affect the conduct of others in the social system. Sociologist Robert O. Schultze puts it in these words:

> . . . a few have emphasized that *act as such* rather than the *potential to act* is the crucial aspect of power. It seems far more sociologically sound to accept a Weberian definition which stresses the potential to act. Power may thus be conceived as an inherently group-linked property, an attribute of social statuses rather than of individual persons. . . . Accordingly, power will denote the *capacity* or *potential* of persons *in certain statuses* to set conditions, make decisions, and/or take actions which are determinative for the existence of others within a given social system.[8]

Thus, elites are people who occupy power roles in society. In a modern, complex society, these roles are institutionalized; the elite are the individuals who occupy positions of authority in large institutions. Authority is the expected and legitimate capacity to direct, manage, and guide programs, policies, and activities of the major institutions of society.

It is true, of course, that not all power is institutionalized. Power can be exercised in transitory and informal groups and in interpersonal interactions. Power is exercised, for example, when a mugger stops a pedestrian on the street and forces him to give up his wallet, or when a political assassin murders a President. But great power is found only in institutional roles. C. Wright Mills, a socialist critic of the structure of power in American society, observed:

> No one . . . can be truly powerful unless he has access to the command of major institutions, for it is over these institutional means of power that the truly powerful are, in the first instance, powerful.[9]

Individuals do not become powerful simply because they have particular qualities, valuable skills, burning ambitions, or sparkling personalities. These assets may be helpful in gaining positions of power, but it is the position itself that gives an individual control over the activities of other individuals. This relationship between power and institutional authority in modern society is described by Mills:

> If we took the one hundred most powerful men in America, the one hundred wealthiest, and the one hundred most celebrated away from the institutional positions they now occupy, away from their resources of men and women and

[8] Robert O. Schultze, "The Bifurcation of Power in a Satellite City," in *Community Political Systems*, ed. Morris Janowitz (Glencoe: Free Press, 1961), p. 20.

[9] C. Wright Mills, *The Power Elite* (New York: Oxford University Press, 1956), p. 9.

money, away from the media of mass communication . . . then they would be powerless and poor and uncelebrated. For power is not of a man. Wealth does not center in the person of the wealthy. Celebrity is not inherent in any personality. To be celebrated, to be wealthy, to have power, requires access to major institutions, for the institutional positions men occupy determine in large part their chances to have and to hold these valued experiences.[10]

Power, then, is an attribute of *roles* in a social system, not an attribute of individuals. People are powerful when they occupy positions of authority and control in social organizations. Once they occupy these positions, their power is felt as a result not only in their actions but in their failures to act as well. Both have great impact on the behaviors of others. Elites "are in positions to make decisions having major consequences. Whether they do or do not make such decisions is less important than the fact that they do occupy such pivotal positions: Their failure to act, their failure to make a decision, is itself an act that is often of greater consequence than the decisions they do make."[11]

People in top institutional positions exercise power whether they act overtly to influence particular decisions or not.[12] When the social, economic, and political values of elite groups, or, more importantly, the structures of the institutions themselves, limit the scope of decision-making to only those issues which do not threaten top elites, then power is being exercised. Political scientists Peter Bachrach and Morton S. Baratz refer to this phenomenon as "*non*–decision-making." A has power over B when he or she succeeds in suppressing issues that might in their resolution be detrimental to A's preferences. In short, the institutional structure of our society, and the people at the top of that structure, encourage the development of some kinds of public issues but prevent other kinds of issues from ever being considered by the American public. Such "non–decision-making" provides still another reason for studying institutional leadership.

POWER AS DECISION-MAKING: THE PLURALIST VIEW

It is our contention, then, that great power is institutionalized—that it derives from roles in social organizations and that individuals who occupy top institutional positions possess power whether they act directly to influence particular decisions or not. But these views—often labeled as "elitist"—are not universally shared among social scientists. We are aware that our institutional approach to power conflicts with the approach of many scholars who believe that power can be viewed only in a decision-making context.

---

[10] Ibid.

[11] Ibid., p. 4.

[12] Peter Bachrach and Morton S. Baratz, "Decisions and Non-Decisions," *American Political Science Review,* 57 (September 1963), 632–42.

[handwritten margin notes: "PLURALISTIC" / "2nd def of power" / "ex. Queen of England"]

This alternative approach to power—often labeled as "pluralist"—defines power as *active participation in decision-making.* Persons are said to have power *only* when they participate directly in particular decisions. Pluralist scholars would object to our presumption that people who occupy institutional positions and who have formal authority over economic, governmental, or social affairs necessarily have power. Pluralists differentiate between the "potential" for power (which is generally associated with top institutional positions) and "actual" power (which assumes active participation in decision-making). Political scientist Robert A. Dahl writes:

> Suppose a set of individuals in a political system has the following property: there is a high probability that if they agree on a key political alternative, and if they all act in some specified way, then that alternative will be chosen. We may say of such a group that it has a high *potential* for control. . . . But a *potential* for control is not, except in a peculiarly Hobbesian world, equivalent to *actual* control.[13]

Pluralists contend that the potential for power is not power itself. Power occurs in individual interactions: "A has power over B to the extent that he can get B to do something that B would not otherwise do."[14] We should not simply assume that power attaches to high office. Top institutional office-holders may or may not exercise power—their "power" depends upon their active participation in particular decisions. They may choose not to participate in certain decisions; their influence may be limited to specific kinds of decisions; they may be constrained by formal and informal checks on their discretion; they may be forced to respond to the demands of individuals or groups within or outside the institutions they lead; they may have little real discretion in their choice among alternative courses of action.

Pluralists would argue that research into institutional leadership can describe at best only the *potential* for control that exists within American society. They would insist that research on national leadership should proceed by careful examination of a series of important national decisions—that the individuals who took an active part in these decisions be identified and a full account of their decision-making behavior be obtained. Political scientist Nelson Polsby, a former student of Robert A. Dahl at Yale, reflects the interests of pluralists in observing specific decisions:

> How can one tell, after all, whether or not an actor is powerful unless some sequence of events, competently observed, attests to his power? If these events take place, then the power of the actor is not "potential" but actual. If these events do not occur, then what grounds have we to suppose that the actor is powerful?[15]

[13] Robert A. Dahl, "Critique of the Ruling Elite Model," *American Political Science Review,* 52 (June 1958), 66 {italics mine}.

[14] Robert A. Dahl, "The Concept of Power," *Behavioral Science,* 2 (1957), 202.

[15] Nelson Polsby, *Community Power and Political Theory* (New Haven: Yale University Press, 1963), p. 60.

And, indeed, much of the best research and writing in political science has proceeded by studying specific cases in the uses of power.

Pluralism, of course, is more than a definition of power and a method of study—it is an integrated body of theory that seeks to reaffirm the fundamental democratic character of American society. Pluralism arose in response to criticisms of the American political system to the effect that individual participation in a large, complex, bureaucratic society was increasingly difficult. Traditional notions of democracy had stressed individual participation of all citizens in the decisions that shape their own lives. But it was clear to scholars of all persuasions that relatively few individuals in America have any *direct* impact on national decision-making.

Pluralism developed as an ideology designed to reconcile the *ideals* of democracy with the *realities* of a large-scale, industrial, technocratic society. Jack L. Walker writes that the "principal aim" of the pluralists "has been to make the theory of democracy more realistic, to bring it into closer correspondence with empirical reality. They are convinced that the classical theory does not account for 'much of the real machinery' by which the system operates."[16]

Pluralists recognize that an elite few, rather than the masses, rule America and that "it is difficult—nay impossible—to see how it could be otherwise in large political systems."[17] However, they reassert the essentially democratic character of America by arguing that competition between leadership groups protects the individual—that is, countervailing centers of power check each other and guard against abuse of power. Leadership groups are not closed; new groups can be formed and gain access to the political system. The existence of multiple leadership groups in society gives rise to a "polyarchy"— *Polyarchy* leaders who exercise power over some kinds of decisions do not necessarily exercise power over other kinds of decisions. Finally, pluralists acknowledge that public policy may not be majority preference, but they claim it is the rough equilibrium of group influence and, therefore, a reasonable approximation of society's preferences.

IDENTIFYING POSITIONS OF POWER

We are committed in this volume to the study of institutional power. It is *not* our purpose to assert the superiority of our approach to power in America over the approaches recommended by others. We do *not* intend to debate the merits of pluralism or elitism as political philosophies. Abstract arguments over conceptualizations, definitions, and method of study already abound in

[16] Jack L. Walker, "A Critique of the Elitist Theory of Democracy," *American Political Science Review,* 60 (June 1966), 286.

[17] Robert A. Dahl, "Power, Pluralism and Democracy," paper delivered at the Annual Meeting of the American Political Science Association, 1966, p. 3.

the literature on power. Rather, working within an *institutional* paradigm, we intend to present systematic evidence about the concentration of resources in the nation's largest institutions, to find out who occupies top positions in these institutions, to explore interlocking and convergence among these top position-holders, to learn how they rose to their positions, to investigate the extent of their consensus or disagreement over the major issues confronting the nation, to explore the extent of competition and factionalism among various segments of the nation's institutional leadership, and to learn how institutional leadership interacts in national policy-making.

We hope to avoid elaborate theorizing about power, pluralism, and elitism. We propose to present what we believe to be interesting data on national institutional elites and to permit our readers to relate it to their own theories of power.

A great deal has been said about "the power elite," "the ruling class," "the liberal establishment," "the military-industrial complex," "the powers that be," and so on. But even though many of these notions are interesting and insightful, we never really encounter a systematic definition of precisely *who* these people are, how we can identify them, how they came to power, and what they do with their power.

We know that power is elusive and that elites are not easy to identify. Scholars have encountered great difficulty in finding a specific working definition of a national elite—a definition that can be used to actually identify powerful people. However, this is the necessary starting place for any serious inquiry into power in America.

Our first task, therefore, is to develop an operational *definition* of a national elite. We must formulate a definition that is consistent with our theoretical notions about the institutional basis of power and that will enable us to identify, by name and position, those individuals who possess great power in America.

Our institutional elites will be individuals who occupy *the top positions in the institutional structure of American society*. These are the individuals who possess the formal authority to formulate, direct, and manage programs, policies, and activities of the major corporate, governmental, legal, educational, civic, and cultural institutions in the nation. Our definition of a national elite, then, is consistent with the notion that great power in America resides in large institutions.

For purposes of analysis, we have divided American society into ten sectors: (1) industrial (nonfinancial) corporations, (2) banking, (3) insurance, (4) investments, (5) mass media, (6) law, (7) education, (8) foundations, (9) civic and cultural organizations, and (10) government.

In the corporate sector, our operational definition of the elite is *those individuals who occupy formal positions of authority in institutions which control more than half of the nation's total corporate revenues*. Our procedure in identifying the largest institutions was to rank corporations by the size of their annual revenues, and to cumulate these revenues, moving from the top of the rankings down, until at least 50 percent of the nation's total revenues in each sector are included (see Table 2–2). Then we identified by name the presidents, officer-directors, and directors of these corporations.

In the financial sector, we identified *those individuals who controlled the* *banks* *ins co.* *nation's largest banks, insurance companies, and Wall Street investment firms.* We ranked these institutions by the size of their assets—banking (Table 3–1), insurance (Table 3–2), and investment firms (Table 3–3)—and identified by name their presidents and directors.

We also included in our definition of the elite *those individuals who occupy* *elite* *formal positions of authority in the mass media, the large prestigious New York and Washington law firms, the well-endowed private universities, the major philanthropic foundations, and the most influential civic and cultural organizations.* The identification of these institutions involved some subjective judgments. These judgments can be defended, but we recognize that other judgments could be made. In the *mass media*, we include ownership of five major television networks (ABC, CBS, NBC, Fox, CNN); the *New York Times*; *Time*, Inc.; *Washington Post–Newsweek*; and seven media conglomerates. Because of the great influence of the news media in America's elite structure, we have devoted a special chapter to "The Media Moguls."

Leadership in a variety of sectors is considered under the general heading of "The Civic Establishment." In *education,* we identify the forty-one colleges and universities with endowment funds totaling $1 billion or more. These universities control two thirds of all endowment funds in higher education, and they are consistently ranked among the nation's most "prestigious" colleges and universities. Our leadership group includes their presidents and trustees, excluding public universities. Our selection of foundations is based on *The Foundation Directory*'s data on the nation's thirty-eight largest foundations. Each of these foundations, and their trustees/directors, control over $1 billion in foundation assets. Identifying top positions in the *law* was an even more subjective task. Our definition of positions of authority in the law includes the senior partners of twenty-nine large and influential New York and Washington law firms. (We also identify Washington's top lobbying firms, but their owners/partners are *not* included in our operational definition of the nation's elite.) Top positions in *civic and cultural affairs* were identified by qualitative evaluations of the prestige and influence of various well-known organizations. The civic organizations are the Council on Foreign Relations, the Trilateral Commission, the Committee on Economic Development, the Business Roundtable, and the Brookings Institution. The cultural organizations are the Metropolitan Museum of Art, the Museum of Modern Art, the Smithsonian Institution, the Lincoln Center for the Performing Arts, and the John F. Kennedy Center for the Performing Arts. The members of the governing boards of trustees or directors were included in our definition of institutional leadership.

In the governmental sectors, the operational definition of the elite is *those individuals who occupy formal positions of authority in the major institutions of the national government.* Positions of authority in government were defined as the President and Vice-President; secretaries, undersecretaries, and assistant secretaries of all executive departments; senior White House presidential advisers and ambassadors-at-large; congressional committee chairpersons and ranking minority committee members in the House and Senate; House and Senate majority and minority party leaders and whips; Supreme Court Justices; and members of the Federal Reserve Board and the Council of Economic Advisers. We also include both civilian offices and top military commands: secretaries, undersecretaries, and assistant secretaries of the Departments of the Army, Navy, and Air Force; all four-star generals and admirals in the Army, Navy, Air Force, and Marine Corps, including the chairman of the Joint Chiefs of Staff; and the Chiefs of Staff and vice-chiefs of staff of the Army and Air Force, the chief and vice-chief of Naval Operations, and the commanding officers of the major military commands.

Any effort to operationalize a concept as broad as a national institutional elite is bound to generate discussion over the inclusion or exclusion of specific sectors, institutions, or positions. (Why law, but not medicine? Why not law firms in Chicago, Houston, or Atlanta? Why not religious institutions or labor unions? Why not governors or mayors of big cities?) There are no explicit guidelines to *systematic* research on national elites. Our choices involve many subjective judgments. Let us see, however, what we can learn about concentration, specialization, and interlocking using the definitions above; perhaps other researchers can improve upon our attempt to operationalize this elusive notion of a national institutional elite. In the analysis to follow, we will present findings for our aggregate elites, and for specific sectors of these elites.

DIMENSIONS OF AMERICA'S ELITE

Our definition of a national institutional elite resulted in the identification of 7,314 elite positions (Table 1–1).

These top positions, taken collectively, control over half of the nation's industrial assets; over one half of all U.S. banking assets; over three quarters of all insurance assets; and they direct Wall Street's largest investment firms. They control the television networks, the influential news leaders, and the major media conglomerates. They control nearly half of all the assets of private foundations and two thirds of all private university endowments. They direct the nation's largest and best-known New York and Washington law firms as well as the nation's major civic and cultural organizations. They occupy key federal governmental positions in the executive, legislative, and judicial branches.

These aggregate figures—roughly 7,300 positions—are themselves

TABLE 1-1

Corporate Sectors	Number of Leadership Positions
1. Industrial corporations (100)	2,143
2. Banks (50)	1,092
3. Insurance (50)	611
4. Investments (15)	479
Total	4,325
Public Interest Sectors	
5. Mass media (18)	220
6. Law (25)	758
7. Education (25)	892
8. Foundations (50)	402
9. Civic and cultural organizations (12)	433
Total	2,705
Governmental Sector	
10. Legislative, executive, judicial	284
Total	**7,314**

important indicators of the concentration of authority and control in American society. Of course, these figures are the direct product of our specific definition of top institutional positions.[18] Yet these aggregate statistics provide us with an explicit definition and quantitative estimate of the size of the national elite in America.

SOME QUESTIONS FOR RESEARCH

Our definition of America's institutional elite provides a starting place for exploring some of the central questions confronting students of power. How concentrated are institutional resources in America? How much concentration exists in industry and finance, in government, in the mass media, in education, in the law, in the foundations, and in civic and cultural affairs? Who are the people at the top of the nation's institutional structure? How did they get there? Did they inherit their positions or work their way up through the

[18] In earlier editions of this volume, using data from 1970–71, we included only 5,416 positions. In recent editions, using data from 1980–81, we added the investment firms and expanded the number of utilities, insurance companies, universities, and foundations. This produced 7,314 positions. Thus, even minor changes in the definition of an elite can produce substantial differences in the overall size of the elite.

ranks of the institutional hierarchy? What are their general attitudes, beliefs, and goals? Do elites in America generally agree about major national goals and the general directions of foreign and domestic policy, and limit their disagreements to the *means* of achieving their goals and the details of policy implementation? Or do leaders disagree over fundamental *ends* and values and the future character of American society?

Are institutional elites in America "interlocked" or "specialized"? That is, is there convergence at the "top" of the institutional structure in America, with the same group of people dominating decision-making in industry, finance, education, government, the mass media, foundations, law, investments, and civic and cultural affairs? Or is there a separate elite in each sector of society with little or no overlap in authority? Are there opportunities to rise to the top of the leadership structure for individuals from both sexes, all classes, races, religions, and ethnic groups, through multiple career paths in different sectors of society? Or are opportunities to acquire key leadership roles generally limited to white, Anglo-Saxon, Protestant, upper-class and upper-middle-class males whose careers are based primarily in industry and finance? Is the nation's institutional leadership recruited primarily from private "name" prep schools and "Ivy League" universities? Do leaders join the same clubs, intermarry, and enjoy the same life styles? Or is there diversity in educational backgrounds, social ties, club memberships, and life styles among the elite?

How much competition and conflict take place among America's institutional elite? Are there clear-cut factions within the nation's leadership struggling for preeminence and power, and if so, what are the underlying sources of this factionalism? Do different segments of the nation's institutional elite accommodate each other in a system of bargaining, negotiation, and compromising based on a widely shared consensus of values?

How do institutional elites make national policy? Are there established institutions and procedures for elite interaction, communication, and consensus-building on national policy questions? Or are such questions decided in a relatively unstructured process of competition, bargaining, and compromise among a large number of diverse individuals and interest groups? Do the "proximate policy-makers"—the President, Congress, the courts—respond to mass opinions, or do they respond primarily to initiatives originating from the elite policy-planning organizations?

2

The Corporate Directors

Control of economic resources provides a continuous and important base of power in any society. A great deal of power is organized into large economic institutions—corporations, banks, insurance companies, and investment firms. These economic organizations decide what will be produced, how much it will cost, how many people will be employed, and what their wages will be. They determine how goods and services will be distributed, what technology will be developed, what profits will be made and how they will be distributed, how much money will be available for capital investment, what interest rates will be charged, and many similarly important questions.

THE CONCENTRATION OF ECONOMIC POWER

Economic power in America is highly concentrated. About 5 million corporate tax returns are received by the U.S. Internal Revenue Service each year. Approximately 22,000 (0.4 percent) of these returns come from corporations that receive over $50 million in annual revenues. Yet these large corporations account for nearly 70 percent of total corporate revenues in the nation (see Table 2–1). In contrast, the nearly 4 million corporations that receive less than $1 million in annual revenues account for only about 5 percent of total corporate revenues.

America's 500 largest corporations—"the Fortune 500"—collectively

TABLE 2–1   The Concentration of Corporate Revenues

	Size of Corporation (in millions of annual revenue)				
	Under $1	$1–5	$4–50	Over $50	Total
Income Tax Returns					
Number (000)	3,791	626	192	22	4,631
Percent	81.9	13.5	4.2	0.4	100.0
Reported Revenues					
$ millions	783	1,326	2,551	10,220	14,890
Percent	5.2	8.9	17.2	68.6	100.0

Source: Statistical Abstract of the United States 1999, p. 546.

take in about $7.2 *trillion* in revenues each year, and these corporations collectively control about $18 *trillion* in total assets. These 500 corporations account for roughly 60 percent of all corporate revenues and all corporate assets in the nation.

The nation's 100 largest nonfinancial corporations are listed in Table 2–2. (The nation's largest banks, insurance companies, and investment firms are listed separately in Chapter 3, "The Money Elite.") The five largest nonfinancial corporations—Exxon Mobil, Wal-Mart, General Motors, Ford Motors, and General Electric—account for over 20 percent of the revenues of nonfinancial corporations in the United States.

America's traditional industrial giants—Exxon Mobil, General Motors, Ford Motors, General Electric, IBM, AT&T, and Philip Morris—continue to occupy dominant places in the corporate world. But in the last decade the booming retail economy has moved Wal-Mart, Kroger, Home Depot, Sears Roebuck, Kmart, Target, Albertson's, J.C. Penney, and Costco—upward in the corporate rankings. Sam Walton's Bentonville, Arkansas, Wal-Mart is now the nation's single largest corporate employer with more than one million people on its payroll. High-tech is the fastest growing sector of the American economy; but established firms like General Electric, IBM, AT&T, and Hewlett-Packard, have managed to stay ahead of newer firms like Compaq, Intel, and Dell.

Thus, there has been both stability and change at the top of the corporate world over the last century. Some of America's industrial giants—Exxon Mobil, General Motors, Ford Motors—have held top positions in the nation's economy throughout the century. In contrast, other leading corporations— U.S. Steel (now USX), Bethlehem Steel, Republic Steel, Anaconda Copper— have been displaced largely as a product of global competition.

The hottest game on Wall Street throughout the 1980s and 1990s has been "M and A" (mergers and acquisitions). Big corporations are getting even bigger by merging with or acquiring other corporations (see Table 2–3). In

TABLE 2–2 The Nation's Largest Nonfinancial Corporations

1	Exxon Mobil	51	Lockheed Martin
2	Wal-Mart	52	Honeywell
3	General Motors	53	Tosco
4	Ford Motors	54	American Express
5	General Electric	55	Sprint
6	Enron	56	Southern
7	IBM	57	Alcoa
8	AT&T	58	Dow Chemical
9	Verizon	59	Microsoft
10	Philip Morris	60	PG&E
11	SBC Communications	61	AutoNation
12	Boeing	62	Georgia-Pacific
13	Texaco	63	TXU
14	Duke Energy	64	El Paso
15	Kroger	65	Briston-Myers-Squibb
16	Hewlett-Packard	66	Phillips Petroleum
17	Chevron	67	Walgreen
18	Home Depot	68	Coca-Cola
19	Compaq Computer	69	PepsiCo
20	Lucent Technologies	70	Tech Data
21	Sears Roebuck	71	Sara Lee
22	Merck	72	SuperValue
23	Procter & Gamble	73	AMR
24	Worldcom	74	Caterpillar
25	Motorola	75	CVS
26	McKesson	76	Viacom
27	Kmart	77	UAL
28	Target	78	Sysco
29	Albertson's	79	Electronic Data Systems
30	USX	80	Cisco Systems
31	Intel	81	Xerox
32	J.C. Penney	82	Federated Department Stores
33	Conoco	83	Raytheon
34	Costco	84	FedEx
35	Safeway	85	Pharmacia
36	Dell Computer	86	TRW
37	Ingram Micro	87	Johnson Controls
38	United Parcel Service	88	IBP
39	Pfizer	89	Minnesota Mining & Mfg.
40	Dynegy	90	Qwest Communications
41	Reliant	91	Weyerhaeuser
42	DuPont	92	Delta Air Lines
43	Delphi Automotive	93	Sun Microsystems
44	Johnson & Johnson	94	Emerson Electric
45	Utilicorp	95	Rite Aid
46	International Paper	96	Valero Energy
47	United Technologies	97	Publix Supermarkets
48	Bellsouth	98	Occidental Petroleum
49	Walt Disney	99	May Department Stores
50	Conagra	100	Goodyear

Source: Derived from data provided in *Fortune,* April 16, 2001.

TABLE 2–3 Big Deals: Largest Corporate Mergers, Acquisitions, Ranked by Value

Rank	Corporation	Merger	Date
1	AOL	Time Warner	2000
2	Exxon Corp.	Mobil Corp.	1998
3	Travelers Group	Citicorp	1998
4	SBC Communications Inc.	Ameritech Corp.	1998
5	Bell Atlantic Corp.	GTE Corp.	1998
6	AT&T Corp.	Tele-Communications Inc.	1999
7	Vodafone Group Plc.	AirTouch Communications	1999
8	AT&T Corp.	MediaOne Group Inc.	1999
9	NationsBank Corp.	BankAmerica Corp.	1998
10	Elf Aquitaine	Total Fina SA	1999
11	British Petroleum Co. Plc.	Amoco Corp.	1998
12	Qwest Communications Intl.	US West Inc.	1999
13	WorldCom Inc.	MCI Communications Corp.	1998
14	Daimler-Benz-AG	Chrysler Corp.	1998
15	Viacom Inc.	CBS Corp.	1999

Source: Data from *Wall Street Journal Almanac 1999*; updated by author.

1990 the total annual value of mergers was $205 billion; by 1998 the total annual value of mergers had grown tenfold to $2,480 billion.[1] The merger of Exxon and Mobil in 1998 was said to partly reconstitute the nineteenth-century Standard Oil Company monopoly of John D. Rockefeller, reversing the nation's most famous antitrust case, *U.S. vs. Standard Oil* (1911). Citicorp made itself the nation's largest banking company, renamed Citigroup, when it acquired Travelers Insurance, and Bank of America kept pace by acquiring NationsBank (see Chapter 3, "The Money Elite"). Chrysler is no longer listed among America's largest corporations because it was swallowed by Germany's Diamler Benz. The largest merger of all, America OnLine (AOL) and Time Warner, created the world's largest media empire (see Chapter 4, "The Media Moguls").

THE GLOBALIZATION OF ECONOMIC POWER

The concentration of economic power in a relatively few large institutions is not an exclusively American phenomenon. On the contrary, the trend toward corporate concentration of resources is worldwide. It is not only large American corporations which have expanded their markets throughout the world, invested in overseas plants and banks, and merged with foreign corporations. Large European and Japanese firms compete very effectively for world busi-

---

[1] Statistical Abstract of the United States 2000, p. 563.

FIGURE 2–1   The Growth of World Trade in the U.S. Economy

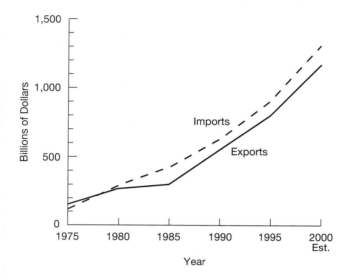

Source: Data from *Statistical Abstract of the United States.*

ness. Just as American companies have greatly expanded investments abroad, so too have foreign companies sharply increased their business in the United States. The result is the emergence of truly supranational corporations, which not only trade worldwide, but also build and operate plants in many nations.

Today, almost one-quarter of the world's total economic output is sold in a country other than the one in which it was produced. The United States currently exports about 11 percent of the value of its gross domestic product (GDP) and imports about 12 percent. Exports and imports were only about 3 percent of GDP as recently as 1970 (see Figure 2–1).

The *world's* largest non-American industrial corporations are listed in Table 2–4. Foreign corporations sell their products in the United States (oil, automobiles, chemicals, electrical products) and also buy American corporations, which become subsidiaries of the foreign multinationals. For example, Royal Dutch Shell owns Shell Oil; British Petroleum owns Standard Oil of Ohio; Tengelmann (Germany) owns A&P supermarkets; Nestlé owns the Libby, Stouffer, and Beech-Nut corporations; Unilever owns the Lever Brothers and Lipton companies; Bayer owns Miles and Cutter Laboratories (Bayer aspirin); and so on.

In brief, the central feature of the American and world economy is the concentration of resources in relatively few large corporations. Most of this concentration occurred many years ago. "The long-established norm of market structure and behavior is that of *oligopoly*, that is, the constrained rivalry of

TABLE 2–4 **World's Largest Non-American Corporations**

Rank	Corporation	Rank	Corporation
1	DaimlerChrysler	16	ING Group
2	Mitsui	17	Sony
3	Mitsubishi	18	Honda Motor
4	Toyota Motor	19	Nissan Motor
5	Itochu	20	Toshiba
6	Royal Dutch Shell	21	Fiat
7	Nippon Telephone	22	Nestlé
8	Marubeni	23	Fujitsu
9	AXA	24	Tokyo Electric
10	British Petroleum	25	Total Fina Elf
11	Volkswagen	26	NEC
12	Siemens	27	Vivendi
13	Hitachi	28	Unilever
14	Matsushita Electric	29	Fortis
15	Nissho Iwai	30	Sinopec

Source: Data derived from *Fortune* "Global 500 List" at www.fortune.com.

a few interdependent sellers who compete mainly by means of product differentiation."[2] In recent years, concentration has continued to increase, although at a slower rate than early in the twentieth century. It is clear that society is *not* going to return to a small, romanticized, perhaps mythical, world of individual enterprise.

INSTITUTIONALIZING THE GLOBAL ECONOMY

Historically, America's corporate and financial elite supported high tariffs in order to protect its domestic marketplace. Tariffs on foreign imports forced up their prices and gave U.S. firms sheltered markets. Not only did this improve the profit margins of U.S. corporations, but also it allowed them to operate less efficiently: management became top heavy; its products, especially automobiles, were frequently poor in quality; and the workforce was larger and wages for workers were higher than they otherwise would be if U.S. firms had to face foreign competition.

But America's corporate and financial elites gradually came to see the economic advantages of expanding world trade. U.S. firms that dominated the domestic market in the 1950s and 1960s (steel, automobiles, aircraft, computers, drugs, electronics, agriculture, and so on) began to look abroad to

[2] Edward S. Herman, *Corporate Control, Corporate Power* (Cambridge, Mass.: Cambridge University Press, 1981), p. 1.

FIGURE 2–2   U.S. Tariff Rates

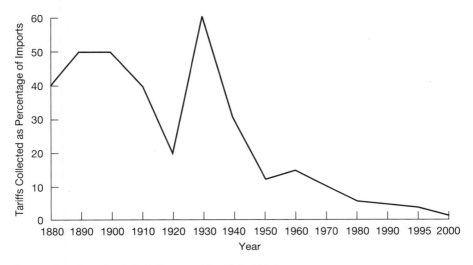

Source: Data from *Statistical Abstract of the United States.*

expand their own sales. American corporations became multinational corporations. They began by expanding their sales and distribution staffs worldwide, and then later began to shift manufacturing itself to low-wage, low-cost countries.

Globalization of economic power required reductions in tariffs and trade barriers around the world. America's corporate and financial elites began to lobby Congress for reductions in U.S. tariffs. The result was a rapid decline in average U.S. tariff rates (see Figure 2–2). In effect, the United States became an open market.

International economic agreements and organizations were arranged in order to facilitate the new global economy. Leadership in global economic policy was provided by the Council on Foreign Relations (CFR) and its multinational arm, the Trilateral Commission (see Chapter 6). The Trilateral Commission was created by CFR BoardChariman David Rockefeller in 1972 to bring together a small group of top economic elites from the United States, western Europe, and Japan.

In addition to initiating annual economic summits of the presidents and prime ministers of the wealthy, industrialized nations, this new global elite put in place a series of policy decisions designed to advance international trade, including the General Agreement on Tariffs and Trade (GATT), the World Trade Organization (WTO), the World Bank and International Monetary Fund (IMF), and the North American Free Trade Agreement (NAFTA) (see Table 2–5).

Table 2–5

Institutionalizing the Global Economy

The World Trade Organization and GATT. The World Trade Organization was created in 1993. Today the WTO includes 130 nations that agree to a governing set of global trade rules. (China and Russia have applied to join.) The WTO is given power to adjudicate trade disputes among countries and monitor and enforce trade agreements, including GATT. GATT, the multinational General Agreement on Tariffs and Trade, was created following World War II for the purpose of encouraging international trade. Over the years GATT has been dominated by banking, business, and commercial interests in Western nations seeking multilateral tariff reductions and the relaxation of quotas. In 1993 the GATT "Uruguay Round" eliminated quotas on textile products; established more uniform standards for proof of dumping; set rules for the protection of intellectual property rights (patents and copyrights on books, movies, videos, and so on); reduced tariffs on wood, paper, and some other raw materials; and scheduled a gradual reduction of government subsidies for agricultural products.

The International Monetary Fund and the World Bank. The IMF's purpose is to facilitate international trade, allowing nations to borrow to stabilize their balance of trade payments. When economically weak nations, however, incur chronic balance of trade deficits and perhaps face deferral or default on international debts, the IMF may condition its loans on changes in a nation's economic policies. It may require a reduction in a nation's government deficits by reduced public spending and/or higher taxes; or it may require a devaluation of its currency, making its exports cheaper and imports more expensive. It may also require the adoption of noninflationary monetary policies. Currently, the IMF as well as the World Bank are actively involved in assisting Russia and other states of the former Soviet Union to convert to free market economies.

The World Bank makes long-term loans, mostly to developing nations, to assist in economic development. It works closely with the IMF in investigating the economic conditions of nations applying for loans and generally imposes IMF requirements on these nations as conditions for loans.

NAFTA. In 1993 the United States, Canada, and Mexico signed the North American Free Trade Agreement. Objections by labor unions in the United States (and independent presidential candidate Ross Perot) were drowned out in a torrent of support by the American corporate community, Democrats and Republicans in Congress, President Bill Clinton, and former President George Bush. NAFTA envisions the removal of tariffs on virtually all products by all three nations over a period of ten to fifteen years. It also allows banking, insurance, and other financial services to cross these borders.

FTAA. Heading the current agenda for institutionalizing global trade is the "Free Trade Area of the Americas." The objective is the negotiation of a tariff-free, rules-based, free trade Western Hemisphere to include thirty-three nations. A meeting of western hemispheric nations in Quebec City in 2001 set a goal for such an agreement for 2005. Recent U.S. presidents, both Democratic and Republican, have pressed Congress for "fast track authority" for trade agreements, essentially requesting that Congress pass presidentially negotiated trade agreements without amendments. So far, Congress has refused to do so.

WHO CONTROLS CORPORATE AMERICA?

In the formal, legal sense, the board of directors "controls" the modern corporation. The typical corporate boardroom consists of about 15 people—presidents, officer-directors, and directors. Collectively the nation's top 100 corporations are formally governed by about 2,500 people—or about one one-thousandths of one percent of the U.S. population. These 2,500 top executives and directors of nonfinancial corporations comprise the first segment of our definition of the nation's elite. "Inside" directors—those who are also top management officers in the corporation—usually dominate board decision-making. Inside directors usually include the chairman, CEO, or president and the top senior vice-presidents. About 40 percent of corporate directors are inside directors. Outside directors—persons who serve on the board but who take no direct part in managing the corporation—usually defer to the judgment of the inside officer-directors. About 60 percent of all directors are "outside" directors. Outside directors are chosen to serve on the board by the inside directors, usually the chairman and chief executive officer (CEO), who also decide on their pay and perks. Most outside directors are themselves current or retired chief executives of other large corporations; their loyalties tend to be with their fellow CEOs running the corporation. Sometimes part of the price of a large loan from a major bank or insurance company to an industrial corporation will include a seat on the board of directors of that corporation. Outside directors representing financial interests do not usually take a direct role in decision-making; they perform a general watch-dog role over their investment. However, *all* directors have a legal responsibility to the owners (stockholders) of the corporation to protect their investment. All directors are formally elected by the stockholders, who cast their votes on the basis of one share equals one vote.

The millions of middle-class Americans who own corporate stock have virtually no influence over the decisions of directors. When confronted with mismanagement, these stockholders simply sell their stock, rather than try to challenge the powers of the directors. Indeed, most stockholders sign over "proxies" to top management so that top management may cast these proxy votes at the annual meetings of stockholders. Management itself usually selects its own "slate" for the board of directors and easily elects them with the help of proxies.

A few outside directors of large corporations represent public relations efforts by top management to improve the image of the corporation. For example, corporations frequently select college presidents, prominent women, and minorities for their boards. It may be true that these corporations really want the counsel of these people; however, one suspects that they also want to promote an image of social responsibility. It is doubtful that these particular people are influential in corporate decision-making.

The globalization of the economy has inspired some American corporations to add top foreign corporate executives to their boards.

Finally, there are the corporate directors—whether inside officers or outsiders—who represent family owners. Family ownership and domination of large corporations has not yet disappeared in America despite marked decline in family control of corporations over the last several decades.

Thus, corporate board members can be divided into types. The following percentage approximations of various types of corporate directors are estimated for the 2,000 members of the 100 largest industrial corporations:[3]

Insiders

Manager-directors	44%

Outsiders

Former managers	6
Financial representatives	8
Ownership representatives	13
Substantial business with corporation	11
Charitable, civic, or educational representatives	5
Other	13
Outsider total	56%

Managers usually triumph in the boardroom. The inside directors, although only a minority of most boards, usually vote as a solid, unified block under the direction of the president. Their block voting strength on the board is augmented by their greater depth of knowledge of the organization, its technology, and its business problems. Insiders work full time on corporate affairs, continuously communicating with each other. Outsiders have no such information or communication base.

Outside directors, with some exceptions, are "invited" to serve on boards by the managers. They are "guests" in the boardroom. They usually have a sense of loyalty to the president who put them on the board. They are passive on most management decisions. "No one likes to be the skunk at the garden party."[4] They may advise on special areas of competence; they may help coordinate decision-making with major suppliers or buyers; and by their presence on the board they may help assure the outside world that the organization is in good hands. The only important exceptions to these usually passive outside managers are those who still represent large stockholder interests.

A brief glimpse inside the boardrooms of IBM and AT&T (see Table 2–6) gives some indication of the principal ties of a large corporation. We have classified these directors as inside and outside, and we have classified

---

[3] Estimates from materials presented in Edward S. Herman, *Corporate Control, Corporate Power*, Chap. 2.

[4] *Business Week*, September 8, 1986, p. 60.

TABLE 2–6   Inside the Board Room

At IBM	
Inside	*Outside Corporate*

Louis V. Gerstner Jr.
   Chairman and CEO
	Cathleen Black
	   President, Hearst Co.

Douglas T. Elix
   Senior Vice-President
	Kenneth I. Chenault
	   President, American Express

Samuel J. Palmisano
   Senior Vice-President
	Juegan Dorman
	   Chairman, Aventis S.A.

J. Thomas Bouchard
   Senior Vice-President
	Minoru Makihara
	   Chairman, Mitsubishi

William A. Etherington
   Senior Vice-President
	Lucio A. Noto
	   Vice Chairman, Exon Mobil

David M. Thomas
   Senior Vice-President
	Alex Trotman
	   Chairman (ret.), Ford Motor

John M. Thompson
   Senior Vice-President
	Ludewijk VanWachem
	   Chairman, Royal Dutch Petroleum

Nicholas M. Donofrio
   Senior Vice-President
	Charles V. Knight
	   Chairman, Emerson Electric

Outside Public Interest

Nannerl O. Keohane
   President, Duke University
John B. Slaughter
   President Emeritus, Occidental College
Charles M. West
   President, M.I.T.

At AT&T	
Inside	*Outside Corporate*

C. Michael Armstrong
   Chairman of the Board and CEO
	Kenneth T. Derr
	   Chairman, Chevron

Amos B. Hostetter
   Chairman, AT&T Internet
	George M. C. Fisher
	   Chairman, Eastman Kodak

John D. Zeglis
   Chairman, AT&T Wireless
	Donald V. Fites
	   Chairman, Caterpillar

	Ralph S. Larsen Chairman, Johnson & Johnson
Outside Public Interest	John C. Malone Chairman, Liberty Media

M. Kathryn Eichoff
   Economics consultant
	Lewis A. Simpson
	   Chairman, GEICO Insurance

Donald F. McHenry
   Former U.S. Ambassador to the U.N.
	Sanford I. Weill
	   Chairman, Citigroup

Michael I. Sovern President Emeritus, Columbia University	

outsiders as those who represent ties to other corporations and banks and those who we believe were appointed to their posts as representatives of the "public interest."

THE MANAGERS: CLIMBING THE CORPORATE LADDER

The top echelons of American corporate life are occupied primarily by people who have climbed the corporate ladder from relatively obscure and powerless bottom rungs. It is our rough estimate that less than 10 percent of the presidents and directors of the top 100 corporations are heirs of wealthy families. The rest—the "managers"—owe their rise to power not to family connections, but to their own success in organizational life. Of course, these managers are overwhelmingly upper middle class and upper class in social origin, and most attended Ivy League colleges and universities. (The social origin and background of top elites are discussed in Chapter 6.) The rise of the manager is a recent phenomenon. As recently as 1950, we estimate that 30 percent of the top corporate elite were heirs of wealthy families. (Indeed, even since 1980, Henry Ford II stepped down as chairman of Ford Motors, and David Rockefeller retired as chairman of Chase Manhattan.) How can we explain the rise to power of the corporate manager?

Today the requirements of technology and planning have greatly increased the need in industry for specialized talent and skill in organization. Capital is something that a corporation can now supply to itself. Thus, there has been a shift in power in the American economy from capital to organized intelligence. This is reflected in the decline of individual- and family-controlled large corporations and in an increase in the percentage of large corporations controlled by management.

Following the Industrial Revolution in America in the late nineteenth century and well into the twentieth century, the nation's largest corporations were controlled by the tycoons who created them—Andrew Carnegie (Carnegie Steel, later United States Steel, and today USX); Andrew Mellon (Alcoa and Mellon banks); Henry Ford (Ford Motors); J.P. Morgan (J.P. Morgan); and, of course, John D. Rockefeller (Standard Oil Company, later broken into Exxon, Mobil, Chevron, Atlantic Richfield, and other large oil companies). But by the 1930s control of most large corporations had passed to professional managers. As early as 1932, Adolf Berle and Gardiner Means, in their classic book *The Modern Corporation and Private Property*, described the separation of ownership from control. The theory of "managerialism" became the conventional wisdom about corporate governance.[5]

---

[5] However, for some Marxists and others on the left, managerialism was denied, because it complicated the theory of class struggle in a capitalist society. They argued that great families retained "latent" power—power to be exercised when something goes seriously wrong. Some Marxists, however, accepted the managerial thesis and simply focused on managers as "the leading echelon of the capitalist class." See Paul A. Baran and Paul M. Sweezy, *Monopoly Capital* (Newark: Monthly Review Press, 1966).

It was recognized early on that corporate managers might run their firms in ways that serve their own best interests rather than those of the owners; for example, paying themselves multimillion-dollar annual salaries and providing themselves with lavish corporate-paid lifestyles. But for decades, individual and institutional stockholders largely ignored this potential principal-agent problem. Stockholders' power was fragmented and dispersed; there was not much they could do, other than sell their stock, even if they knew that managers were taking personal advantage of their position. But perhaps a more important reason that managers were largely unchallenged was that the American economy prospered from the 1940s through the 1970s. Governance of the U.S. corporation seemed to be working well, rewarding both managers and owners.

Liberal economist John Kenneth Galbraith once summarized the triumph of managerialism:

> Seventy years ago the corporation was the instrument of its owners and a projection of their personalities. The names of these principals—Carnegie, Rockefeller, Harriman, Mellon, Guggenheim, Ford—were well known across the land. They are still known, but for the art galleries and philanthropic foundations they established and their descendants who are in politics. The men who now head the great corporations are unknown. Not for a generation did people outside Detroit in the automobile industry know the name of the current head of General Motors. In the manner of all men, he must produce identification when paying by check. So with Ford, Standard Oil, and General Dynamics. The men who now run the large corporations own no appreciable share of the enterprise. They are selected not by the stockholders but, in the common case, by a board of directors which narcissistically they selected themselves.[6]

How does one climb the corporate ladder? It is not easy, and most who begin the climb fall by the wayside at some point in their careers.

> Just to be in the running, a career riser must discipline himself carefully. He must become a seasoned decision-maker. He must cultivate an aura of success and sustain his upward momentum on the executive ladder. He must be loyal to a fault, tolerably bright, fairly creative, politically agile, always tough, sometimes flexible, unfailingly sociable and, in the minds of his company's directors, seem superior to a dozen men who are almost as good. He must also be lucky.[7]

Today, more than ever before, getting to the top requires the skills of a "technocrat"—knowledge of bureaucratic organization, technical skills and information, extensive formal education (including postgraduate degrees), and proven ability to work within legal constraints and governmental regulations. Very few sons and no daughters are taking over the presidencies of large corporations owned by their families. Fewer than 10 of the nation's 500 largest

---

[6] John Kenneth Galbraith, *The New Industrial State* (Boston: Houghton Mifflin, 1967), p. 323.

[7] Howard Morgans, former president of Procter & Gamble, as quoted in "Proud to Be an Organization Man," *Forbes*, May 15, 1972, p. 241.

corporations are headed by men whose families had previously run the corporation.[8] Top corporate management is drawn from the ranks of upper-middle-class, well-educated, white, male management, financial, and legal experts.

Perhaps the most significant change over the years has been the rising number of top corporate and governmental executives who have acquired graduate degrees. Today over half of the corporate presidents of the 500 largest corporations have advanced degrees, including M.B.A.s (masters of business administration), law degrees, and Ph.D.s. (See Chapter 7.)

An increasing number of top corporate leaders are coming out of finance and law, as opposed to production, operations, advertising, sales, engineering, or research. Lawyers and accountants now head two out of every five large corporations. This is further evidence that finance, taxation, and governmental regulation are the chief problems confronting large corporations. The problems of production, sales, engineering, and transportation have faded in relation to the pressing problems of money and power.

Getting to the top by climbing the ladder of the giant corporation is not only difficult, it is also risky. The chances of any one individual making it to the top are infinitesimal.

> Yet hundreds of thousands of executives willingly devote entire careers to working their way up through these giant corporations. On the lower rungs of the ladder, when they are in their 20s, all of them dream of reaching the top. As they advance into their 30s, and receive more responsibility and more money, the dream flowers brightly. Some time in their 40s and 50s, however, most realize they aren't going to make it. They are sorely disappointed, but it's too late to change. Comfortable and secure, they stay. Then each year there are perhaps a dozen or so—the lucky men who go all the way.[9]

THE INHERITORS: STARTING AT THE TOP

Unquestionably, the Rockefellers, Fords, du Ponts, Mellons, and other families still exercise considerable influence over America's economic resources. However, research on family holdings in large corporations is not easy. Table 2–7 lists major family holdings of large corporations as revealed in a variety of sources. But it is not possible to tell from such a list whether a family really "controls" the operations of a corporation, or whether control has been passed on to the managers. It is possible for families who no longer hold active management positions in a corporation to exercise "latent" power—that is, to use their control blocs of stock as a restraint on management. Sometimes families interfere only when something goes seriously wrong.

---

[8] Charles G. Burch, "A Group Profile of the Fortune 500 Chief Executives," *Fortune*, May 1976, p. 174. See also *Business Week*, October 23, 1987, p. 37.

[9] "Proud to Be an Organization Man," p. 244.

TABLE 2–7 Historic Family Ties to Corporations

Corporation	Family
DuPont	du Pont
Ford Motor Co.	Ford
Alcoa	Mellon
Wal-Mart	Walton
Exxon	Rockefeller
Mobil	Rockefeller
Sears, Roebuck & Co.	Rosenwald
IBM	Watson, Fairchild
Dow Chemical Co.	Dow
Corning Glass Works	Houghton
International Paper Co.	Phipps
W.R. Grace & Co.	Grace, Phipps
Weyerhaeuser	Weyerhaeuser
Winn-Dixie, Inc.	Davis
Campbell Soup Company	Dorrance
H.J. Heinz Co.	Heinz
Firestone Tire & Rubber	Firestone
Olin Chemical	Olin
Ralston Purina Co.	Danforth
Hilton Hotels	Hilton
Howard Johnson Co.	Johnson
Great Atlantic & Pacific Tea Co. (A&P)	Hartford
Woolco	Woolworth
McDonnell Douglas Aircraft	McDonnell
International Harvester	McCormick
Coca-Cola	Woodruff
Eli Lilly & Co.	Lilly
Duke Power Co.	Duke
Rockwell Mfg. Co.	Rockwell
Gerber Products Co.	Gerber
Deere & Company	Deere
Borden Co.	Borden

The Ford Family. Until 1980, Henry Ford II, grandson of the Ford Motor Company founder, served as chairman of the board. "The first thing you have to understand about the company is that Henry Ford is the boss. . . . He *is* the boss, he always was the boss since the first day I came in and he always will be the boss." These are the words of Arjay Miller, who spent twenty-three years climbing the rungs of Ford management to become president of the company, only to find that Henry Ford II actually ran things. Miller eventually resigned to become dean of the Graduate School of Business at Stanford University.[10]

---

[10] Quoted in Victor Lasky, *Never Complain, Never Explain* (New York: Richard Marek, 1981), p. 86.

Henry Ford II grew up in a very narrow society; he was a member of a rich, insulated family that was dominated by his grandfather—known to be an exceedingly suspicious, prejudiced, and willful man. Young Ford attended Hotchkiss School and later Yale University. However, he failed to graduate in 1940 after admitting that he had cheated on a term paper. He enlisted in the U.S. Navy and served until his father died in 1943; President Roosevelt directed the secretary of the navy to release Ford to return to the family business.

Ford started in the automobile industry at the age of twenty-five as vice-president of Ford Motors, serving under his aged grandfather. A year later he took over the presidency. His initial decisions were to replace the one-person autocratic rule of the company with a modern management structure, recruiting bright, young management types (the famous Ford "Whiz Kids," including Robert S. McNamara, who later resigned as Ford president to become secretary of defense; Lee Iacocca; Arjay Miller; and Charles B. Thornton, later to become chairman of Litton Industries). He also initiated a modern labor relations program and ended the company's traditional hostility toward labor unions. As commonplace as these policies appear today, they were considered advanced, enlightened, and liberal for the Ford Motor Company at the time.

Over the years Ford proved himself a capable director of the company, despite some occasional and even colossal mistakes. (The Edsel fiasco cost the company over $300 million.) Ford worked long hours at the company headquarters in Detroit. He personally approved style changes in Ford cars and test-drove them himself. He was active on the board of the Ford Foundation and conscientiously reviewed research and grant proposals with other board members. His younger brothers, Benson and William Clay, eventually became Ford vice-presidents and board members. (William Clay Ford married the daughter of tire manufacturer Harvey S. Firestone, Jr., and purchased the Detroit Lions professional football team.)

Henry Ford II helped launch the National Urban Coalition and organized the National Alliance of Businessmen to provide more jobs for minorities. He was a prime mover in Detroit's urban renewal and redevelopment program, Renaissance Center. It was Ford himself who convinced his old rival, General Motors, as well as Amoco, Kmart, Parke-Davis, and Western International Hotels, to invest in the central city project. When cost overruns forced up the price of the project, Ford "arm-twisted" many Ford suppliers—U.S. Steel, Firestone, Budd Company—to come up with the additional funds.

Like many people born to wealth and power, Ford's personal style was far from that of the bland organizational person. He was frequently unpredictable, sometimes abrasive, often profane; he expressed his opinions directly. His public and private actions were often controversial. (He divorced his wife of many years and married a beautiful, young Italian actress in 1965; in 1980, he divorced her to marry an American model.)

The Ford Foundation was created before the death of the elder Henry

Ford. Originally, it supported charities in the Detroit area; its assets were primarily Ford stock. As the company prospered, the value of the foundation assets increased. In 1951, Henry Ford II asked Robert Hutchins, chancellor of the University of Chicago, to take over the foundation and make it a national force in civic affairs. Hutchins immediately funded some projects that "the Chairman" did not like; Hutchins was cut loose to become head of the Fund for the Republic, a smaller, Ford-funded foundation. The Ford Foundation supported moderate black civil rights organizations, including the Urban League, with Henry Ford II's approval. In 1966, McGeorge Bundy, Presidents Kennedy and Johnson's national security adviser, became the Ford Foundation head.

Bundy gradually sold off the Ford stock from the foundation assets. Bundy and Henry Ford clashed over the liberal programs of the Foundation. Finally, in 1976, Ford resigned from his directorship of the Ford Foundation. In his resignation letter, he pointedly advised the foundation to direct more attention to strengthening the capitalist system. "The Foundation is a creature of capitalism. . . . I'm just suggesting to the trustees and the staff that the system that makes the Foundation possible very probably is worth preserving."[11]

By 1980, Henry Ford II faced many troubles. The Pinto car had to be recalled for a faulty gas tank—the largest recall in auto history. Brother Benson Ford died of a heart attack. The break with Lee Iacocca was troublesome. Henry went through another divorce and remarriage. His nephew, Benson Ford, Jr., sued him over his father's will and demanded a seat on the Ford board, which Henry denied him. And in 1980, the Ford Motor Company lost $1.5 billion—the largest annual loss until then in the history of any American corporation. (Of course, General Motors lost money that year, and Chrysler would have gone bankrupt without favorable U.S. government loan guarantees.) Henry Ford II resigned as chairman of the board of Ford Motors.

William Clay Ford Jr., the fourth-generation favored son of the family, became Chairman of the Board of Ford Motors in 1999 at age 44. Ford prepped at Hotchkins and attended Princeton. After graduation he went directly into Ford's top management. But not all of the company's managers believed that he was ready for leadership of the now worldwide industrial giant. Yet with three family members on the Board of Directors—his father, William Clay Ford; his cousin Edsel B. Ford; and himself—and the Ford family continuing to hold the largest block (40 percent) of Ford stock, "Bill" Ford easily assumed the driver's seat. His leadership was immediately tested when allegations arose that Ford Explorer models had design flaws that contributed to the failure of their Firestone tires and contributed to many injuries and deaths on the road. (Ford and Firestone are currently engaged in a bitter feud over responsibility.) Chairman "Bill" Ford says that his job is to provide "the long-term direction of the Company," and his CEO, up-from-the-ranks

[11] *Newsweek,* January 24, 1977, p. 69.

Lebanese immigrant Jacques Nasser, is charged with the responsibility for day-to-day operations. (Nasser was assigned responsibility for taking the heat on the Firestone issue; William Clay Ford's mother is Martha Firestone.) Ford perceives himself as an environmentalist, even though his company's gas-guzzling SUVs now account for 50 percent of its revenues. His vision is to transform the vast Rouge factory complex that his great-grandfather built into a global showcase. His motto is "sustainability": he apparently believes that Ford Motors must accommodate itself to environmental concerns over the long run.

PAYCHECKS OF THE CORPORATE CHIEFS

Top corporate executives in the United States reward themselves with truly astronomical paychecks. The average CEO of a major U.S. corporation is currently paid over $12 *million* annually. That is 475 times more than the average blue-collar worker. And the recent trend has been skyward; since 1990 the average CEO paycheck has risen from $2 million to over $12 million.

American corporate executives pay themselves many times more than executives of corporations located anywhere else in the world. The ratio of CEO pay to the average manufacturing employee (475 in the United States) is only 13 in Germany and 11 in Japan. Indeed, the huge differential between American and German executive salaries has reportedly complicated the global merger of Daimler-Benz and Chrysler.

Corporate executive "compensation packages" combine annual salary and stock options. Stock options vary from year to year. *Forbes* magazine reports that Computer Associates' owner and CEO, Charles B. Wang, took $650 million total compensation out of his corporation in 2000, creating a new record.[12] Other executives in the *Forbes* top list gave themselves more "modest" packages: Louis V. Case, AOL, $117 million; Louis V. Gerstner, Jr., IBM, $107 million; John F. Welch, Jr., General Electric, $107 million; Stanford P. Weill, Citigroup (see Chapter 3), $85 million; Michael D. Eisner, Walt Disney (see Chapter 5), $50 million.

CORPORATE COUNTERREVOLUTIONS

Traditionally, the top managers of large corporations were considered impregnable; nothing short of bankruptcy could dislodge them. Corporate managers ran the American economy, perpetuating themselves in office; they ruled without much interference from outside directors, stockholders, employees, or consumers. But beginning in the 1980s, new challenges to the

[12] As reported at www.forbes.com. See also "Executive Paywatch" at www.aflcio.com.

imperial position of top management arose, most notably from: (1) a new activism by outside directors and large stockholders, checking the power of corporate chief executives and occasionally forcing their retirement; and (2) a rise in "hostile takeovers" led by corporate raiders who acquire corporate stock and voting power in order to force the ouster and replacement of existing management.

The new activism by outside directors and large stockholders, particularly institutional investors—pension funds, mutual funds, insurance companies, and banks—is partly attributable to the failure of some American corporations to remain competitive in global markets.[13] Traditionally, poor economic performance by management resulted in the sale of the corporation's stock by institutional investors, who simply shifted their investment to more profitable corporations. The chief executives of poorly performing corporations might suffer some public embarrassment from falling prices of their companies' stock, perhaps even some shouted insults at annual stockholders' meetings, but their positions of power generally remained secure. However, as institutional stock ownership has grown to over half of all stockholding in the nation, top corporate managers have come face to face with more informed and aggressive representatives of owners.[14] Mutual and pension fund managers as well as managers of banks and insurance companies are more likely than small individual investors to take action against the managers of poorly performing corporations in which they have invested funds. Traditionally, fund managers routinely voted with management, but today they are taking a much more aggressive role in corporate governance. Because the funds now own so much stock, it is not always possible for them to "dump" it without suffering heavy losses, and fund managers have a legal responsibility to protect their own investors. Hence, these managers, acting on behalf of stockholders, are clipping the powers of the corporate chiefs and even on occasion getting some fired. According to *Fortune* magazine: "The fact is, the institutions' fingers are on the most celebrated CEO ousters."[15]

THE BATTLE FOR IBM

Consider the rise and fall of John F. Akers, former chairman and chief executive officer of IBM, once America's premier corporation. Akers attended Yale University, majored in engineering, and served four years as a U.S. Navy pilot. He joined IBM in 1960 as a sales representative and rose rapidly up the corporate ladder, becoming a vice-president in 1982. But already IBM was facing

---

[13] See Margaret M. Blair, "Who's in Charge Here?" *Brookings Review* (Fall 1991), pp. 8–13.

[14] Institutional ownership of stock grew from 15 percent of all outstanding sharers of U.S. corporations in 1965, to 30 percent in 1980, to 50 percent in 1992. See *Fortune*, January 11, 1993, p. 36.

[15] *Fortune*, January 11, 1993, p. 35.

tough competition from Japan and from newer, leaner, aggressive U.S. companies like Microsoft, Apple, and Wang. IBM continued to focus its business on large, expensive "mainframe" computers, while the market turned increasingly to smaller, cheaper, personal desktop computers.

Akers was made president of IBM in 1983. He tried to steer "Big Blue" in new directions and to cut costs. Reorganizations and layoffs resulted in thousands of lost jobs in a company that once prided itself on employee morale. But the red ink continued to flow, and stockholders were crushed. IBM stock fell over 70 percent in value (from a 1987 high of $175 to a 1993 low of $48). While many individual and institutional stockholders were publicly critical of Akers, he defiantly held on to his job, claiming the backing of his board. But finally in early 1993, following a report of the corporation's record $5-billion annual loss for 1992, the IBM board forced Akers's resignation following an acrimonious meeting.[16] Prior to resignation Akers had been co-chairman of the Business Roundtable (see Chapter 6) and a director of the New York Times Company, Pepsico, the Metropolitan Museum of Art, the California Institute of Technology, and the United Way of America.

Louis V. Gerstner, Jr., made his career as a corporate "fixer"—a manager skilled at turning around the fortunes of depressed companies. So when the IBM board ousted Akers, it sought out Gerstner—an outsider who would bring new thinking to the stodgy corridors of Big Blue and resuscitate the sick giant.

Gerstner earned an engineering degree at Dartmouth before going on to Harvard Business School for his M.B.A. He began his career in 1965 as a corporate fixer with a leading management consulting firm—McKinsey & Company. In 1978 he accepted a senior management position with American Express and was named president six years later. He is credited with having introduced the glitzy gold card program that jacked up the company's revenues. In 1989, following one of the largest corporate mergers in history—R.J. Reynolds (tobacco) and Nabisco (foods) merged as RJR-Nabisco, currently the nation's twelfth-ranked industrial corporation—Gerstner was lured away from American Express to run the new food and tobacco giant. Its principal owners, the financial firm of Kohlberg, Kravis and Roberts, had funded the merger with billions in junk bonds, nearly sinking the new company with a huge debt load. But in four years, Gerstner cut costs, introduced new products, and reduced the debt load by half. He won the dubious reputation as one of the nation's toughest "slash and burn" CEOs, ruthlessly firing managers and selling off divisions that failed to produce profits.

The IBM board's public search for a new CEO generated an embarrassing squabble between insiders and outsiders. Insiders wanted someone with a technical background who was knowledgeable about the computer industry. Several well-known "techies" turned the job down; rescuing IBM may be the

---

[16] *Time,* February 8, 1993, p. 54.

toughest job in corporate America. IBM's outside board member James E. Burke, former chairman of Johnson & Johnson (drugs), finally convinced the board to hire a nontechnical outsider to "bury the old culture" at IBM.[17] Gerstner was recruited from RJR-Nabisco to bring new life to America's largest computer manufacturer.

Gerstner lived up to his "slash and burn" reputation, shrinking the IBM workforce and making significant cost reductions. More importantly, he expanded the corporation's focus well beyond large mainframe computers to network computing, PCs, and "integrated business solutions." IBM's stock rose again to over $100 per share. The Corporation acquired several software companies, including the highly successful Lotus Development Corp. And in 1997 IBM's supercomputer, "Deep Blue," defeated World Chess Champion Garry Kasparov, the first time a computer had won against a world champion. In 2001, eight years after his arrival as IBM's chairman, Gerster had established his full control over the corporation.

HOSTILE TAKEOVERS

The threat of hostile takeovers represents another challenge to management control of corporate America. A hostile takeover involves the purchase of enough stock in a publicly held corporation to force the ouster and replacement of existing corporate management.

A hostile takeover begins with a corporate "raider" buying the stock of a corporation on the open market, usually with money borrowed for this purpose. The raider may wish to keep his early purchases secret for a while to avoid rapid rises in the price of the stock; but federal Securities and Exchange Commission rules require disclosure when a person acquires 5 percent of a corporation's stock. The raider may then offer a takeover bid to existing management. Management may reject the bid outright or try to buy back the stock purchased by the raider at a higher price, that is, to offer the raider "greenmail." If the raider and management cannot reach agreement, the hostile takeover proceeds. The raider arranges to borrow additional money—perhaps several billion dollars—to make a purchase offer to the target corporation's stockholders, usually at a price higher than the current stock exchange price. Management may search for a "White Knight"—someone willing to offer even more money to purchase the corporation from its stockholders but who promises to keep the existing management. If the raider wins control of the corporation, he replaces management.

Following a successful takeover, the corporation is heavily laden with new debt. The raider may have borrowed billions to buy out shareholders. The investment firms that provide the loans to finance the corporation's pur-

---

[17] *Business Week*, April 5, 1993, p. 20.

chase may issue "junk bonds" with high interest rates to attract investors to these risky ventures. The corporation must pay off these bonds with its own revenues. Additionally there may be many millions of dollars in bond-sale commissions and attorneys' fees to pay out. The raider may be forced to sell off parts of the corporation or some of its valuable assets in order to help pay off part of the debt. Thus, the target corporation itself must eventually bear the burden of the takeover battle.

Of course, the raider originally targets the corporation because its stock price is low compared to the value of its assets and/or its potential for future profits. The raider believes that the low price of the stock is a product of poor management performance. The raider hopes that with new management the corporation can improve its performance, pay off its debt, and produce greater profits. And the raider must convince the investment firms who provide the takeover money of the accuracy of his predictions.

Why does a corporation emerge as a target of a hostile takeover? Why have takeovers become so pervasive in the last decade? One explanation is inflation; the cost of replacing existing assets far exceeds the value placed on these assets. It is therefore cheaper to buy existing plants, buildings, machinery, inventories, and the like than to produce new ones. It is cheaper to buy known oil reserves held by oil companies than to search for new oil. Another explanation focuses on mismanagement by isolated, arrogant, lazy American management. Managers not only have allowed American industry to fall behind foreign competition, but they have also failed to put the assets of their corporations to their most productive use. Return on invested capital and world market shares have dwindled. The corporate raiders offer a way to "throw the rascals out" of the boardroom and reinvigorate American enterprise.

Government antitrust and tax policies combine to encourage mergers and takeovers. Tax policies contribute by allowing corporations to deduct from their taxable income the interest on loans used to acquire other companies. Both the U.S. Department of Justice and the Federal Trade Commission are responsible for enforcing the nation's antitrust laws. These laws forbid "monopoly" and "combinations in restraint of trade" (Sherman Antitrust Act, 1887), "unfair method of competition" and "efforts to reduce competition" (Federal Trade Commission Act, 1914), and the acquisition by one corporation of another "where the effect of such acquisition is to substantially lessen competition" (Clayton Act, 1914). But the interpretations placed on these laws in recent years have given increasing attention to *world* market conditions. It is argued that increasing concentrations of corporate assets in the United States through mergers do *not* "substantially lessen competition" because these firms are competing in a world market against giant Japanese and European multinational corporations. Indeed, in such a world market, it is even argued that the U.S. government should *encourage* mergers of U.S. firms in order to strengthen them against foreign competition.

Are corporate takeovers good or bad for America? There is no easy answer to this important question. The raiders claim that their activities force improvements in efficiency and productivity. Even the potential threat of a takeover forces corporate managers to streamline their operations, eliminate waste, increase revenues, raise profits, and distribute profits to their shareholders rather than spend them on the comforts of management. The raiders argue that American management has grown soft, lazy, and self-satisfied; that, as a result, the American corporation has lost its competitive edge in the world marketplace.

Opponents of the corporate-takeover movement argue that fear of the raider forces management to focus on near-term profits at the expense of long-range research and development. Management must keep the current price of its stock high in order to deter a takeover attempt. Even worse, management often resorts to "poison pills" to deliberately weaken its own corporation to make it unattractive to raiders; it may increase its debt, buy other poorly performing corporations, devalue stockholders' voting powers, or provide itself with "golden parachutes" (rich severance benefits) in the event of ouster. The corporate raiders enrich the shareholders and speculators, but they do so at the expense of the industry itself.

The debt incurred in corporate takeovers is a concern to employees, consumers, and taxpayers. While the original stockholders are paid handsomely by the raider, the corporation must labor intensively to pay off the debt incurred. The corporation may be broken apart and its separate pieces sold, which may disrupt and demoralize employees. Consumers may be forced to pay higher prices. If the corporation cannot meet the high interest payments, bankruptcy threatens. The corporation's heavy interest payments are tax-deductible, thus depriving the U.S. Treasury of corporate tax revenues. And the diversion of American capital from productive investments to takeovers threatens to weaken national productivity.

THE LIMITS OF CORPORATE POWER

Elites do not like to acknowledge their own power. Kenneth Olsen, CEO of Digital Equipment, offered a typical elite response to the question of power: "I've got no power. All I can do is encourage people, motivate people to do things. I've got no power over them."[18] Why do elites say things like this? It is not merely modesty nor intent to deceive. "Power" in a democratic society has acquired a pejorative meaning—tyranny, arbitrariness, absolute rule. And this connotation conflicts with the requirements for successful corporate leader-

[18] Quoted in *Forbes*, May 30, 1988, p. 120. Inasmuch as Olsen was deposed as CEO by his board in 1992, his earlier disclaimer of power appears prophetic in retrospect.

TABLE 2–8 Pressures on the Corporate Elite

Compared with five years ago, would you say that the following individuals or institutions have gained influence over decisions in companies such as yours, lost influence, or kept their influence?

	Gained Influence	Lost Influence	Kept Influence	Not Sure
Institutions holding big stock blocs	47%	2%	42%	9%
Raiders and potential raiders	58	2	24	16
Investment bankers	46	13	36	5
Stock analysts	48	4	43	5
Government regulators	41	20	34	5
Environmentalists	37	14	40	9
Consumer groups	28	14	49	9
Labor unions	2	54	34	10

Let me read you a list of people, institutions, and other factors that might be the source of pressure on companies to focus on the short term, rather than on long-term growth. Tell me which three or four you believe exert the most pressure on companies to focus on the short term.

Banks holding debt	12%
Bond-rating services	14
Boards of directors	15
Financial press	34
Institutional shareholders	58
Investment bankers, takeover advisers	45
Securities analysts	65

Source: Survey of 400 chief executives of corporations in the top 1,000, reported by *Business Week*, October 23, 1987, p. 28.

ship today. Hence, corporate elites deny they have power, but they acknowledge that they have the principal responsibility for "how the company is run."

Yet top corporate elites feel more constrained today in the exercise of their authority than in the past. Many believe that the era of the all-powerful CEOs is over. No large corporation can be directed from the top in the fashion a generation ago of William Paley's CBS, Armand Hammer's Occidental Petroleum, or Harold Geneen's ITT.

The greatest constraint on corporate power is the global market. Thirty years ago the American market was isolated; each sector of industry was a self-contained oligopoly with three to eight major manufacturers competing in a limited fashion. Top corporate elites were relatively unconstrained in deciding about products and prices, technologies and innovations, capital flows and investments. But today, global competition severely limits American corporate decision-making. The United States remains the world's largest market, but large shares of the U.S. market have been captured by foreign competition in nearly every industrial sector.

Top corporate elites believe their own power is more limited today than a few years ago. They believe other elites have gained in power relative to themselves. They acknowledge that labor unions have lost influence in American life, but they believe that institutional investors and bankers, Wall Street analysts, government regulators, and most of all, corporate raiders, are gaining power (see Table 2–8).

America's corporate elite has come under severe criticism for its failure to plan for the long term, to direct funds into research, and to develop strategies to confront global competition. It is charged with myopic concern with short-term profits, tomorrow's stock prices, and next quarter's earnings.

Elites agree that the criticism is justified, but they claim that their failure to focus on long-term growth strategies is a result of pressures from institutional investors, Wall Street analysts, and corporate raiders.

SUMMARY

Economic power in America is highly concentrated. A relatively small number of corporations—500 out of 5 million—account for roughly 60 percent of all corporate revenues and assets in the nation. Indeed, the nation's five largest nonfinancial corporations account for over 20 percent of the revenues of all nonfinancial corporations in America. This concentration of economic power is increasing gradually over time, in part as a product of acquisitions and mergers.

Economic power is gradually becoming globalized. World trade is expanding rapidly; today about one-quarter of the world's output is sold in a country other than the country that produced it.

America's corporate elite strongly supports globalization. Over the years, the United States has become an open market for goods produced all over the world. American corporations, once protectionist in their views, came to support the elimination of tariffs and trade barriers in the United States and throughout the world. Leadership in global economic policy was formed with the creation of the Trilateral Commission in 1972. The global elite saw the advantages of becoming institutionalized. The World Trade Organization grew out of the General Agreement on Tariffs and Trade. The World Bank and International Monetary Fund were also created to stimulate global trade. The current model for global trade is the North American Free Trade Agreement. Currently, corporate elites in the United States are seeking to expand it to a hemispheric "Free Trade Area of the Americas."

Power over corporate assets rests in the hands of about 1,500 officers and directors of the nation's 100 largest nonfinancial institutions. These managers, not the stockholders or the employees, decide major policy questions, choose the people who will carry out these decisions, and even select their own replacements.

Most of these corporate chiefs have climbed the corporate ladder to their posts. They owe their rise to power to their skills in organizational life and to their successful coping with the new demands for expertise in management, finance, technology, and planning. Individual capitalists are no longer essential in the formation of capital assets. Most industrial capital is raised either within the corporation itself or from institutional borrowing.

Corporate boardrooms are inhabited by "inside" directors (top officers of the corporation, including the CEO) and "outside" directors (often current or retired CEOs of other corporations). Outside directors may also represent financial institutions with a large stake in the corporation, and they may represent family owners. Virtually all large corporations also appoint a few notable "public interest" representatives to their boards. But corporate decision-making is usually dominated by the inside manager-directors rather than the outside directors.

America's corporate chiefs pay themselves extraordinarily well—about 475 times more than their average worker—a ratio that exceeds any other executive-worker pay ratio in the world.

In recent years challenges to managerial control of the corporation have arisen from (1) a new activism by outside directors and large stockholders, and (2) the threat of hostile takeovers often led by corporate "raiders." Slow growth and global competition have inspired outside directors and large stockholders to oust some prominent corporate chieftains. Corporate raiders claim to reinvigorate American enterprise and competition by ousting poorly performing managers and reorganizing corporate assets to maximize their value. But critics claim that takeover activity wastes capital resources, demoralizes managers and workers, and burdens corporations with excessive debts.

3

The Money Elite

The concentration of financial assets in America is even greater than the concentration of the assets of industrial corporations. Banks, insurance companies, and investment firms occupy a strategic position in the American economy. They decide whether, when, and under what terms American corporations, as well as state and local governments, can borrow money, sell stock, and expand or contract the money supply. These institutions are responsible to the independent Federal Reserve System and the Securities and Exchange Commission, both of which function largely beyond the control of Congress and the president, and both of which are composed of bankers and investors. The nation's elite includes the top officers and directors of the largest banks, insurance companies, investment firms, and the Federal Reserve Board.

THE CONCENTRATION OF FINANCIAL RESOURCES

There are more than 12,000 banks serving the nation, but the twenty-five largest banks control more than half of all the banking assets in the United States (see Table 3–1). Giant banking mergers in the last decade have resulted in a greater concentration of banking assets than at any time in recent history. Today three banking corporations—Citigroup, J.P. Morgan Chase, and Bank of America—control about one-third of all of the nation's banking assets. The

TABLE 3–1   The Nation's Largest Banks

1	Citigroup[1]	14	Bank of New York Co.
2	J.P. Morgan Chase	15	Wachovia Corp.
3	Bank of America Corp.	16	Firstar Corp.
4	Wells Fargo	17	Mellon Financial Corp.
5	Bank One Corp.	18	Providian Financial
6	First Union Corp.	19	State St. Corp.
7	FleetBoston Financial	20	BB&T Corp.
8	U.S. Bancorp	21	Fifth Third Bancorp
9	National City Corp.	22	Comerica
10	Suntrust Banks	23	Southtrust Corp.
11	Keycorp	24	Regions Financial
12	MBNA	25	Amsouth Bancorp.
13	PNC Financial Svcs. Group		

[1]Includes Travelers Insurance.

Source: Derived from data provided in *Fortune*, April 16, 2001.

TABLE 3–2   The Nation's Largest Insurance Companies

Life

1	Metropolitan	6	Massachusetts Mutual
2	Prudential	7	AFLAC
3	New York Life	8	Unumprovident
4	Northwestern Mutual	9	Guardian Life
5	American General	10	Canseco

Property

1	State Farm	6	Liberty Mutual
2	American International	7	Nationwide
3	Berkshire Hathaway	8	Hartford
4	Allstate	9	St. Paul
5	Loews	10	USAA

Health

1	Aetna	6	Tenet
2	United Health Group	7	Humana
3	Cigna	8	Wellpoint
4	HCA	9	Health Net
5	Pacificare	10	Anthem

Source: Derived from data provided in *Fortune*, April 16, 2001.

TABLE 3–3   The Nation's Largest Investment Firms

1	Morgan Stanley Dean Witter	6	Paine Webber
2	Merrill Lynch	7	Charles Schwab
3	Goldman Sachs	8	A.G. Edwards
4	Lehman Brothers	9	Franklin Resources
5	Bear Stearns	10	Raymond James Financial

Source: Derived from data provided in *Fortune*, April 16, 2001.

merger of J.P. Morgan and Chase Manhattan, and the merger of Bank of America with NationsBank, consolidated the nation's financial industry. The megafinancial giant, Citigroup, was created first through the merger of Citi-Corp with the Wall Street investment firms of Salomon Brothers and Smith Barney, followed by its acquisition of Travelers Insurance. Former Secretary of the Treasury Robert Rubin was named the first cochairman of the new giant of the financial world.

More than 2,000 insurance companies operate in the United States, but more than half of all insurance assets in the nation are controlled by the companies listed in Table 3–2. Indeed, just two companies (Prudential and Metropolitan) control over one-quarter of all insurance assets.

Mergers have reduced the total number of all Wall Street investment firms to those listed in Table 3–3. These firms decide whether, when, and under what terms corporations can sell stocks, bonds, and other securities. Moreover, these financial institutions have increasingly undertaken to challenge the traditional dominance of "inside" directors of industrial corporations for control of decision-making (see "Corporate Counter-Revolutions" in Chapter 2).

THE BANKING BOARDROOMS

The boardrooms of the nations' largest banks, insurance companies, and investment firms resemble corporate boardrooms, not only in their size and extravagant furnishings, but also in the people who occupy the plush leather chairs. Consider the boardroom of Citigroup in 2000 (Figure 3–1). It is presided over by Chairman and CEO Stanford I. Weill, who himself serves on the Board of Directors of AT&T, Du Pont, and United Technologies. The Chairman of the Executive Committee is former Secretary of Treasury Robert Rubin, himself a director of Ford Motor and former senior partner of Goldman Sachs. Former CIA Director John M. Deutch sits on the board of Citigroup as well as a number of large industrial corporations. Former President Gerald R. Ford sits on the board in an advisory capacity. We will return to the issue of interlocking directorates in Chapter 7.

FIGURE 3–1   Inside the Boardroom at Citigroup

Sanford I. Weill.   Chairman of the Board and CEO of Citigroup. Former chairman of Travelers Insurance, American Express, and Shearson Lehman brothers (investments). A director of AT&T, Du Pont, and United Technologies. A member of the Business Roundtable and a trustee of Cornell University.

Robert E. Rubin.   Chairman of the Executive Committee of Citigroup. Former Secretary of the Treasury and former senior partner Goldman Sachs. A director of Ford Motor Co.

C. Michael Armstrong.   Chairman and CEO of AT&T. Former Chairman and CEO of Hughes Electronics. A trustee of Johns Hopkins University and a member of the Council on Foreign Relations.

Alain J. P. Belda.   Chairman and CEO of Alcoa.

Kenneth J. Bialkin.   Senior Partner in Skadden Arps. A director of Travelers Insurance in the Municipal Assistance Corporation of New York ("Big Mac"). A member of the Council on Foreign Relations.

Kenneth T. Derr.   Chairman and CEO of Chevron. A director of AT&T and Potlatch Corp. A member of the American Petroleum Institute and the Business Council.

John M. Deutch.   Former Director of the CIA. A director of Cummins Engine, Raytheon, CMS Energy, and Araid Pharmaceuticals.

Rubin Mark.   Chairman and CEO of Colgate Palmolive and a director of Time Warner.

Michael T. Masin.   Vice-chairman of GTE. Former partner at O'Melvany & Myers. A director of Puerto Rico Telephone Company and a trustee of the Museum of Modern Art.

Richard D. Parsons.   President of Time Warner. A director of Philip Morris and Estee Lauder.

Andrall E. Pearson.   Chairman and CEO of Tricon Global Restaurants. Former president and CEO of Pepsico.

Franklin A. Thomas.   Former president of the Ford Foundation. A director of Alcoa, Cummins Engine, Lucent Technologies, Pepsico, and Conoco.

Edgar S. Woolard, Jr.   Former Chairman of the Du Pont Corporation. A director of Apple Computer and a member of the Business Council.

Gerald R. Ford.   Advisory Director of Citigroup. Former President of the United States.

BANKING "REFORM"

The financial industry is consolidating itself into ever larger concentrations of money and power. In 1999 Congress paved the way to consolidation by passing banking "reform." The Financial Services Modernization Act of 1999 is not the type of legislation that very many people outside elite circles know about. Yet it is likely to have major consequences for consumers as well as for the structure of the nation's elite system.

During the Great Depression of the 1930s, banks, investment firms, and insurance companies came under intense criticism as contributors to the nation's economic instability. The result, early in the administration of President Franklin D. Roosevelt, was the Glass-Steagall law, officially the Banking Act of 1933, that forced a separation between the banking and securities industries. The act was intended to protect bank depositors from having their funds intermingles with those of stock market speculators or speculated with by banks themselves.

In recent decades, megamergers of giant financial groups successfully circumvented the act. (For example, Citibank first merged with the Salomon Brothers and Smith Barney investment firms, and then later with Travelers Insurance, to create the megacorporation Citigroup. Former Secretary of the Treasury Robert Rubin was named cochairman of Citigroup following the merger.) But these key sectors of America's national elite still resented the Glass-Steagall law and began to call for its outright repeal in the 1980s. Progress was slowed, however, due to squabbling among banks, investment firms, and insurance companies over specific provisions of what they referred to as "banking reform." But by 1999, a general settlement had been reached; the Glass-Steagall Act was repealed and the "financial services" industry was freed of many bothersome government restrictions. The Financial Services Modernization Act is designed to allow the creation of giant financial supermarkets that will provide one-stop services to consumers—commercial banking; mortgage loans; life, health, home, and auto insurance; corporate and bond stock underwriting; and mutual fund, stock, and bond brokerage services.

Banking "reform" was accompanied by one of the largest spending sprees in American politics. Between 1993 and 1998, banks, investment firms, and insurance companies made nearly $250 million in soft money, PAC, and individual campaign contributions. More than $100 million was spent by these industries in the 1998 midterm congressional election alone (see Table 3–4). Both Democratic and Republican candidates prospered, but Republicans, having control of both houses of Congress in 1994, received the bulk of this largesse. About 40 percent of these contributions went to members of the committees that dealt directly with the content of the repeal bill—the House Banking and Senate Banking Committees. And, not surprisingly, the top indi-

TABLE 3–4   Political Contributions by the Financial Industry

(Congressional campaign contributions, 1998, prior to the passage of the Financial Services Modernization Act of 1999[a])

Company	Total
Investment Firms	
Goldman, Sachs & Co.	$1,912,866
Citigroup[b]	1,051,608
Merrill Lynch	1,025,141
Morgan Stanley Dean Witter	889,294
Bear Stearns	832,181
Paine Webber	715,927
M.A. Berman Co.	660,850
Chicago Mercantile Exchange	648,300
J.W. Childs Associates	572,250
Investment Co. Institute	564,937
Total: Securities	51,660,995
Insurance Companies	
American Financial Group	1,472,645
Blue Cross/Blue Shield	1,415,690
National Association of Life Underwriters	1,355,500
Citigroup[b]	1,085,708
AFLAC	1,000,470
American Council of Life Insurance	841,005
American International group	768,465
Independent Insurance Agents of America	661,514
Cigna	615,960
Alfa Mutual Insurance	532,000
Total: Insurance	41,711,427
Banks	
BankAmerica	1,732,650
American Bankers Association	1,466,786
Bank One	1,259,588
J.P. Morgan & Co.	659,344
Chase Manhattan	633,061
America's Community Bankers	590,176
Citigroup[b]	471,430
Independent Bankers Association	469,804
First Union	429,352
Wells Fargo	387,503
Total: Banking	20,875,266

[a] Top ten campaign contributors, 1998, in each sector.

[b] Based on FEC data. Totals include contributions from subsidiaries.

Source: Center for Responsive Politics, based on Federal Election Commission data.

vidual recipient (of nearly $2 million) was U.S. Senator Phil Gramm (R-Tex.), chairman of the Senate Banking Committee.

The top corporate contributors from the banking, securities, and insurance industries in the 1998 congressional elections represent the core of America's financial elite (see Table 3–4). In addition to their campaign contributions, these industries incurred more than $250 million in direct lobbying expenses over the two years prior to the passage of banking "reform."[1]

THE FEDERAL RESERVE BOARD

Money is far too important to be left to democratic governments. All of the advanced industrial democracies have created central banks to control the supply of money. These central banks function largely independently of their governments.

It became apparent in the United States at the beginning of the twentieth century that the control of money would have to be removed from direct government control and placed in the hands of bankers themselves. Moreover, it was generally agreed that bankers' power over money would have to be unrestricted by Congress or the president.

The Federal Reserve Act of 1913 created the Federal Reserve System. Its purpose is to decide on the nation's monetary policy and credit conditions, to supervise and regulate all banking activity, and to provide various services to banks. Federal Reserve banks are banks' banks; only banks may open accounts at Federal Reserve Banks.

The Federal Reserve System is fully independent—its decisions need not be ratified by the president, Congress, the courts, or any other governmental institution. It does not depend on annual federal appropriations, but instead it finances itself. Theoretically, Congress could amend or repeal the Federal Reserve Act of 1913, but to do so would be politically unthinkable. The only changes to the Act throughout the century have been to *add* to the powers of "the Fed." In the International Banking Act of 1978, the Fed was directed by the Congress to encourage economic growth, maintain high levels of employment, keep inflation low, and maintain moderate long-term interest rates.

The Federal Reserve System is governed by its seven-member Board of Governors, who are appointed for *fourteen-year terms.* Members are appointed by the president, with the consent of the Senate, but they may not be removed from the board except for "cause." No member has ever been removed since the creation of the Board in 1913. The powerful Chairman of the Board (see

---

[1] Center for Responsive Politics, 1999, according to figures reported by lobbyists under the terms of the 1995 Lobby Registration Act.

"Alan Greenspan: Ruling over Money") serves only a four-year term, but the chairman's term overlaps that of the president, so that new presidents cannot immediately name their own chair. The board oversees twelve Federal Reserve Banks that serve various regions of the nation. Each Federal Reserve Bank has nine directors—six elected by member banks in the district and three appointed by the board of governors. Thus, control of the nation's money supply and the regulation of banks rest in the hands of bankers themselves.

CONTROLLING THE MONEY SUPPLY

Banks create money when they make loans. They simply create "demand deposits" and make them available to borrowers. Currency (cash) in circulation, together with demand deposits, constitute the nation's principal money supply—"M_1." Demand deposits far exceed currency in circulation. (Only about 5 percent of the money supply is in the form of cash.) Most money transactions consist of checks or electronic transfers; in normal times people are satisfied to accept these paper or electronic promises of banks in lieu of currency. But at times in the past, large numbers of people have demanded that their deposits be given to them in currency—creating a "run" on a bank. Inasmuch as the bank simply created these deposits, it cannot possibly pay all of its depositors (or even a significant portion of them) in currency. The bank fails, and depositors lose their money.

The Federal Reserve System was created by bankers primarily to stabilize the banking system and control the supply of money. The Fed requires all banks to maintain a reserve in currency or in deposits with a Federal Reserve Bank. If the "reserve ratio" is set at 20 percent, for example, a bank may only create demand deposits up to five times the amount of its reserve. (If it has $100 million in reserve, its total demand deposits cannot exceed $500 million.)

If the Fed decides that there is too much money in the economy (inflation), it can raise the reserve requirement, for example from 20 to 25 percent, reducing what a bank can create in demand deposits to only four times its reserve. (If a bank has $100 million in reserve, its total demand deposits would be limited to $400 million.) In this way the Fed can expand or contract money supply as it sees fit.

The Fed can also alter the money supply by changing the interest it charges member banks to borrow reserve. A bank can expand its deposits by borrowing reserve from the Fed, but it must pay the Fed an interest rate, called the "discount rate," in order to do so. The Fed regularly raises and lowers the discount rate, thereby making it easier or harder for banks to borrow reserve. Raising the discount rate tends to contract money supply; lowering it expands the money supply.

The Fed is also authorized to buy and sell U.S. Treasury bonds and notes in what is called "open market operations." Indeed, the assets of the Fed consist of U.S. bonds and notes. Each day the Open Market Desk of the Fed buys and sells billions of dollars worth of government bonds. If it sells more than it buys, it reduces its own reserve and hence its ability to lend reserve to banks; this contracts the money supply. If it buys more than it sells, it adds to its own reserve, enabling it to lend reserve to member banks and expand the money supply.

ALAN GREENSPAN: RULING OVER MONEY

Alan Greenspan was first appointed chairman of the Federal Reserve Board in 1987 by President Ronald Reagan. (Greenspan replaced the long-serving chair Paul Volcker, whose tight-money policies in the early 1980s ultimately brought down the high rates of inflation that had plagued the nation for most of the 1970s; Volcker went on to serve as chairman of the World Bank.) Born in New York City, Greenspan studied music at the prestigious Julliard School and enjoyed a brief but successful career as a professional saxophone player in a big swing band before returning to the classroom at New York University. He received an M.A. in economics in 1950 under the tutelage of Arthur F. Burns, who served as chair of the Federal Reserve from 1970 to 1978. After graduation, Greenspan formed his own economic consulting company, Townsend-Greenspan, which provided economic forecasts for some of America's largest corporations. In his spare time, Greenspan completed his Ph.D. at New York University and became a fan of the social philosopher and writer Ayn Rand. Greenspan embraced Rand's vision of a society in which every person could realize his or her own potential in any chosen field without government interference or regulation.

Greenspan began his public service in the Nixon Administration, serving on commissions and task forces, including the Commission on an All-Volunteer Armed Force. In 1974 President Nixon appointed Greenspan to chair the Council of Economic Advisers, a position Greenspan continued to hold under President Gerald Ford. When the Carter Administration came to Washington in 1977, Greenspan returned to running his private company.

In the early 1980s, Fed chair Paul Volcker instituted a tight-money policy that ultimately brought down the high rates of inflation which had plagued the nation for most of the 1970s. The Reagan Administration eventually complained that Volcker's stringent anti-inflationary policies were slowing economic growth. In August 1987 the Democrat Volcker handed in his resignation and Reagan nominated Republican Greenspan to follow him.

Like Reagan, Greenspan opposed higher taxes, but who the president had hoped would be a loyal Republican soldier often acted independently and disagreed with the administration over expanding the money supply. Greenspan's management of the Fed has been widely praised by both Democrats and Republicans. He has earned credibility with his fellow economists by avoiding the Washington political game. He is credited for his quick reaction to the stock market crash on October 19, 1987, when he ensured that Federal Reserve Banks would have enough money on hand to prevent panic following the record drop in stock prices. During the 1991 recession, Greenspan pushed interest rates down to a twenty-year low and cut required Federal Reserve funds in half in order to ease credit. As independent as the Fed itself, he frequently criticized Presidents Reagan and Bush and the Congress regarding huge federal deficits.

Having supervised the Fed over the nation's longest continuous period of economic growth and the emergence of federal budget surpluses, President Bill Clinton was obliged to reappoint Greenspan in 1999. The Fed chairman moved quickly in early 2001 to reduce interest rates when economic growth appeared to slow. He reduced them to an all-time low in 2001 following the September 11 terrorist attack.

THE SECURITIES AND EXCHANGE COMMISSION

The Securities and Exchange Commission (SEC) was created not so much to regulate the stock market but rather to try to restore public confidence in it after the great market crash of 1929. Indeed, most major investment firms strongly supported the Securities and Exchange Act of 1934. President Franklin D. Roosevelt appointed a notorious stock market manipulator (and FDR's principal campaign contributor) Joseph P. Kennedy, President John F. Kennedy's father, to serve as the first Chairman of the SEC.

The SEC is comprised of five commissioners, appointed by the president for five years for staggered terms and subject to Senate confirmation. No more than three commissioners may belong to the same political party. Most appointees over the years have come from the ranks of loyal party supporters; few have been moneyed elites themselves. (A possible exception is the chairman, currently Arthur Leavitt, a former Wall Street investment banker, chairman of the American Stock Exchange, and editor of the Washington insider newsletter *Roll Call*.) But, unlike the Federal Reserve Board, the largely ministerial duties of the Securities Exchange Commission do not really require heavyweight commissioners.

The SEC's principal responsibility is to insure full disclosure of information to the investing public on the part of corporations offering to sell stock to the public. It can investigate violations of securities laws, but it has only civil, not criminal, enforcement authority. (Any evidence of fraud that it discovers is forwarded to the Justice Department for further investigation and prosecution.) The SEC also insures customer accounts at investment firms against the failure (bankruptcy) of these firms. Of course, it does *not* cover investor losses from market declines.

THE SUPERRICH: DISTINGUISHING WEALTH FROM POWER

It is a mistake to equate *personal* wealth with economic power. Persons with relatively little personal wealth can exercise great power if they occupy positions
that give them control of huge institutional resources. A president of a large
corporation who came through the ranks of management may receive an
income of only $5 million or $10 million a year, and possess a net worth of
only $10 million or $20 million. Yet these amounts are relatively small when
you consider that this person may control a corporation with annual revenues
of $2 *billion* and assets worth $10 *billion* or $20 *billion*. (The contrast is even
greater in government, where $80,000-a-year bureaucrats manage govern-
ment expenditures of $50 *billion* a year!) The important point is that personal
wealth in America is insignificant in comparison to corporate and governmental wealth.

One must occupy top *positions* in large corporate *institutions* to exercise
significant economic power. The mere possession of personal wealth, even a
billion dollars, does not guarantee economic power. Indeed, among America's billionaires—individuals with personal wealth in excess of $1 *billion*—
there are people such as widows, retirees, and other inheritors who have never
played any role in the family business. There are also many "independent
operators" who have acquired great wealth in, say, independent oil operations
or land speculation, but who do not occupy high positions in the corporate
world. Of course, there are many billionaires whose personal wealth has come
to them through their personal ownership of corporate shares. Familiar
names—Ford, Rockefeller, du Pont, Mellon—are liberally sprinkled among
the nation's top personal wealth-holders. However, their personal wealth is a
byproduct of their role, or their ancestor's role, in the corporate structure.

Socialist critics of America often fail to comprehend the insignificance
of personal wealth in relation to corporate and governmental resources. They
direct their rhetoric against inequality in personal income in the nation, when
in fact the greatest inequities occur in the comparisons between corporate
and government resources and the resources of individuals.

The relationship between personal wealth and institutional power is
described well by economist Adolf A. Berle:

> As of now, in the United States and in Western Europe, the rich man has little
> power merely because he is rich. . . . {He} amounts to little unless he connects
> himself with effective institutions. He must master past institutions or must cre-
> ate new ones. . . . However large his bank account, he can do nothing with it but
> consume. He can build or buy palaces, amuse himself at Mediterranean or
> Caribbean resorts, become a figure in Monte Carlo, Miami, or Las Vegas. He can
> amuse himself by collecting books or purchasing bonds. He can give libraries or
> laboratories to universities and have his name put on them. He can receive the
> pleasant but powerless recognition of decorations, honorary degrees, and even
> titles of nobility. None of these things entitle him to make decisions affecting

TABLE 3–5   Total Wealth of the 400 Richest Americans

	1982	1988	1992	2000
Total net worth ($ billions)	$ 92	$220	$288	$1,200
Median net worth ($ millions)	$150	$375	$450	$1,450
Number of billionaires	13	51	71	274

Source: Derived from data in *Forbes*, www.forbes.com/lists.

other men or to give orders (outside his household) with any likelihood they will be fulfilled. . . .

So, if he wishes a power position, he must find it outside his bank account. He can, it is true, use the bank account to buy into, or possibly create, an institution. He can buy control of a small corporation. (Few rich men are left who are capable of buying individual control of really large ones.) He can undertake the management of that corporation. Then he can derive power from the institution—if, and only if, he is capable of handling it. Whatever power he has comes from the corporation or other institutions, and from such intellectual or organizing skill as he may have—not from his wealth, which is largely irrelevant.[2]

Even though personal wealth is not the equivalent of economic power, it is still interesting to observe the increasing concentration of wealth in America over the past several decades. *Income* inequality in general has grown: the income share of the top 5 percent of income recipients in the United States has grown from 14.4 percent in 1972 to 21 percent in 2000. Inequality of *wealth* is much greater and growing even faster. *Forbes* magazine regularly tracks the richest Americans—"the *Forbes* 400." In 1982 there were only 13 billionaires on the *Forbes* list; the total net worth of the entire list was only $92 billion dollars. In 2000 there were 274 billionaires, and the total net worth of the list was an astonishing $1.2 trillion (see Table 3–5).

A list of the richest Americans (see Table 3–6, pages 52–53) includes at least two categories—descendants of old and established families whose wealth is inherited from large corporate enterprises, and newly rich individuals whose wealth is derived from "independent" oil operations, real estate speculation, fast foods and discount merchandising, or more recently the aerospace and computer industries. In 1918, the first year for which a reasonable estimate of the nation's wealthiest Americans is available, virtually all of the names on the list were newly rich, having acquired great wealth within a single generation. These were the great entrepreneurs of America's Industrial Revolution—Rockefeller, Carnegie, Frick, Harkness, Ford, Vanderbilt, Morgan, and so on. Only a few of the wealthiest Americans in the early twentieth century were inheritors: for example, the Astors, whose original fortune

[2] Adolph A. Berle, *Power* (New York: Harcourt Brace Jovanovich, 1967), p. 92.

was made in the North American fur trade; and the du Ponts, who manufactured gunpowder in Delaware even before the Revolutionary War. However, by mid-century, the great families of the Industrial Revolution had become the nation's established wealth-holders. Their wealth was tied to the large corporations and banks which their ancestors had founded.

It is widely believed that great personal wealth in America today is inherited and that opportunities to acquire great personal fortunes dried up after the Industrial Revolution. C. Wright Mills wrote that "Wealth not only tends to perpetuate itself, but . . . tends also to monopolize new opportunities for getting great wealth. . . . In none of the latest three generations has a majority of the very rich been composed of men who have risen."[3] But Mills and other Marxist critics of American society are *wrong!* All of the available evidence points to considerable social mobility among the wealthiest Americans.

Today most of America's top wealth-holders are self-made single-generation tycoons. On the lists of billionaires and centimillionaires, the names of self-made men and women outnumber heirs to family fortunes, and first- and second-generation immigrants abound. Moreover, in every successive list of top wealth-holders over the decades there are as many dropouts and newcomers as holdovers. It is true that America's great nineteenth-century industrial fortunes have held together remarkably well, despite inheritance taxes and family dispersions.[4] But in each generation, America produces a new crop of superrich entrepreneurs.

Representative of the newly rich in 1968 were the seven wealthiest Americans—J. Paul Getty and H.L. Hunt, whose fabulous fortunes were amassed in independent oil operations; Howard Hughes, whose fortune was made in the aerospace industry, as well as David Packard and William Hewlett; Edward H. Land, an inventor whose self-developing camera was the foundation of the Polaroid Corporation; and Daniel K. Ludwig, who wisely purchased war-surplus oil tankers in anticipation of U.S. dependence on foreign oil.

By 1987 additional new names on the roster of the superrich emerged from the burgeoning computer industry—William Gates, the "boy wonder" billionaire who dropped out of Harvard to found Microsoft; and Ross Perot, who founded his own software company, Electronic Data Systems. Other newly rich included the Bechtels, whose giant construction firm is the world's largest privately owned enterprise; Ray Kroc, who founded McDonald's; Forest Mars, the original creator of the Milky Way bar and other candies; the Bass brothers, independent oil operators; and Sam Walton, who opened his first Wal-Mart Store in rural Arkansas in 1962.

By 2000, the list of the wealthiest Americans was dominated by newly rich entrepreneurs from the computer world—William Gates and his partners from Microsoft, and the founders of Oracle, Intel, Qwest, Dell, Hewlett-

---

[3] C. Wright Mills, *The Power Elite* (New York: Oxford University Press, 1956), p. 105.
[4] See Michael Patrick Allen, *The Founding Fortunes* (New York: Dutton, 1987).

TABLE 3–6 America's Superrich

1918 "Wealthiest Americans"	1968 "Centimillionaires"	1987 "Billionaires"	2000 "50 Wealthiest Americans"
J.D. Rockefeller (oil)	J.P. Getty (oil)	S.M. Walton (retail)	William H. Gates (computers—Microsoft)
H.C. Frick (coke, steel)	H. Hughes (aerospace)	J.W. Kluge (communications)	Joseph Ellison (computers—Oracle)
A. Carnegie (steel)	H.L. Hunt (oil)	H. Ross Perot (computers)	Paul Allen (computers—Microsoft)
G.W. Baker (banking)	E.H. Land (Polaroid)	D. Packard (aerospace)	Warren Buffet (investments—Berkshire Hathaway)
W. Rockefeller (oil, RRs)	D.K. Ludwig (shipping)	S.I. Newhouse, Jr. (publishing)	Gordon Moore (computers—Intel)
E.S. Harkness (oil)	Alisa M. Bruce (Mellon)	D.E. Newhouse (publishing)	Philip Anschutz (computers—Qwest)
J.O. Armour (meat packing)	P. Mellon (Mellon)	Lester Crown (defense)	Stephen Ballmer (computers—Microsoft)
H. Ford (cars)	R.K. Mellon (Mellon)	K.R. Murdoch (publishing)	Alice Walton (retail stores—Wal-Mart)
W.K. Vanderbilt (RRs)	N.B. Hunt (oil)	W.E. Buffet (stock market)	Helen Walton (retail stores—Wal-Mart)
Ed. H.R. Green (banking)	J.D. McArthur (insurance)	L.H. Wexner (retail)	Jim Walton (retail stores—Wal-Mart)
Mrs. E.H. Harriman (RRs)	W.L. McKnight (3M)	J.A. Pritzker (real estate)	John Walton (retail stores—Wal-Mart)
V. Astor (real estate)	C.S. Mott (GM)	R.A. Pritzker (real estate)	Robson Walton (retail stores—Wal-Mart)
J. Stillman (banking)	R.E. Smith (oil)	E.M. Bronfman (liquors)	Michael Dell (computers—Dell)
T.F. Ryan (transit, tobacco)	H.F. Ahmanson (banking)	Barbara C. Anthony (inherited)	Sumner Redstone (media—Viacom)
D. Guggenheim (mining)	C. Allen, Jr. (banking)	Ann C. Chambers (publishing)	John Kluge (media—Metromedia)
C.M. Schwab (steel)	Mrs. W.V. Clark, Sr. (Avon)	Ted Arison (cruises)	Charles Ergen (media—satellites)
J.P. Morgan (banking)	J.T. Dorrance, Jr. (soup)	A.A. Taubman	Rupert Murdock (publishing)
Mrs. R. Sage (banking)	Mrs. A.I. du Pont (Du Pont)	H.L. Hillman (inherited)	Barbara Cox Anthony (publishing)
C.H. McCormick (farm machinery)	C.W. Englehard, Jr. (mining)	M.H. Davis (oil)	Ann Cox Chambers (publishing)
J. Widener (transit)	S.M. Fairchild (cameras)	W.R. Hewlett (aerospace)	Abigail Johnson (insurance—Fidelity)
A.C. James (mining, RRs)	L. Hess (oil)	Harry Helmsley (hotels)	Henry Nicholas (communications—Broadcom)
Nicholas F. Brady (transit)	W.R. Hewlett (aerospace)	P.F. Anschutz	Henry Samueli (communications—Broadcom)
J.H. Schiff (banking)	D. Packard (aerospace)	Anheuser Busch, Jr. (beer)	Charles Schwab (investments—Charles Schwab)
J.B. Duke (tobacco)	A. Houghton (Corning Glass)	J.T. Dorrance, Jr. (soup)	Robert "Ted" Turner (media—Turner Communications)

G. Eastman (cameras)	J.P. Kennedy (investments)	M.J. Petrie (retail)	William Hewlett (computers—Hewlett-Packard)
P.S. du Pont (gunpowder)	Eli Lilly (drugs)	E.M. Kauffman (drugs)	Theodore Waitt (computers—Gateway)
L.F. Swift (meat packing)	F.E. Mars (candy)	Ray Lee Hunt (oil)	David R. Huber (fiber optics)
J. Rosenwald (mail orders)	S.E. Newhouse (newspapers)	E.J. DeBartolo (real estate)	James Goodnight (computers)
Mrs. L. Lewis (oil)	Marjorie M. Post (foods)	W.H. Gates, III (computers)	Kirk Kerkorian (casinos, investments)
H. Phipps (steel)	Mrs. J. Mauze (Rockefeller)	D.L. Bren (real estate)	Craig McCaw (telephones)
	D. Rockefeller	S.J. LeFrak (real estate)	Forrest Mars (candy)
	J.D. Rockefeller	R.M. Bass (oil)	John Mars (candy)
	L. Rockefeller	E.L. Gaylord	Daniel Smith (fiber optics)
	N. Rockefeller	F.E. Mars, Sr. (candy)	David Filo (computers—Yahoo)
	W. Rockefeller	F.E. Mars, Jr. (candy)	Thomas Siebel (systems)
	Cordelia S. May (Mellon)	J.F. Mars (candy)	Jerry Yang (computers—Yahoo)
	R.M. Scaife (Mellon)	J.M. Vogel	John Morgridge (computers—Cisco)
	D. Wallace (Reader's Digest)	H.C. Simmons (investments)	Robert Pritzker (investments)
	Mrs. C. Payson (Whitney)	Sol Goldman	Thomas Pritzker (investments)
	J.H. Whitney	Margaret H. Hill (Hunt oil)	Eli Broad (real estate)
		Sid R. Bass (oil)	Donald Newhouse (publishing)
		Lee M. Bass (oil)	George Soros (investments)
		L.A. Tisch (theaters, CBS)	Lee Bass (oil)
		P.R. Tisch (theaters, CBS)	Jeffrey Bezos (computers—Amazon)
		David Rockefeller	John Simplot (potatoes)
		L.N. Stern	Alfred Lerner (banking)
		C.H. Lindner, II	Pierre Omidyar (computers—eBay)
		Roger Milliken	Edgar Bronfman (Seagram)
		Joan B. Kroc (McDonald's)	Sid Bass (oil)
			Philip Knight (sportswear—Nike)

Lists ranked in order of estimated wealth.

Sources: 1918—*Forbes Magazine,* March 2, 1918, reprinted in *Forbes Magazine,* Fall 1983; 1968—*Fortune,* May 1968; 1987—*Forbes Magazine,* October, 1987; 2000—*Forbes* People list, 2001, at www.Forbes.com.

Packard, Gateway, Yahoo, Cisco, and eBay. (Their wealth was exaggerated by the spectacular run-up of technology stock prices in the late 1990s; it remains to be seen whether all of them will remain among the wealthiest Americans in future years.) Among the inheritors on the list now are the Walton, Cox, Mars, and Bass families. But even these families are relative newcomers, having acquired their wealth in the second half of the twentieth century.

America's wealthy are wealthier than ever. In 1968 it required only $100 million ("centimillionaire" status) to be listed among the nation's wealthiest. By 1987 it required $1 billion; indeed, *all* of the nation's "billionaires" are listed for that year in Table 3–6. But in 2000, *Forbes* lists over one hundred billionaires. To make the top 50 on the list on Table 3–6, a person had to possess a net wealth of nearly $5 billion. (William Gates' fortune is estimated to be $68 billion.) Ross Perot, the Koch family, the Bechtel family, and Hollywood's David Geffen, all with only $3 to $4 billion, did not make the top 50 list.

SUMMARY

America's financial assets are heavily concentrated in the nation's largest banks, insurance companies, and investment firms. Indeed, just 25 banks, out of more than 12,000 serving the nation, control over half of all banking assets in the United States.

The concentration of financial assets in America will likely accelerate as result of "banking reform"—the Financial Services Modernization Act of 1999. This Act allows megamergers of banks, bank holding companies, insurance companies, and investment firms. The financial giant Citigroup may be a forerunner of future concentrations of money and power.

Control of the nation's money supply is vested in the Federal Reserve System—the Fed—and its powerful Board of Governors. This central banking system functions independently of Congress or the president. It determines interest rates, regulates financial activity, and provides various services to banks throughout the nation. Fed governance is largely in the hands of bankers themselves. The Securities and Exchange Commission plays a lesser role in the nation's financial affairs, principally ensuring full disclosure of information to the investing public on the part of corporations offering to sell stock.

Personal wealth does not necessarily guarantee economic power. Personal wealth must be institutionalized in order for the wealthy to exercise real power in America. The nation's top wealth-holders include both old and established families whose wealth has been passed down through generations and newly rich individuals whose wealth is derived from expanding new enterprises. Indeed, there are as many newly rich people among America's top wealth-holders as there are inheritors.

4

The Governing Circles

Govn not limited

If there ever was a time when the powers of government were limited—when government did no more than secure law and order, protect individual liberty and property, enforce contracts, and defend against foreign invasion—that time has long passed. Today it is commonplace to observe that governmental institutions intervene in every aspect of our lives—from the "cradle to the grave." Government in America has the primary responsibility for providing insurance against old age, death, dependency, disability, and unemployment; for organizing the nation's health-care system; for providing education at the elementary, secondary, collegiate, and postgraduate levels; for providing public highways and regulating water, rail, and air transportation; for providing police and fire protection; for providing sanitation services and sewage disposal; for financing research in medicine, science, and technology; for delivering the mail; for exploring outer space; for maintaining parks and recreation; for providing housing and adequate food for the poor; for providing job training and manpower programs; for cleaning the air and water; for rebuilding central cities; for maintaining full employment and a stable money supply; for regulating business practices and labor relations; for eliminating racial and sexual discrimination. Indeed, the list of government responsibilities seems endless, yet each year we manage to find additional tasks for government to do.

THE CONCENTRATION OF GOVERNMENTAL POWER

Government in the United States grew enormously throughout most of the twentieth century, both in absolute terms and in relation to the size of the national economy. The size of the economy is usually measured by the gross domestic product (GDP), the dollar sum of all the goods and services produced in the United States in a year. Governments accounted for only about 8 percent of the GDP at the beginning of the century, and most governmental activities were carried out by state and local governments. Two world wars, the New Deal programs devised during the Great Depression of the 1930s, and the growth of the Great Society programs of the 1960s and 1970s all greatly expanded the size of government, particularly the federal government. The rise in government growth relative to the economy leveled off during the Reagan presidency (1981–89), and no large new programs were undertaken in the Bush and Clinton years. An economic boom in the 1990s caused the GDP to grow rapidly, while government spending grew only moderately. The result was a modest *decline* in governmental size in relation to the economy. Today, federal expenditures amount to about 20 percent of GDP, and total governmental expenditures are about 30 percent of GDP (see Figure 4–1).

FIGURE 4–1   The Growth of Government

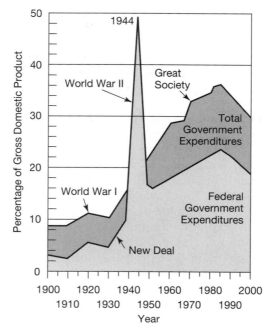

Source: Budget of the United States Government, 2000.

Not everything that government does is reflected in governmental expenditures. *Regulatory activity,* for example, especially environmental regulations, imposes significant costs on individuals and businesses; these costs are not shown in government budgets.

We have defined our governmental elite as the top executive, congressional, and judicial officers of the *federal* government; the President and Vice-President; secretaries, undersecretaries, and assistant secretaries of executive departments; senior White House presidential advisers; congressional committee chairpersons and ranking minority members; congressional majority and minority party leaders in the House and Senate; Supreme Court Justices; and members of the Federal Reserve Board and the Council of Economic Advisers. And we add to this definition of political elites the "fat cat" contributors who keep them in power.

THE FAT CAT CONTRIBUTORS

More money was spent on political campaigning in 2000 than in any election year in American history. An estimated $3 *billion* was spent by all presidential and congressional candidates, Democratic and Republican parties, political action committees sponsored by interest groups, and independent political organizations in federal, state, and local elections combined. The costs of elections rises in each election cycle (see Figure 4–2). The largest increases in campaign finance came not from regulated "hard money" contributions to candidates, but rather from large unregulated "soft money" contributions to the parties.

FIGURE 4–2 Campaign Fund Raising, President and Congress

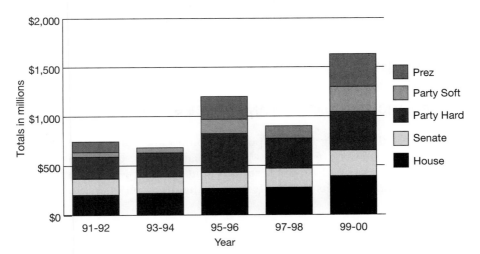

Virtually all of the top "fat cat" campaign contributors from the *corporate, banking, and investment* worlds have been previously listed among the nation's largest corporate (Chapter 2) and monied (Chapter 3) institutions. AT&T, Philip Morris, Citigroup, and Goldman Sachs regularly appear each election cycle among contributors of $2 to $3 million or more (see Table 4–1). One notable newcomer among top corporate "fat cat" contributors in 2000 is Bill Gates's Microsoft Corporation. In the past, Gates tried to avoid politics altogether; Microsoft was notably absent from previous lists of top campaign contributors. But Gates learned a hard lesson when Clinton's Justice Department under Attorney General Janet Reno launched its costly antitrust suit against Microsoft. (See "The New Tycoons" in Chapter 7.)

While contributions from the corporate, banking, and investment institutions are usually divided between the parties (albeit weighted toward Republicans), contributions from *unions* are almost exclusively directed toward Democrats. Indeed, union contributions are the single largest source of campaign money for the Democratic Party, followed by contributions from Hollywood's entertainment industry.

Contributions from wealthy individuals failed to match institutional contributions. While more than 100 institutions contributed $1 million or more in 2000, only two individuals contributed over this amount. (Peter Buttenwieser of Buttenwieser & Associates of Philadelphia and S. Daniel Abraham of Slim-Fast Foods both contributed over $1 million to Democrats.)

Expenditures for congressional campaigns also reached a new high. The U.S. Senate race in New York, featuring former First Lady Hillary Clinton against relative newcomer Republican Rick Lazio, set a new combined spending record for congressional elections at more than $85 million. A new individual congressional spending record of $65 million was set by multibillionaire investment banker (Goldman Sacks) Democrat Jon Corzine, who dug into his own fortune to win a U.S. Senate seat from New Jersey.

The *average* candidate for a U.S. Senate seat raised and spent over $5 million. And the *average* candidate for a U.S. House seat raised and spent about $800,000. This means that the average incumbent member of Congress must raise about $8,000 *per week*, every week of their term in office.

THE POLITICIANS: AMBITION AND OFFICE SEEKING

Ambition is the driving force in politics. Politics attracts people for whom power and celebrity are more rewarding than money, leisure, or privacy. "Political office today flows to those who want it enough to spend the time and energy mastering its pursuit. It flows in the direction of ambition—and talent."[1]

---

[1] Alan Ehrenhalt, *The United States of Ambition: Politicians' Power and Pursuit of Office* (New York: Random House, 1991), p. 22.

TABLE 4–1   Fat Cat Campaign Contributors, 2000

Rank	Contributor	Total Contributions	To Dems.	To Repubs.
1	American Fedn. of St./Cnty./Munic. Employees	$6,935,989	98%	2%
2	Service Employees International Union	$4,961,010	95%	5%
3	AT&T	$4,667,844	38%	61%
4	Microsoft Corp	$4,309,856	46%	54%
5	Communications Workers of America	$3,871,185	99%	0%
6	National Assn. of Realtors	$3,834,600	41%	59%
7	Goldman Sachs Group	$3,646,382	68%	32%
8	United Food & Commercial Workers Union	$3,578,452	99%	1%
9	Intl. Brotherhood of Electrical Workers	$3,561,860	97%	3%
10	Citigroup Inc.	$3,559,566	53%	47%
11	Philip Morris	$3,460,200	18%	81%
12	SBC Communications	$3,418,466	46%	54%
13	Verizon Communications	$3,357,420	36%	64%
14	Carpenters & Joiners Union	$3,183,383	92%	8%
15	United Parcel Service	$3,133,119	26%	73%
16	American Federation of Teachers	$3,110,055	99%	1%
17	Assn. of Trial Lawyers of America	$3,030,750	88%	12%
18	Laborers Union	$2,929,275	93%	7%
19	National Rifle Assn.	$2,885,377	8%	92%
20	MBNA America Bank	$2,733,000	17%	83%
21	National Education Assn.	$2,584,478	92%	7%
22	Sheet Metal Workers Union	$2,551,584	99%	1%
23	Machinists/Aerospace Workers Union	$2,546,138	99%	1%
24	Teamsters Union	$2,517,240	93%	7%
25	Ernst & Young	$2,497,761	42%	58%
26	National Auto Dealers Assn.	$2,410,200	32%	68%
27	Federal Express Corp.	$2,388,428	34%	66%
28	Enron Corp.	$2,365,458	28%	72%
29	National Assn. of Home Builders	$2,336,799	37%	63%
30	Lockheed Martin	$2,333,794	39%	61%
31	Emily's List	$2,328,840	100%	0%
32	Credit Suisse First Boston	$2,325,705	29%	70%
33	Bristol-Myers Squibb	$2,300,792	14%	86%
34	United Auto Workers	$2,248,755	99%	0%
35	Morgan Stanley, Dean Witter & Co.	$2,225,823	39%	60%
36	BellSouth Corp.	$2,219,752	41%	59%
37	Freddie Mac	$2,198,839	48%	52%
38	AFL-CIO	$2,173,638	96%	4%
39	Global Crossing	$2,142,386	50%	50%
40	Pfizer Inc.	$2,136,647	14%	86%
41	Blue Cross/Blue Shield	$2,125,552	27%	73%
42	American Medical Assn.	$2,077,644	47%	52%
43	National beer Wholesalers Assn.	$2,059,061	19%	80%
44	Bank of America	$1,889,318	59%	40%
45	Time Warner	$1,860,237	73%	27%
46	National Assn. of Letter Carriers	$1,830,700	86%	13%
47	Union Pacific Corp	$1,805,144	16%	84%
48	General Electric	$1,793,879	39%	61%
49	Joseph E Seagram & Sons	$1,791,060	62%	38%
50	Andersen Worldwide	$1,781,412	29%	70%

continued

TABLE 4–1 continued

Rank	Contributor	Total Contributions	To Dems.	To Repubs.
51	Marine Engineers Union	$1,776,082	60%	40%
52	Deloitte & Touche	$1,761,826	29%	71%
53	American Online	$1,724,286	50%	50%
54	AFLAC Inc.	$1,716,010	45%	55%
55	Merrill lynch	$1,713,377	34%	65%
56	American Bankers Assn.	$1,677,707	35%	65%
57	Pricewaterhouse Coopers	$1,677,281	26%	74%
58	Anheuser-Busch	$1,656,525	49%	51%
59	Credit Union National Assn.	$1,649,439	47%	53%
60	Boeing Co.	$1,624,958	43%	57%
61	WorldCom Inc.	$1,607,681	32%	68%
62	American Hospital Assn.	$1,601,769	50%	49%
63	Prudential Insurance	$1,576,150	45%	54%
64	Fannie Mae	$1,558,357	54%	46%
65	Walt Disney Co.	$1,547,189	59%	41%
66	Eli Lilly & Co.	$1,539,285	19%	81%
67	Plumbers/Pipefitters Union	$1,520,107	96%	3%
68	International Assn. of Fire Fighters	$1,516,150	86%	14%
69	Lehman Brothers	$1,512,700	30%	70%
70	Painters & Allied Trades Union	$1,502,650	99%	1%
71	American International Group	$1,491,662	47%	53%
72	Williams & Bailey	$1,468,300	100%	0%
73	Glaxo Wellcome Inc.	$1,461,758	12%	88%
74	UST Inc.	$1,456,096	10%	89%
75	American Financial Group	$1,442,105	33%	67%
76	Slim-Fast Foods	$1,435,700	99%	1%
77	United Transportation Union	$1,430,800	86%	14%
78	Paine Webber	$1,418,900	33%	67%
79	Loral Spacecom	$1,386,150	98%	2%
80	Mirage REsorts	$1,377,656	44%	56%
81	Exxon Mobil Corp.	$1,373,310	10%	89%
82	American Airlines	$1,373,047	37%	62%
83	Ironworkers Union	$1,351,915	91%	8%
84	American Dental Assn.	$1,341,617	45%	55%
85	BP Amoco Corp.	$1,341,264	30%	70%
86	Southern Co.	$1,318,925	27%	73%
87	Saban Entertainment	$1,318,400	100%	0%
88	United Steelworkers	$1,285,050	98%	1%
89	US West Inc.	$1,277,295	34%	66%
90	Bank One Corp.	$1,249,158	34%	66%
91	Northwest Airlines	$1,243,055	48%	51%
92	Chase Manhattan	$1,239,519	47%	52%
93	KPMG LLP	$1,211,464	30%	70%
94	Schering-Plough Corp.	$1,192,576	24%	76%
95	Buttenwieser & Assoc.	$1,186,500	100%	0%
96	Verner, Liipfert et al.	$1,185,289	56%	43%
97	General Dynamics	$1,184,705	40%	60%
98	Angelos Law Office/Baltimore Orioles	$1,168,440	100%	0%
99	Limited Inc.	$1,140,719	34%	66%
100	National Assn. of Convenience Stores	$1,135,334	13%	87%

Source: Based on data released by the FEC, January 2, 2001.

Political ambition is the most distinguishing characteristic of elected officeholders. The people who run for and win public office are not necessarily the most intelligent, best informed, wealthiest, or most successful business or professional people. At all levels of the political system, from presidential candidates, members of Congress, governors and state legislators, to city councils and school board members, it is the most politically ambitious people who are willing to sacrifice time, family and private life, and energy and effort for the power and celebrity that comes with public office.

Politics is becoming increasingly professionalized. "Citizen-statesmen"—people with business or professional careers who get into politics part-time or for short periods of time—are being driven out of political life by career politicians—people who enter politics early in life as a full-time occupation and expect to make it their career. Politically ambitious young people seek out internships and staff positions with members of Congress, with congressional committees, in state legislators' or governors' offices, or mayors' or council chambers. Others volunteer to work in political campaigns. Many find political mentors, as they learn how to organize campaigns, contact financial contributors, and deal with the media. By their early thirties, they are ready to run for local office or the state legislature. Rather than challenge a strong incumbent, they may wait for an open seat to be created by retirement, reapportionment, or its holder seeking another office. Or they may make an initial attempt against a strong incumbent of the opposition party in order to gain experience and win the appreciation of their own party's supporters for a good effort. Over time, running for and holding elective office becomes their career. They work harder at it than anyone else, in part because they have no real private sector career to return to in case of defeat.

The prevalence of lawyers in politics is an American tradition. Among the nation's Founders—the fifty-five delegates to the Constitutional Convention in 1787—some twenty-five were lawyers. The political dominance of lawyers is even greater today, with lawyers filling nearly two thirds of U.S. Senate seats and nearly half of the seats in the U.S. House of Representatives.

It is sometimes argued that lawyers dominate in politics because of the parallel skills required in law and politics. Lawyering is the representation of clients; a lawyer employs similar skills whether representing clients in private practice or representing constituents in Congress. Lawyers are trained to deal with statutory law, so they may at least know how to find United States Code (the codified laws of the United States government) in a law library when they arrive in Congress to make or amend these laws.

But it is more likely that the people attracted to politics decide to go to law school, fully aware of the tradition of lawyers in American politics. Moreover, political officeholding, at the state and local level as well as in the national government, can help a struggling lawyer's private practice through free public advertising and opportunities to make contacts with potential clients. Finally, there are many special opportunities for lawyers to acquire public office in "lawyers only" posts in federal, state, and local government as judges and prosecuting attorneys. The lawyer-politician is not usually a top professional lawyer. (We will examine the "superlawyers"—the nation's legal elite—in Chapter 6). Instead, the typical lawyer-politician uses his or her law career as a means of support—one that is compatible with political office seeking and officeholding.

A significant number of top politicians have inherited great wealth. The Roosevelts, Rockefellers, Kennedys, Bushes, and others have used their wealth and family connections to support their political careers. However, it is important to note that *a majority of the nation's top politicians have climbed the ladder from relative obscurity to political success.* Many have acquired some wealth in the process, but most political leaders started their climb from very middle-class circumstances. Thus, as in the corporate world, we find more "climbers" than "inheritors" at the top in the world of politics.

BILL CLINTON: THE POLITICAL CLIMBER

Born Billy Blythe in rural Hope, Arkansas, three months after his father's death in an automobile accident, Bill Clinton learned that persistence and tenacity were the keys to success and acclaim. His strength was always his ability to mold himself into what others expected him to be.

Young Bill held so many class offices in high school that the principal told him he wasn't allowed to take on any more. He assumed his stepfather's name at age fifteen, even though he would later talk about the older man's alcoholism and abuse. He won first place in the state band's saxophone section, but his sights were set on politics, not music. As a delegate to Boys' Nation, he won a handshake from President John F. Kennedy in 1963. He chose to study international relations at private, prestigious Georgetown University in Washington. No sooner had Clinton arrived at the capital, he called on his state's U.S. senator, William J. Fulbright, chairman of the Senate Foreign Relations Committee, presenting his job recommendations from hometown politicians. Fulbright took the young college student under his wing as a legislative aide. Clinton soon began reflecting his new mentor's opposition to the Vietnam War.

Fulbright himself had been a Rhodes scholar at Oxford, and when Clinton graduated with his international affairs degree from Georgetown, Fulbright recommended Clinton for the same honor. At Oxford Clinton never finished a degree, but he cultivated friendships that would later enhance his public career. In London he helped organize anti–Vietnam War demonstrations, even while he worried that his antiwar activities might someday come back to haunt his political ambitions. When he received a draft notice, he promptly enrolled in the ROTC program at the University of Arkansas, making himself temporarily ineligible for the draft. Later, draft calls were cut back as President Richard Nixon de-escalated the war and a lottery system was instituted. Clinton drew a high number making him unlikely to be drafted. Soon after, he wrote to the ROTC withdrawing his name, "Thank you for saving me from the draft. . . ," acknowledging that his real plans were to go to Yale Law School, which he entered in 1970. He met his future wife, Hillary Rodham, a classmate at Yale Law School, daughter of a wealthy Chicago family, and a graduate of Wellesley.

Upon graduation from Yale Law School, Clinton turned down offers to return to Washington as a congressional staff aide. He was anxious to launch his own political career, and he knew that the road to elective office ran through his home state. Within a year he was running for a seat in Congress. Trying to capitalize on the Watergate scandal, he challenged a veteran Republican congressman. With long 60s-style hair, a Yale and Oxford background, and liberal friends coming from Washington to help in the campaign, including Hillary Rodham, he could have lost by a wide margin in conservative Arkansas. But instead, he came within a few votes of defeating a strong incumbent, in part as a result of the Watergate scandal that swept many Democrats into Congress in 1974, and in part a result of his own tireless campaigning.

Clinton's strong showing in the congressional race won him political recognition statewide. When the state's elected attorney general decided to run for Congress in 1976, Clinton mounted a successful campaign to replace him. In 1978, when Governor David Pryor left office to run for the U.S. Senate, Clinton jumped into the open gubernatorial contest. His relatively easy victory (he won 60 percent of the vote in a five-man Democratic primary, and 63 percent of the vote in the general election) made him the nation's youngest governor at age thirty-two. Viewing himself as a vanguard of a new generation, he set about pushing a broad program of liberal reform for Arkansas, increasing taxes and expenditures. But as a Yale-educated Rhodes scholar, he created an image of an arrogant, isolated, crusading, liberal politician, out of touch with his more conservative Arkansas constituency. Clinton was defeated in his 1980 reelection bid by a conservative Republican banker.

Clinton's defeat "forever influenced the way he approached government and politics."[2] He proceeded to remold himself into a political moderate, calling for "workfare" to replace welfare, supporting the death penalty, and working to create a favorable business climate in Arkansas. He cut his hair and his wife began using her married name, so as not to offend social conservatives. He told his state's voters that he had been humbled by his earlier loss and he promised "to listen to the people." He was elected governor once again in 1982, winning 42 percent of the vote in a five-man Democratic primary and 54 percent against the Republican governor in the general election. He would go on to win two more two-year terms by more substantial margins.

By most accounts, Bill Clinton became a successful governor. He focused his energies on two areas—economic development and education. He raised

---

[2] *New York Times,* July 16, 1992, p. A14.

taxes for education and forced both students and teachers to take compe-
tency tests. He declared himself an environmentalist but granted concessions
to his state's giant chicken industry in the interest of the economy. His many
compromises and accommodations led to his "slick Willie" label by the
Arkansas Democrat Gazette.

   Michael Dukakis's disastrous defeat in 1988 reinforced Bill Clinton's
view that only a moderate Democrat could succeed in winning the presidency.
Just as he had shaped his image to better fit his Arkansas constituents, he
molded his national image as a "new" Democrat—concerned with economic
growth, favoring workfare over welfare, tough on crime, and willing to stand
up to traditional core Democratic interest groups—labor unions, minorities,
and government employees. He served for a while as chairman of the centrist
Democratic Leadership Conference (DLC), denounced by Jesse Jackson as
"Democrat for the Leisure Class." He used the DLC as a platform to promote
a winning Democratic presidential profile—a moderate, pro-business, pro-
investment Democrat capable of winning back the support of the white middle class. He espoused "neo-liberal" ideas about government's role in
promoting and "investing" in American industry, and he began winning constituents among Wall Street and business interests. He perfected his down-
home "aw shucks" Elvis-style mannerisms. He sought to control his
motor-mouth delivery of programmatic facts and figures. (In his long-winded
1988 Democratic convention speech, he had drawn cheers with the words "In
conclusion.") He honed his skills as an organizer and fund-raiser. He promised everything to everybody: "We can be pro-growth and pro-environment,
we can be pro-business and pro-labor, we can make government work again by
making it more aggressive and leaner and more effective at the same time,
and we can be pro-family and pro-choice."[3]

   Success in politics is often a product of good fortune. Few would have
predicted in 1991 that George Bush's all-time high presidential popularity
after the Gulf War would plummet with the onset of an economic recession.
Indeed, the real heavyweights in the Democratic party—Mario Cuomo, Bill
Bradley, Richard Gephardt, Lloyd Bentsen, Jesse Jackson—all decided early
not to try to challenge the popular incumbent President. But Bill Clinton had
little to lose; in fact, a good run at the presidency in 1992 might gain him
national prominence and a real chance to capture the office in 1996. Yet as
the recession lengthened into 1992 and Bush's popularity drastically declined,
Clinton's teenage dreams of becoming President took on real meaning.

   Early in the Democratic primaries, Bill Clinton almost lost the prize he
had sought for a lifetime when Genifer Flowers held a nationally televised
press conference to expose a long-term affair with the governor. Rumors of
marital infidelity had shadowed Clinton for many years. The same problem
had driven Gary Hart out of the presidential race in 1988. But a tenacious Bill

---

[3] *Time*, November 2, 1992, p. 33.

Clinton decided to confront the "bimbo" issue head-on early in the campaign. So when Don Hewitt, liberal producer of *60 Minutes*, offered Clinton a Sunday night prime-time interview just after the Superbowl, the candidate accepted. With Hillary at his side, Clinton told a huge nationwide audience that his marriage had survived shaky moments but it was rock solid now.

The Democratic convention was a celebration of Clinton's good fortune. When the temperamental Ross Perot unexpectedly withdrew from the race, millions of his disillusioned supporters were set adrift at precisely the moment that Clinton was broadcasting his message of change to national audiences. Perot's moderate, middle-class, independent supporters flocked to Clinton's banner. They had lost confidence in Bush's handling of the economy and were prepared to overlook Clinton's character flaws. The choice of Al Gore as running mate, a man of presidential stature in his own right, seemed to demonstrate Clinton's good judgment and self-confidence. It also balanced the ticket with a Vietnam War veteran and committed family man. By the end of the Democratic convention, Clinton had soared to a twenty-point lead in the polls.

The voter's anxieties about the economy determined the election outcome. While Clinton emerged only five percentage points ahead of Bush in the popular vote, the nation's desire for change was clearly evident in the combined votes for Clinton and Perot. Fully 62 percent of the voters chose to vote against their incumbent President. Clinton prevailed because he skillfully presented himself to the voters as an agent of change.

Clinton stumbled badly early in his first term. His first major battle—to retain homosexuals in the military—proved a disaster. Military chiefs, including the popular General Colin Powell, resisted, and Clinton was forced to retreat. He succeeded in getting the Democratic-controlled Congress to pass a large tax increase, raising the top marginal income tax rate from 31 to 39.6 percent. But in his second year, a massive national health-care program developed under Hillary's direction failed, and Clinton's approval ratings sagged. The sweeping Republican congressional victory in 1994 appeared to foreshadow a one-term presidency for Clinton. But characteristically he mounted another political "comeback." He vetoed several Republican balanced-budget plans, and when the government temporarily "shut down," Clinton shifted the blame to the Republican Congress. He cast himself as a defender of "Medicare, Medicaid, education, and the environment" against the mean-spirited Republican Speaker Newt Gingrich. Clinton's approval ratings began a long rise.

Clinton had relatively little difficulty in defeating the old Republican standard-bearer, Bob Dole, to win a second term in 1996. The economy was in a strong recovery, and voters showed little interest in the aging Dole's promises of tax reductions. Clinton again campaigned as a centrist. He modestly observed in his election-might victory speech: "Tonight we proclaim that the vital American center is alive and well." But even if he had sought to return to a liberal agenda, it is not likely that a Republican Congress would have allowed him to get very far. Critics of President Clinton describe his second term as "risk adverse," adrift, and even aimless. Yet the nation's booming economy in the 1990s kept Clinton's approval ratings high. It also provided a solution to what had been the nation's most vexing problem: continuing deficit spending. Robust economic growth increased federal tax revenues enough to produce a balanced federal budget, a goal that had eluded presidents and congresses for over a quarter-century.

Bill Clinton is the second president in the nation's history (following Andrew Johnson in 1867) to be impeached by the U.S. House of Representatives. (President Richard Nixon resigned just prior to an impeachment vote in 1974.) The 1998 House impeachment vote split along partisan lines (228 to 106, with all but five Republicans voting "yes" and all but five Democrats voting "no.") It followed a report to the House by Independent Counsel Kenneth Starr that recommended impeachment for perjury, obstruction of justice, witness tampering, and "abuse of power."

The Starr Report describes in graphic and lurid detail Clinton's sexual relationship with young White House intern Monica Lewinsky. It cites as impeachable offenses Clinton's lying about their relationship to his staff, friends, and the nation; his misleading testimony in a sworn statement in the earlier Paula Jones case; his conversations with close friend Vernon Jordan about finding Lewinsky a job; his attempts to impede Starr's investigation; and his evasive testimony before Starr's grand jury:

QUESTION: "I have a question regarding your definition [of sexual relations] then. And my question is, is oral sex performed on you within that definition . . . ?"

ANSWER: "As I understood it, it was not, no."

QUESTION: "Well, the grand jury would like to know, Mr. President, why it is you think that oral sex performed on you does not fall within the definition of sexual relations?"

ANSWER: "Because that is—if the deponent is the person who has oral sex performed on him, then the contact is with—not with anything on that list, but with the lips of another person."[4]

The American people apparently did not believe that Clinton's misconduct should result in his impeachment and removal from office:

QUESTION: Do you approve or disapprove of the House decision to vote in favor of impeaching Clinton and sending the case to the Senate for trial? Yes–35%   No–63%[5]

---

[4] Congressional *Quarterly Weekly Report*, Sept. 26, 1998, pp. 2607–2613.
[5] Gallup poll reported in *USA Today*, December 21, 1998.

On the contrary, Clinton's approval rating rose to an all-time high (68 percent) during the impeachment proceedings. The Senate "trial" on February 12, 1999, also divided along party lines. But removing Clinton from office failed to win even a majority of Senate votes, far less than the required two-thirds. All 45 Democrats were joined by 5 Republicans to create a 50–50 tie vote that left Clinton tarnished but still in office.

Clinton himself seems aware that he will never be ranked among the great presidents. "Greatness," he believes, is as much a product of the times as the man. Clinton faced no really great national or international challenges during his presidency; an opposition-controlled Congress limited his policy options; and good economic times dampened the public's enthusiasm for new government programs.[6]

It is not clear whether his policy centrism was pragmatic and skillful, or unprincipled and opportunistic. Perhaps he deserves praise for fiscal responsibility—initially raising taxes, presiding over economic growth with low inflation, and eventually presenting balanced federal budgets to the nation. On the other hand, perhaps his personal conduct contributed to the nation's cultural amoralism—its willingness to overlook character defects in its leadership as long as the good times roll on.

THE BUSH FAMILY DYNASTY

The Bushes are inheritors in politics. President George W. Bush's grandfather, U.S. Senator Prescott Bush, was the managing partner in the once great Wall Street investment firm of Brown Brothers, Harriman & Co., as well as chairman of the board of Yale Corporation, which governs Yale University, and Republican U.S. senator from Connecticut from 1962 to 1972. George Herbert Walker Bush was born in 1924 and spent his boyhood in upper-class Greenwich, Connecticut. He attended the Greenwich Country Day School before entering Phillips Academy in Andover, Massachusetts, where he was captain of the soccer team and president of his senior class.

"Poppy"

At age seventeen, in the dark days of World War II, George Bush set aside his admission to Yale in order to join the Navy. His worried father asked President Roosevelt to ignore the age requirements and allow George to be commissioned as an ensign. As the youngest pilot in the U.S. Navy, Bush was assigned to the light aircraft carrier U.S.S. *San Jacinto* in 1943. He flew fifty-eight combat missions. He was awarded the Distinguished Flying Cross and three Air

---

[6] See Bert A. Rockman, "Cutting with the Grain: Is There a Clinton Leadership Legacy?" in Colin Campbell and Bert A. Rockman, eds., *The Clinton Legacy* (New York: Chatham House, 2000), p. 288.

Medals for action in the Pacific. His torpedo bomber was shot down, his two crewmen were killed, and he was rescued at sea by a submarine. He returned home on leave to marry Barbara Pierce, daughter of the publisher of *Redbook* and *McCall's* magazines.

George Bush entered Yale in September of 1945. He captained the baseball team and graduated in three years, Phi Beta Kappa in economics. His father wanted him to join his investment banking firm in New York, but at twenty-five George wanted to strike out on his own. "On his own" turned out to be a job as vice-president of Dresser Industries, a Texas oil-drilling equipment firm of which his father was a director. George Bush quickly became very successful in the Texas oil business. He formed several oil companies with financing from his uncle, Herbert Walker: Bush-Overby, Zapata Petroleum, and Zapata Offshore Oil. He served as a director of the First International Bank of Houston and London as well as of Eli Lilly, Texas Gulf, and Purolator. By the early 1960s Bush was a multimillionaire Texas oilman still in his thirties. Having conquered the world of business, he turned to politics.

Bush did not have the same easy success in politics that he enjoyed in business. In 1964 he plunged into a campaign to unseat Ralph Yarborough, U.S. senator from Texas and ally of President Lyndon Johnson. Bush fell victim to the Johnson landslide in that year but captured a larger share of the vote than any previous Republican candidate in Texas. In 1966, Bush returned to the political fray to win election to Congress from a wealthy suburban Houston district. After serving two terms in the House, he set out again in 1970 to defeat Ralph Yarborough and win a Senate seat. But Yarborough was upset in the Democratic primary by another wealthy oilman, conservative Democrat Lloyd Bentsen. The Bush-Bentsen race was hard fought and expensive for both sides; Bush was edged out in a very close election.

President Richard Nixon named George Bush to the post of United Nations ambassador in 1970, where he served for two years. Following Nixon's reelection, the President named Bush as chairman of the Republican National Committee, a job which became very difficult as the Watergate scandal mushroomed. But most of the Watergate evils occurred under the Committee to Reelect the President (CREEP—an organization which was separate from the Republican National Committee), and George Bush was successful in keeping the regular Republican organization free of scandal and his own name untarnished. A grateful President Gerald Ford asked Bush to pick his own post in the new administration, and Bush chose the newly created ambassadorship to the People's Republic of China. In 1975 President Ford asked him to return from China to head the Central Intelligence Agency.

George Bush inherited the support of the Eastern Establishment wing of the Republican party. These internationalist Wall Street Republicans had formed the foundation of Eisenhower's administration and had been led for many years thereafter by Nelson Rockefeller. Following Gerald Ford's defeat at the hands of Jimmy Carter, Bush began his own bid for the presidency. He hoped to combine his Eastern Establishment support with his Texas oil friends, thus bringing together the new wealth of the Sunbelt and the old wealth of the East. He recruited his friend, Houston attorney James A. Baker, Ford's campaign manager, as his own and conducted a vigorous nationwide campaign. But Ronald Reagan had spent years building his political base among the southern and western Sunbelt Republicans. Following a New Hampshire debate in which Bush looked stiff and inflexible and Reagan relaxed and amiable, Bush narrowly lost the 1980 New Hampshire presidential primary. Although Bush went on to win primaries in Massachusetts, Connecticut, and Pennsylvania, he was "stunned" again by Reagan's victory in Bush's home state of Texas. Despite his many years in Texas, George Bush was unable to escape his Eastern preppy background to win the hearts of Texans. At the Republican National Convention, Ronald Reagan turned to George Bush as his vice-presidential running mate to balance the Reagan ticket with his foreign policy experience and appeal to Republican moderates.

George Bush was a supremely loyal Vice-President. He steadfastly refused to differ with his President—even when he was being skewered by the media for the Iranian arms-for-hostages dealings. Indeed, George Bush was portrayed as a terminal second banana with no principles or passions of his own, forever to be overshadowed by Ronald Reagan. *Newsweek* magazine even devoted its cover to branding Bush as a "wimp."[7]

But George Bush's loyalty to his President paid off handsomely. Ronald Reagan recovered his popularity in his final year. Eight years of peace and prosperity were rewarded at the polls. Bush was perceived as the legitimate heir to the Reagan legacy, both in the primary elections where he swept away his Republican challengers, and in the general election where Michael Dukakis failed to convince Americans that their well-being was a temporary illusion.

George Bush's presidential performance was schizophrenic—strength, perseverance, and victory in foreign and military affairs, and weakness, vacillation, and defeat on domestic matters. He became President at a turning point in world history—the collapse of communism in Eastern Europe, the end of the Soviet-led Warsaw Pact anti-Western military alliance, and the disintegration of the Soviet Union itself. He was given the opportunity to declare Western victory in the decades-long Cold War and to lay the foundation for a "new world order" in which the United States occupied the predominant global position. His finest hour was his resolute performance in the Persian Gulf. He assembled a worldwide political coalition, including the Soviet Union, China, and Western and Arab nations, against Saddam Hussein's invasion and occupation of Kuwait. He wisely left the strategic planning and implementation of military operations to a highly capable team—Defense Secretary Richard Cheney, Joint Chiefs of Staff Chairman Colin Powell, and

---

[7] *Newsweek*, October 19, 1987.

field commander General Norman Schwarzkopf. He avoided the mistakes of Vietnam—gradual escalation of force, prolonged operations, accumulating casualties, muddled negotiations, moratoriums of bombings, political interference in military operations. He sought a rapid, decisive military victory with the use of overwhelming force. He resisted efforts to stall the attack or engage in endless negotiations or allow intermediaries to compromise the outcome. He sought to limit casualties among Americans and coalition forces and perhaps ended the war too soon. But his overall performance as Commander-in-Chief earned him the highest public approval rating ever attained by an American President.

By contrast, in the domestic policy arena, George Bush was a failure. He lacked his predecessor Ronald Reagan's ideological commitments. He was never able to use his Gulf War popularity to seize the initiative in domestic affairs. He offered few domestic policy ideas to Congress. On key issues he collapsed in the face of congressional pressure. He campaigned on as firm a promise as any candidate could make on taxes: "Read my lips! No new taxes!" Yet in his second year in office he agreed to support an increase in income-tax rates. He took a strong rhetorical stand against "quotas" in civil rights legislation, yet later signed a bill almost identical to an earlier one he had vetoed. And when recession struck the nation's economy, he responded with too little too late, leaving the impression that he was "out of touch" with the concerns of the American people.

Bush's public approval ratings plummeted throughout the spring of 1992. Although the economy began a slow recovery, the media focused on the nation's economic ills. Ross Perot detached millions of middle-class voters from Bush by turning the spotlight on the government's huge deficits. Democrat Bill Clinton dodged attacks on his own character and captured the image of change. Bush's reelection campaign was in shambles; James Baker left his post as secretary of state to try to rescue his old friend. But Bush turned in a lackluster performance in the first two presidential debates, and a final mini-surge in his campaign fell short. The nation clearly wanted change as 62 percent of the voters chose either Clinton or Perot over Bush. The voters did not so much express confidence in Clinton as dissatisfaction with Bush and his neglect of their domestic discontents.

"Dubya"

George W. followed in his father's footsteps to Yale University, but he was not the scholar-athlete that his father had been. Rather, he was a friendly, likable, heavy drinking president of his fraternity. Upon graduation in 1968, he joined the Texas Air National Guard, completed flight school, but never faced combat in Vietnam. He earned an MBA degree from the Harvard Business School and returned to Texas to enter the oil business himself. Later in his career he would acknowledge his "youthful indiscretions," including a drunk driving arrest in 1976.

Although his famous name attracted investors in a series of oil companies he managed, virtually all of them lost money (including the Harvard Management Company that invests that university's endowment funds). Even a deal with the government of oil-rich Bahrain, negotiated while his father was president, failed to bail out Bush's Harken Energy Company. But Bush was able to sell off his oil interests and reinvest the money in the Texas Rangers baseball team; he eventually sold his interest in the Rangers in a deal that netted him over $15 million.

George W. Bush had never held public office before running for governor of Texas in 1994. But he had gained valuable political experience serving as an unofficial adviser to his father during his presidential campaigns. He went up against the sharp-tongued incumbent Democratic Governor Ann Richards, who ridiculed him as the "shrub" (little Bush). Bush heavily outspent Richards and won 54 percent of the vote, to become Texas's second Republican governor in modern times.

George W's political style fitted comfortably with the Texas "good old boys" in both parties. Although the Texas legislature was controlled by Democrats, Bush won most of his early legislative battles. He supported legislation that gave law-abiding adult Texans the right to carry concealed handguns. A strong economy allowed him to improve public services yet keep Texas among the few states without an income tax. He supported educational reform by opposing the practice of "social promotion" and requiring third-, fifth-, and eighth-grade pupils to pass statewide tests before advancing to the next grade.

Bush's style was to meet frequently and privately with his Democratic opponents and to remain on friendly personal terms with them. He was willing to accept legislative compromises and tried to avoid controversies wherever possible. He helped to lead the gradual realignment of Texas away from its traditional Democratic roots and toward its current Republican coloration.

Bush versus Gore

George W. Bush and Al Gore were both born into family traditions of wealth, privilege, and public service. Both attended prestigious private prep schools—Bush, Andover; Gore, St. Albans. Both attended Ivy League universities—Bush, Yale; Gore, Harvard.

By traditional expectations, Democratic Vice-President Al Gore's election should have been a "slam dunk." The nation was enjoying economic prosperity, low unemployment, low inflation, budget surpluses, and relative peace. Traditionally, under such conditions, Americans have kept the incumbent party in the White House.

But the campaign started off very badly for Al Gore. The Veep was perceived as a stiff, wooden prop for his boss, the flawed yet charismatic Bill Clinton. Gore trailed George W. Bush badly in opinion polls for the first eight months of the election year. He tried to "reinvent" himself several times—self-consciously projecting different images of himself at different times. His "image adviser" recommended that he give up formal suits and ties for more relaxed sweaters and open-collar shirts and that he become an "Alpha male"—spirited and aggressive rather than subdued and wonkish. Yet throughout the Spring he seemed unable to shed the image of a loyal, decent, yet colorless backup to the more magnetic Clinton.

George W. Bush's campaign rested largely on his personal appeal to voters—his warmth, good humor, and general likability. Early on, he settled on the theme of "*compassionate conservatism*," trying to appeal to independents, minorities, and especially women. Bush partially dispelled the notion that he lacked sufficient "gravitas" (wisdom and experience) in the televised presidential debates. Although out-pointed by Gore, he succeeded in convincing most viewers that he had a good grasp of the issues. Gore appeared overly aggressive, perhaps even rude, especially in the first debate. Bush retook the lead in the polls following the debates. But each day there seemed to be large gyrations in the polling figures.

As the campaign progressed, Gore distanced himself from Clinton, apparently in an effort to direct the campaign away from his former boss's scandals. But in doing so, he failed to take full credit for the nation's years of prosperity under Clinton. Overall, Gore won on the issues—the economy, education, Social Security, health care, and so forth. But Bush was judged by the voters to be more "likable."[8]

Americans were given a dramatic reminder in 2000 that the president of the United States is *not* elected by nationwide popular vote but rather by a majority of the electoral votes of the states. Democrat Al Gore won 500,000 more popular votes nationwide than Republican George W. Bush, out of more than one hundred million votes cast. But Bush won the majority of the states' electoral votes—271 to 267—the narrowest margin in American history.

Early on election night the television networks "called" the key battleground states for Gore, in effect declaring him the winner. But by 9 P.M. Florida was yanked back into the undecided column; the electoral college vote looked like it was splitting down the middle. Around 1 A.M., Florida was "called" for Bush, and the networks pronounced him the next president of the United States. Gore telephoned Bush to concede, but shortly thereafter, upon hearing that the gap in Florida was closing fast, Gore withdrew his concession. For the second time, the television networks put Florida back into the "too close to call" column.

Teams of lawyers descended on Florida for the first post-election presi-

[8] CNN/*USA Today* Poll, October 17, 2000.

dential contest in over a century. Each side called on their legal and political heavyweights. The Bush campaign sent a team of attorneys headed by former Secretary of State James Baker, and the Gore campaign sent an eighteen-person team headed by former Secretary of State Warren Christopher. The battle of the ballots would consume over a month.

In the end it was the most elitist branch of the U.S. government, the Supreme Court, that actually chose the president. Only the High Court seemed to possess sufficient legitimacy to resolve the first contested presidential election in over a century. The Supreme Court's decision on December 12 in *Bush vs. Gore* rested on constitutional issues, but the 5–4 division of the Court raised the question of the Court's political impartiality. The Supreme Court's majority held that "the use of standardless manual recounts violates the Equal Protection and Due Process Clauses" of the Constitution. And three justices in the majority held that the Florida Supreme Court "plainly departed from the legislative scheme" previously enacted by the Florida Legislature and therefore violated Article II of the Constitution. The Court divided along ideological lines. The five justices in the majority included acknowledged conservatives Renquist, Scalia, and Thomas, together with moderates O'Conner and Kennedy. The minority included the acknowledged liberals, Stevens, Breyer, and Ginsburg, together with Souter. Yet despite the prolonged contest, the bitter feelings of many of the participants, and the apparently ideological split, George W. Bush was recognized as the legitimate president of the United States immediately after the Supreme Court's historic decision.

EXECUTIVE DECISION-MAKERS: THE SERIOUS PEOPLE

The politician is a professional office-seeker. The politician knows how to run for office—but not necessarily how to run the government. After victory at the polls, the prudent politician turns to "serious" people to run the government.[9] The corporate and governmental experience and educational credentials of

---

[9] Pulitzer Prize–winning writer David Halberstam reports a revealing conversation between newly elected President John F. Kennedy and Robert A. Lovett in December 1960, a month before Kennedy was to take office: "On the threshold of great power and great office, the young man seemed to have everything. He was handsome, rich, charming, candid . . . [But] he had spent the last five years, he said ruefully, running for office, and he did not know any real public officials, people to run a government, *serious men*. The only ones he knew, he admitted, were politicians. . . . Politicians *did* need men to serve, to run the government." Robert Lovett was "the very embodiment of the Establishment." His father had been chairman of the board of Union Pacific Railroad and a partner of the great railroad tycoon, E. H. Harriman. Lovett urged Kennedy to listen to the advice of Lovett's partner and former governor of New York and ambassador to the Soviet Union, Averell Harriman; to see "Jack McCloy at Chase" (then chairman of the board of Chase Manhattan), and "Doug Dillon too" (to become Kennedy's secretary of the treasury); to look up a "young fellow over at Rockefeller, Dean Rusk" (to become Kennedy's secretary of state); and to get "this young man at Ford, Robert McNamara" (to become Kennedy's secretary of defense). Kennedy gratefully accepted the advice: he turned to these "serious men" to run the government. David Halberstam, *The Best and Brightest* (New York: Random House, 1969), pp. 3–4.

these "serious" decision-makers greatly exceed those of most members of Congress or other elected officials. When presidents turn from the task of *running for office* to the task of *running a government*, they are obliged to recruit higher quality leadership than is typically found among political officeholders.

The responsibility for the initiation of national programs and policies falls primarily upon the top White House staff and the heads of executive departments. Generally, Congress merely responds to policy proposals initiated by the executive branch. The President and his key advisers and administrators have a strong incentive to fulfill their responsibility for decision-making. In the eyes of the American public, they are responsible for everything that happens in the nation, regardless of whether they have the authority or capacity to do anything about it. There is a general expectation that every administration, even one committed to a "caretaker" role, will put forth some sort of policy program.

The President and Vice-President, White House presidential advisers and ambassadors-at-large, Cabinet secretaries, undersecretaries, and assistant secretaries constitute our executive elite. Let us take a brief look at the careers of some of the people who have served in key Cabinet positions in recent presidential administrations.

SECRETARIES OF STATE

John Foster Dulles. (1953–60). Senior partner of Sullivan & Cromwell, and member of the board of directors of the Bank of New York, Fifth Avenue Bank, American Bank Note Co., International Nickel Co. of Canada, Babcock and Wilson Corp., Shenandoah Corp., United Cigar Stores, American Cotton Oil Co., United Railroad of St. Louis, and European Textile Corp. He was a trustee of the New York Public Library, Union Theological Seminary, the Rockefeller Foundation, and the Carnegie Endowment for International Peace; also a delegate to the World Council of Churches.

Dean Rusk. (1961–68). President of the Rockefeller Foundation.

William P. Rogers. (1969–73). U.S. attorney general during Eisenhower administration; senior partner in Royall, Koegal, Rogers and Wells (one of the twenty largest Wall Street law firms).

Henry Kissinger. (1973–77). Special assistant to the president for national security affairs; former Harvard professor of international affairs, and project director for Rockefeller Brothers Fund and for the Council on Foreign Relations.

Cyrus Vance. (1977–80). Senior partner in the New York law firm of Simpson, Thacher & Bartlett. A member of the board of directors of IBM and Pan American World Airways; a trustee of Yale University, the Rockefeller Foundation, and the Council on Foreign Relations; former secretary of the army under President Lyndon Johnson.

Alexander M. Haig, Jr. (1981–82). President of United Technologies Corporation, and former four-star general, U.S. Army. He was former Supreme Allied Commander, NATO forces in Europe; former assistant to the President under Richard

Nixon; former deputy assistant to the President for national security under Henry Kissinger; former deputy commandant, U.S. Military Academy at West Point; former deputy secretary of defense.

George P. Shultz. (1982–89). President of the Bechtel Corporation. Former secretary of the treasury, former secretary of labor, and former director of Office of Management and Budget under President Richard Nixon. Earned Ph.D. in economics from M.I.T. Former dean of the school of business, University of Chicago. Former director of General Motors, Borg-Warner, and Dillon, Read & Co.

James A. Baker III. (1989–92). Houston attorney and oil man who previously served as secretary of the treasury and White House chief of staff in the Reagan administration.

Warren Christopher. (1993–1997). California attorney (former law clerk for U.S. Supreme Court Justice William Douglas); partner, O'Melvany & Meyers; Deputy Secretary of State under President Carter; a director of California Edison, First Interstate Bancorp, Lockheed, and chairman of the Board of Trustees of the Carnegie Corp.

Madeleine Albright. (1997–2001). Georgetown University professor; U.S. Ambassador to the United Nations; member of the Council on Foreign Relations.

SECRETARIES OF TREASURY

George M. Humphrey. (1953–57). Former chairman of the board of directors of the M.A. Hanna Co.; member of board of directors of National Steel Corp., Consolidated Coal Co. of Canada, and Dominion Sugar Co.; trustee of M.I.T.

Robert B. Anderson. (1957–61). Secretary of the navy, 1953–54; deputy secretary of defense, 1945–55; member of board of directors of Goodyear Tire and Rubber Co. and Pan American World Airways; member of the executive board of the Boy Scouts of America.

Douglas Dillon. (1961–63). Chairman of the board of Dillon, Read & Co. (one of Wall Street's largest investment firms); member of New York Stock Exchange; director of U.S. and Foreign Securities Corp. and U.S. International Securities Corp.; member of board of governors of New York Hospital and the Metropolitan Museum of Art.

David Kennedy. (1969–71). President and chairman of the board of Continental Illinois Bank and Trust Co.; director of International Harvester Co., Commonwealth Edison, Pullman Co., Abbott Laboratories, Swift and Co., U.S. Gypsum, and Communications Satellite Corp.; trustee of the University of Chicago, the Brookings Institution, the Committee for Economic Development, and George Washington University.

John B. Connally. (1971–72). Secretary of the navy, governor of Texas, administrative assistant to Lyndon B. Johnson; attorney for Murcheson Brothers Investment (Dallas); former director of New York Central Railroad.

George P. Shultz. (1972–74). Secretary of labor and director of the Office of Management and Budget; former dean of the University of Chicago Graduate School of Business; former director of Borg-Warner Corp., General American Transportation Co., and Stein, Roe & Farnham (investments).

William E. Simon. (1974–77). Director of Federal Energy Office, and former deputy secretary of the treasury; formerly a senior partner of Salomon Brothers (one of Wall Street's largest investment firms specializing in municipal bond trading).

Warner Michael Blumenthal. (1977–79). President of the Bendix Corporation; former vice-president of Crown Cork Co.; trustee of Princeton University and the Council on Foreign Relations.

G. William Miller. (1979–81). Chairman and chief executive officer of Textron Corporation. Former partner in Cravath, Swaine & Moore (one of the nation's twenty-five largest and most prestigious law firms); a former director of Allied Chemical and Federated Department Stores; former chairman of the Federal Reserve Board.

Donald T. Regan. (1981–85). Chairman of the board and chief executive officer of Merrill Lynch & Co. Inc. (the nation's largest investment firm); former vice-chairman of the New York Stock Exchange; trustee of the University of Pennsylvania and the Committee for Economic Development; member of the policy committee of the Business Roundtable.

James A. Baker III. (1985–89). Wealthy Houston attorney whose father owned Texas Commerce Bank. Former undersecretary of commerce in the Ford administration and campaign chairman for George Bush's unsuccessful presidential race in 1980. President Reagan's White House chief of staff in his first term.

Nicholas Brady. (1989–93). Former chairman of Dillon, Read & Co.; a director of Purolator, NCR, Georgia International, ASA, and Media General.

Robert E. Rubin. (1995–2001). Chairman of the Wall Street investment firm Goldman Sachs. Trustee, Carnegie Corp.

SECRETARIES OF DEFENSE

Charles E. Wilson. (1953–57). President and chairman of the board of directors of General Motors.

Neil H. McElroy. (1957–59). President and chairman of the board of directors of Procter & Gamble; member of the board of directors of General Electric, Chrysler Corp., and Equitable Life Assurance Co.; member of the board of trustees of Harvard University, the National Safety Council, and the National Industrial Conference.

Thomas S. Gates. (1959–60). Secretary of the navy, 1957–59; chairman of the board and chief executive officer, Morgan Guaranty Trust Co.; member of the board of directors of General Electric, Bethlehem Steel, Scott Paper Co., Campbell Soup Co., Insurance Co. of North America, Cities Service, SmithKline and French (pharmaceuticals), and the University of Pennsylvania.

Robert S. McNamara. (1961–67). President and chairman of the board of directors of the Ford Motor Co.; member of the board of directors of Scott Paper Co.; president of the World Bank, 1967–81.

Clark Clifford. (1967–69). Senior partner of Clifford & Miller (Washington law firm); member of board of directors of the National Bank of Washington and the

Sheridan Hotel Corp.; special counsel to the President, 1949–50; member of the board of trustees of Washington University in St. Louis.

Melvin Laird. (1969–73). Wisconsin Republican congressman, and former chairman of Republican conference in the House of Representatives.

James R. Schlesinger. (1973–77). Director, Central Intelligence Agency; former chairman of Atomic Energy Commission; formerly assistant director of the Office of Management and Budget; economics professor; and research associate of the RAND Corp.

Harold Brown. (1977–81). President of the California Institute of Technology. A member of the board of directors of International Business Machines (IBM) and the Times-Mirror Corp. Former secretary of the air force under President Lyndon Johnson, and U.S. representative to the SALT I talks under President Richard Nixon.

Caspar W. Weinberger. (1981–89). Vice-president and director of the Bechtel Corporation, the world's largest privately owned corporation. A member of the board of directors of Pepsico and Quaker Oats Co. Former secretary of Health, Education, and Welfare under President Richard Nixon; former director of the Office of Management and Budget; former chairman of the Federal Trade Commission. A former San Francisco attorney and California state legislator.

Richard B. Cheney. (1989–93). Congressman and chairman of the House Republican Conference; assistant to the President, Gerald Ford; chairman of the Cost of Living Council; director of Office of Economic Opportunity under President Richard Nixon. Attorney.

Les Aspin. (1993–94). Ph.D. Economics. U.S. Army 1966–68; House of Representatives, 1970–92; chairman of the House Armed Forces Committee, 1985–92.

William J. Perry. (1994–1997). Ph.D. Mathmatics. Former director of Electronic Defense Laboratories of GTE; former director of Stanford University Center for International Security; former Deputy Secretary of Defense.

William S. Cohen. (1997–2001). Attorney. U.S. Senator from Maine.

THE BUSH RESTORATION

The Bush Cabinet brings familiar faces back to Washington. Indeed, insiders in the Ford, Reagan, and especially Bush (the elder) administrations must feel very comfortable with the return of so many of their friends. Among eighteen Cabinet-level officials (which include the Vice-President, fourteen department heads, plus the National Security Adviser, White House Chief of Staff, and Director of the Office of Management and Budget), eleven have served in high places in previous Republican administrations (see Table 4–2). Perhaps stocking the cabinet with old Washington hands is designed to compensate for Bush's own perceived lack of experience and preference for delegating decisions.

TABLE 4-2 The Bush Restoration

Position	Education	Occupation	Career Highlights	Corporate Connections[1]
President George W. Bush	B.A., Yale; M.B.A, Harvard	Oil co exec.; Mgr./Dir. Texas Rangers	Gov. Texas, 1994–2000	Harkin Energy,* Texas Rangers,* Enron, Philip Morris, AT&T, Microsoft
Vice-President Richard Cheney	B.A., M.A., U. of Wyoming	Oil co exec.	White House staff, 75–77; U.S. Rep. WY, 79–89; Sec't Defense, 89–93	Halliburton Oil,* Enron, Philip Morris, AT&T, Microsoft
Secretary of State Colin Powell	B.S., CUNY; M.B.A., George Washington U.	Army officer	Nat'l. Sec. Adv, 87–89; Chrm JCS, 89–94; founder, America's Promise, 95–00	AOL Time Warner,* Gulfstream Aerospace,* General Dynamics*
Secretary of Treasury Paul H. O'Neill	B.A., Fresno State U.; M.P.A. U. of Indiana	Aluminum co. exec.	OMB staff, 67–77; vice-president International Paper, 77–87; Chairman & CEO, Alcoa, 87–00	Alcoa,* International Paper,* Lucent Technologies,* Eastman Kodak*
Secretary of Defense Donald Rumsfeld	A.B., Princeton	Drug co. exec.	U.S. Rep. IL, 63–69; Assistant to President, 69–75; Secretary of Defense, 75–77; President, G.D. Searle, 77–85	G.D. Searle,* Tribune Co,,* Motorola,* Gulfstream Aerospace,* General Dynamics,* Sears Roebuck,* Allstate,* Kellog*
Attorney General John Ashcroft	B.A., Yale; J.D., U. of Chicago	Attorney	Atty. Gen., MO, 76–85; Gov.r, MO, 85–93; U.S. Senator, MO, 94–00	AT&T, Microsoft, Monsanto, Enterprise Rent-A-Car
Secretary of Commerce Donald L. Evans	B.S, M.B.A., U. of Texas	Oil co. exec.	Chrm., Bush–Cheney 2000	Tom Brown Inc.,* Sharp Drilling*

Secretary of HUD Mel Martinez	B.A., J.D., Florida State U.	Attorney	Chrm., Orange County FL Commission, 95–00	none
Secretary of Labor Elaine Chao	B.A., Mount Holyoke; M.B.A., Harvard	Banker; Pres. of Civic Org.	Director, Peace Corp., 91–92; President, United Way, 92–96	Northwest Airlines,* Clorox,* HCA,* Bank of America,* Dole Food*
Secretary of Transportation Norman Y. Mineta	B.S., U. of California	Aircraft co. exec.	Mayor, San Jose, CA, 71–74; U.S. Rep. CA, 75–95; V.P. Lockheed Martin, 95–00; Sec't. of Commerce, 00	Lockheed Martin,* Northwest Airlines, United Airlines, Union Pacific, Boeing
Secretary of Interior Gale Norton	B.A., J.D., U. of Denver	Attorney	Staff, Dep't. of Interior, 85–90; Attorney General, CO, 91–99	Delta Petroleum, N.L. Industries, British Petroleum, Ford Motor
Secretary of HHS Tommy G. Thompson	B.A., J.D., U. of Wisconsin	Attorney	Governor, WI, 87–00	Philip Morris, AOL Time Warner, General Electric, Merck
Secretary of Education Roderick Paige	B.A., Jackson State U; M.A., Ph.D., U. of Indiana	Educator	Houston School Superintendent, 94–00	None
Secretary of Agriculture Ann M. Veneman	B.A., U.Cal.-Davis; J.D., U. Cal-Berkeley	Attorney	Dep't. Sec't., Dep't. of Agric., 81–93; Sec't. of Agric. for CA, 95–99	Monsanto,* Pharmacia
Secretary of Energy Spencer Abraham	B.A., Michigan State U; J.D., Harvard	Attorney	U.S. Senator, MI, 94–00	General Motors, Ford, Lear Corp., Daimler Chrysler

continued

TABLE 4-2 continued

Position	Education	Occupation	Career Highlights	Corporate Connections[1]
Secretary of VA Anthony Principi	B.A., U.S. Naval Acad.; J.D., Seton Hall	Attorney	U.S. Navy, 67–80; Dep't. Sec't, VA, 89–93	Federal Network,* Lockheed Martin,* QTC Medical*
National Security Advisor Condoleeza Rice	B.A., U of Denver; M.A. Notre Dame; Ph.D, U. of Denver	Educator	Hoover Institute (think tank): Provost, Stanford U.	Chevron,* Charles Schwab,* TransAmerica*
Chief of Staff Andrew Card	B.S., U of South Carolina;	Lobbyist	State leg., MA, 75–82; Asst. to pres., 83–92; Sec't. of Transportation, 92; Pres., Automobile Mfgs. Assn., 92–00	General Motors,* Citigroup,* General Electric,* Merck*
Director, OMB Mitchell Daniels	B.A., Princeton; J.D., Georgetown	Drug co. exec.	V.P., Eli Lilly	Eli Lilly,* Citigroup,* General Electric,* Merck*

1 Corporate connections provided by the Center for Responsive Politics. Connections include services as officer or director (shown with asterisk*), together with major stock holdings and/or heavy campaign contributions.

Business executives have returned to high places in Washington, after a relative absence during the Clinton years (see Table 4–3). Vice-President Richard Cheney served as president of the giant oil conglomerate, Halliburton; Secretary of Treasury Paul H. O'Neill was president of International Paper and later chairman and CEO of Alcoa; Secretary of Defense Donald Rumsfeld (who also ran the Pentagon in the Ford administration) was president and CEO of the international drug company G.D. Searle; Secretary of Commerce Don Evans was an oil company executive; OMB Director Mitchell Daniels was vice-president of the giant drug company Eli Lilly; and White House Chief of Staff Andrew Card was president and chief lobbyist for the Automobile Manufacturers Association.

After a nearly complete absence of military experience at the top of the Clinton administration, Bush's team includes four veterans: Former Chairman of the Joint Chiefs of Staff General Colin Powell is, of course, the most prominent military presence. Others who served tours of duty in the services include Secretary of Defense Donald Rumsfeld (Navy), Secretary of Transportation Norman Mineta (Army), and Anthony Principi (Navy). Even George W. himself served in the Texas Air National Guard, and former Wisconsin Governor and HUD Secretary Tommy Thompson served in the Army Reserve.

Yet it is also clear that Bush has tried to reach out and bring highly qualified minorities into his administration. Secretary of State Colin Powell was an easy choice; the popular General might have won the same office in a Gore

TABLE 4–3   Profile of Administration Leadership

	Truman through Carter	Reagan	Bush	Clinton	Bush
Education					
Advanced degree	69%	68%	80%	89%	83%
Law degree	40	26	40	67	50
Ivy League degree	48	58	50	50	28
Ph.D.	19	16	25	22	12
No college degree	0	0	0	0	0
Women	4%	5%	10%	17%	18%
Blacks	4%	5%	5%	17%	18%
Occupations					
Law	28%	11%	40%	5%	28%
Business	28	32	55	5	39
Government	16	16	5	67	6
Education	19	16	25	11	12
Military	3	5	10	0	12

Source: For Truman through Carter, see Phillip H. Burch, Jr., *Elites in American History,* Vol. 3 (New York: Holmes and Meier, 1980).

administration. Likewise, African American Condoleeza Rice was a highly qualified choice as National Security Adviser; she had established stellar credentials in the national security field (a field not occupied by many women) at the Hoover Institute and Stanford University. By placing African American Roderick Paige at the head of the Department of Education, Bush signaled that improvement of minority education would be a priority in his administration. As governor of Texas, Bush was more successful at bringing Hispanics into his top circles than most other Republican governors (with the possible exception of his brother Jeb Bush, Governor of Florida). Hispanics are well represented on the White House staff , and Mel Martinez heads up HUD.

Women occupy roughly the same proportion of top positions as they have in previous administrations. Three women head cabinet departments—Secretary of Labor Elaine Chao, Secretary of Interior Gale Norton, and Secretary of Agriculture Ann Veneman. And Condoleeza Rice's appointment represents the real breakthrough for women on the National security Council.

The quality of Bush's initial appointments to top positions suggests that he is seeking legitimacy by bringing into high office people who have already won respect in business and government. The quality of his appointments and the authority he appears to have given them would be consistent with the image he projected in the campaign. He does not see himself as a policy expert, but openly acknowledges his dependence on getting good advice from knowledgeable people.

THE CONGRESSIONAL ESTABLISHMENT

Although policy initiatives are usually developed outside Congress, Congress is no mere "rubber stamp." Key members of Congress do play an independent role in national decision-making; thus, key congressional leaders must be included in any operational definition of a national elite.

Political scientists have commented extensively on the structure of power *within* the Congress. They generally describe a hierarchical structure in both houses of the Congress—a "congressional establishment"—which largely determines what the Congress will do. The congressional establishment has survived periodic efforts at decentralization. It is composed of the Speaker of the House and president pro tempore of the Senate; House and Senate majority and minority leaders and whips; and committee chairpersons and ranking minority members of House and Senate standing committees. Party leadership roles in the House and Senate are major sources of power in Washington. The Speaker of the House and the majority and minority leaders of the House and Senate direct the business of Congress. Although they share this task with the standing committee chairpersons, these leaders are generally "first among equals" in their relationships with committee chairpersons.

TABLE 4–4   The Congressional Establishment 107th Congress (2001–2003)

Senate Leadership	
Majority Leader	Thomas Daschle (D-SD)
Majority Whip	Henry Reid (D-NV)
President pro tempore	Robert C. Byrd (D-WV)
Republican Leader	Trent Lott (R-MS)
Republican Whip	Don Nickles (R-OK)

House Leadership	
Speaker of the House	Dennis Hastert (R-IL)
Majority Leader	Dick Armey (R-TX)
Majority Whip	Tom DeLay (R-TX)
Minority Leader	Dick Gephardt (D-MO)
Minority Whip	David Bonier (D-MI)

Key Senate Committees		
	Democratic Chair	**Republican Ranking**
Appropriations	Byrd (WV)	Stevens (AK)
Foreign Relations	Biden (DE)	Helms (NC)
Judiciary	Leahy (VT)	Hatch (UT)
Finance	Baucus (MT)	Grassley (IA)
Armed Services	Levin (MI)	Warner (VA)
Budget	Conrad (ND)	Dominici (NM)

Key House Committees		
	Republican Chair	**Democratic Ranking**
Rules	Hansen (UT)	Rahall (WV)
Appropriations	Young (FL)	Obey (WI)
International Relations	Hyde (IL)	Lantos (CA)
Judiciary	Sensenbrenner (WI)	Conyers (MI)
Ways and Means	Thomas (CA)	Rangel (NY)
Armed Services	Stump (AZ)	Skelton (MO)
Budget	Nussle (IA)	Sporatt (SC)

But the committee system also creates powerful congressional figures, the chairpersons of the most powerful standing committees—particularly the Senate Foreign Relations, Appropriations, Judiciary, Finance, Armed Services, and Budget committees, and the House Rules, Appropriations, International Relations, Judiciary, Armed Services, Budget, and Ways and Means committees (see Table 4–4).

Viewed within the broader context of a *national elite*, congressional leaders appear "folksy," parochial, and localistic. Because of the local constituency of members of Congress, they are predisposed to concern themselves with local interests. Members of Congress are part of local elite structures "back home"; they retain their local businesses and law practices, club memberships, and religious affiliations. Members of Congress represent many small segments of the nation rather than the nation as a whole. Even top congressional leaders from safe districts, with many years of seniority, cannot completely shed their local interests. Their claim to *national* leadership must be safely hedged by attention to their local constituents. Consider, for example, the parochial backgrounds of the following top congressional leaders.

TED KENNEDY: THE POLITICAL INHERITOR

The Kennedy dynasty began with the flamboyant career of Joseph P. Kennedy, a son of a prosperous Irish saloon-keeper and ward boss in Boston. Joseph Kennedy attended Boston Latin School and Harvard, receiving his B.A. in 1912. He started his career in banking, moved into stock market operations, dabbled in shipbuilding, formed movie-making companies (RKO and later Paramount), and married the daughter of the mayor of Boston. "Old Joe" made the major part of his fortune in stock market manipulations. With his associate, William Randolph Hearst, Kennedy provided key financial backing for the 1932 presidential campaign of Franklin D. Roosevelt. FDR later made Kennedy head of the Securities and Exchange Commission. But making a market speculator head of a commission that was designed to protect investors caused such public outcry that Kennedy was forced to resign after one year. FDR then appointed Kennedy head of the Maritime Commission, but rumors of extravagant subsidies to shipbuilding friends forced his resignation after only two months on the job. In 1937, FDR appointed him ambassador to England. His diplomatic career lasted three years and ended over differences with FDR regarding U.S. assistance to the Allies. Old Joe is said to have advised FDR of the likelihood of German victory and the advantages of placating Hitler.

Joseph P. Kennedy, Sr., was the father of nine children. (Joseph P., Jr., was killed as a World War II Navy pilot; President John F. Kennedy was assassinated; Senator Robert F. Kennedy was assassinated; Kathleen died in a plane crash; Rosemary is living in an institution for the mentally retarded; Eunice is married to Sargent Shriver, former director of the Peace Corps and the War on Poverty and replacement for Senator Thomas Eagleton as the Democratic vice-presidential nominee in 1972; Patricia, formerly married to actor Peter Lawford; Jean, wife of Stephen Smith; and the youngest, Edward M. "Ted" Kennedy.)

Although born to great wealth and accustomed to an upper-class style of living (he received his first communion from Pope Pius XII), Ted Kennedy acquired the sense of competition fostered in the large Kennedy household. In 1951, suspended from Harvard for cheating on a Spanish examination, he joined the Army and served two years in Germany. He was readmitted to Harvard, where he played on the Harvard football team and graduated in 1956.

Despite his family background, Harvard Law School rejected Ted Kennedy's application for admission. He enrolled instead in the University of Virginia Law School and completed his law degree in 1959. Following graduation and work on his brother's 1960 presidential campaign, he was appointed assistant district attorney for Suffolk County, Massachusetts.

When he was just thirty years old, the minimum age for a U.S. senator, he announced his candidacy for the Massachusetts Senate seat formerly held by his brother, who was then President. In the Democratic primary he faced Edward J. McCormack, nephew of the then Speaker of the House, John W. McCormack. During a televised debate, McCormack said to Kennedy, "You never worked for a living. You never held elective office. You lack the qualifications and maturity of judgment. . . . If your name were not Kennedy, your candidacy would be a joke." But Kennedy won overwhelmingly and went on to defeat the Republican candidate, George Cabot Lodge. (George Cabot Lodge was the son of U.S. Ambassador to South Vietnam and former U.S. Senator Henry Cabot Lodge, Jr. In 1916, Kennedy's grandfather, Boston Mayor John F. Fitzgerald, had been defeated in a race for the same Senate seat by Lodge's great-grandfather, Senator Henry Cabot Lodge.)

Kennedy performed better in the Senate than many had expected. He cultivated Senate friends, appeared at fund-raising dinners, and informed himself about several important policy fields. He worked hard learning about national health problems and problems of the elderly. In 1969 he was elected Senate Democratic whip by his colleagues.

His personal life, however, was marred by accident, tragedy, and scandal. He nearly died in a 1964 plane crash in which he suffered a broken back. An athletic and handsome six foot two inches, Kennedy was frequently the object of romantic gossip at Washington cocktail parties. On July 19, 1969, a young woman, Mary Jo Kopechne, died when the car Kennedy was driving plunged off a narrow bridge on Chappaquiddick Island after a late-night party. Missing for ten hours after the accident, Kennedy later made a dramatic national television appearance, saying that the tragedy had been an accident and that he had been too confused to report the tragedy until the next day. The official inquest has been kept secret, and many feel that there are still unresolved discrepancies in Kennedy's story.[10] Kennedy pled guilty to the minor charge of leaving the scene of an accident. Senate Democrats removed Kennedy from his position as majority whip. But the national news media never pressed the Chappaquiddick incident and continued favorable reporting of the still charismatic senator.

Kennedy deliberately avoided the Democratic presidential nomination in both 1972 and 1976. His advisers argued that the public's memory of

---

[10] See Robert Sherrill, "Chappaquiddick + 5," *New York Times Magazine,* July 14, 1974.

Chappaquiddick was still too fresh for Kennedy to enter a campaign battle in which the issue of his personal life would certainly be raised. However, in late 1979, with Jimmy Carter standing at a near all-time low for presidents in the opinion polls, Kennedy announced his presidential candidacy. Most observers thought that Kennedy was unbeatable, but Carter was temporarily saved by the Iranian seizure of American embassy employees in Iran as hostages. Shortly thereafter, Soviet troops invaded neighboring Afghanistan. Support for the President was equated with support for America, and Carter benefited from a "rally round the flag" effect. The media focus was on the President, and the international news simply obliterated the Kennedy campaign. But Ted Kennedy reestablished his leadership of liberal Democrats and polished his own charismatic image with a dramatic and inspiring speech at the 1980 Democratic National Convention. It was clearly Ted Kennedy's finest public performance.

Kennedy avoided subsequent presidential races, citing family affairs as his reason. And indeed, his family situation might have caused him political problems had he chosen to run. He was divorced from his wife, Joan, and many stories were published in women's magazines portraying her as a victim of Ted's heavy drinking and "womanizing." At the same time, he felt responsible for the many sons and daughters of his deceased brother Robert as well as his own children. Several of these "third-generation" Kennedys suffered serious personal problems.[11]

Kennedy's personal life appeared to stabilize following his marriage to a Washington attorney in 1992. He won his seventh Senate term in 2000 with 73 percent of the vote in Massachusetts. The 2000 election produced a Senate evenly divided between Democrats and Republicans, and when Vermont's Senator Jim Jeffords switched his affiliation to the Democratic Party in 2001, Kennedy assumed the chairmanship of the Senate Labor and Human Resources Committee.

Clearly, Ted Kennedy is an inheritor rather than a climber in the world of politics. His success rests upon his image and style more than upon his substantive contributions to public policy. He was elected to the Senate solely because he was a Kennedy, an inheritor of a famous political image. The image survived tragedy and scandal, and he remains the recognized leader of the liberal wing of the Democratic party.

HILLARY CLINTON: POWER AND AMBITION

Hillary Rodham Clinton has scratched and clawed her way to power throughout her lifetime. Along the way she has endured personal humiliation and

---

[11] See Peter Collier and David Horowitz, *The Kennedys: An American Dream* (New York: Summit, 1984).

political defeat. Yet her brilliance, tenacity, and tough-mindedness have made her a leading political figure in the U.S. Senate and the nation.

Hillary Rodham grew up in suburban Chicago, the daughter of a wealthy businessman who sent his daughter to prestigious private Wellesley College. A "Goldwater Girl" in high school, Hillary quickly reversed political direction to become a leader in radical and antiwar politics on campus. A 1969 honors graduate with a counterculture image—horn-rimmed glasses, long straggling hair, no makeup—she was chosen by her classmates to give a commencement speech—a largely inarticulate rambling about "more immediate, ecstatic, and penetrating modes of living." (Years later her views would coalesce around the New Age writings of leftist Jewish thinker Michael Learner, who coined the phrase *the politics of meaning*.) At Yale Law School, she met a long-haired, bearded Rhodes scholar from Arkansas, Bill Clinton, who was even more politically ambitious than Hillary. Both Bill and Hillary received their law degrees in 1973, but Bill returned to Arkansas to build a career in state politics, while Hillary went to Washington as an attorney, first for the liberal lobbying group the Children's Defense Fund, and later for the staff of the House Judiciary Committee seeking to impeach President Nixon.

Hillary and other Yale grads traveled to Arkansas to help Bill run unsuccessfully for Congress in 1974. Hillary decided to stay with Bill in Little Rock; they married before his next campaign, a successful run for state attorney general in 1976. Hillary remained Hillary Rodham, even as her husband went on to the governorship in 1978. She taught briefly at the University of Arkansas Law School and eventually joined Little Rock's influential Rose law firm. She kept her Washington ties with the Children's Defense Fund. She also became a director of Wal-Mart Stores, TCBY Enterprises, the LaFarge Corporation, and the federal government's Legal Services Corporation. Her husband's 1980 defeat for reelection as governor was blamed on his liberal leanings; in his 1982 comeback Bill cut his hair and repackaged himself as a moderate and centrist. Hillary cooperated by becoming Mrs. Bill Clinton, shedding her hornrims for contacts, blonding her hair, and echoing her husband's more moderate line. These tactics helped propel them back into the governor's mansion.

Hillary was far from the traditional governor's wife. She chaired the governor's task force on education and drew up his key educational reform package. She became a full partner in the Rose law firm, regularly earning over $200,000 a year (while Bill earned only $35,000 as Arkansas governor). She won national recognition as one of the "100 most influential lawyers in the United States" according to the American National Law Journal. She chaired the American Bar Association's Commission on Women and the Profession.

Hillary's support for Bill's presidential ambitions was absolutely crucial to this success. Married life in the governor's mansion was at best "rocky," as Bill and Hillary would later acknowledge on national television. Rumors of Bill's "womanizing" had long circulated in Little Rock, and they broke into the national news early in the presidential race when Genifer Flowers held a press conference describing a long-term affair with the governor and playing tapes of their telephone conversations. The focus was on Hillary in an interview on *60 Minutes* in early 1992. In a very convincing performance, Hillary acknowledged that their marriage had been "shaky" but was "rock solid" now.

Hillary's prominent role in the Clinton presidency was no surprise to those who followed her career. Her social consciousness, upper-class liberalism, and "burning desire to make the world better for everybody" were evident in her early radical critique of the "prevailing acquisitive and competitive corporate life" in America. Her "politics of meaning" combine a progressive social agenda with a strong dose of moralism. Reportedly very influential in all aspects of the Clinton presidency, she undertook the leadership of the President's Task Force on Health Care Reform in 1993. However, the defeat of Hillary's health-care plan caused her temporarily to assume a less public role in Washington politics. In her 1996 book, *It Takes A Village*, she advocated universal health-care, gun control, a higher minimum wage, and a federal overhaul of the nation's educational system. She received an $8 million advance for her autobiography just prior to leaving the White House.

During the Monica Lewinsky affair in 1998, Hillary again "stood by her man." Reportedly, she initially believed Bill's denials; she issued a statement blaming the reports of the affair on "a vast right-wing conspiracy." Later, on learning the truth, she appeared angry and upset, yet she declined to publicly criticize her husband. Indeed, her support for Bill was no doubt critical to his remaining in office. Her popularity with the American people reached an all-time high during the affair and the subsequent impeachment proceedings. She was widely admired by women for her steadfastness under pressure.

In 2000 Hillary became the first First Lady to run for public office—the New York Senate seat vacated by retiring Democrat Daniel Patrick Moynihan. When New York City's Republican Mayor, Rudolph Guliani, dropped out of the race, Hillary faced a relative unknown, Congressman Rick Lazio. Nevertheless, the nationally spotlighted race set a new record in campaign spending. Hillary won comfortably with 55 percent of the vote. She rates high in presidential preference polls among Democrats, but she may not make a run for the White House until 2008.

THE JUDGES

Nine people—none of whom is elected and all of whom serve for life—possess ultimate authority over all the other institutions of government. The Supreme Court of the United States has the authority to void the acts of popularly elected Presidents and Congresses. There is no appeal from their decision about what is the "supreme law of the land," except perhaps to undertake the difficult task of amending the Constitution itself. Only the good judgment of the Justices—their sense of "judicial self-restraint"—limits their power. It was the Supreme Court, rather than the President or Congress, that took the lead in important issues such as eliminating segregation from public life, ensuring voter equality in representation, limiting the powers of police, and declaring abortion to be a fundamental right of women.

Social scientists have commented frequently on the class bias of Supreme Court Justices: "White; generally Protestant . . . ; fifty to fifty-five years of age at the time of his appointment; Anglo-Saxon ethnic stock . . . ; high social status; reared in an urban environment; member of a civic-minded, politically active, economically comfortable family; legal training; some type of public office; generally well educated."[12] No blacks had served on the Supreme Court until the appointment of Associate Justice Thurgood Marshall in 1967. No women had served until the appointment of Sandra Day O'Connor in 1981. (See Table 4–5.) Of course, social background does not necessarily determine judicial philosophy. But as John R. Schmidhauser observes, "If . . . the Supreme Court is the keeper of the American conscience, it is essentially the conscience of the American upper-middle class sharpened by the imperative of individual social responsibility and political activism, and conditioned by the conservative impact of legal training and professional attitudes and associations."[13]

Clarence Thomas: Up from Pinpoint.   Not all Justices, however, conform to the upper-class portrait. No member of the nation's governing elite has ever had a steeper climb to the top than Justice Clarence Thomas. Born to a teenage mother who earned $10 a week as a maid, Clarence Thomas and his brother lived in a dirt-floor shack in Pinpoint, Georgia, where they were raised by strict, hard-working grandparents who taught young Clarence the value of education and sacrificed to send him to a Catholic school. He excelled academically and went on to mostly white Immaculate Conception Seminary College in Missouri to study for the Catholic priesthood. But when he overheard a fellow seminarian express satisfaction at the assassination of Dr. Martin Luther King, Jr., Thomas left the seminary in anger and enrolled at Holy Cross College, where he helped found the college's Black Student Union, and went on to graduate with honors and win admission to Yale Law School.

Upon graduating from Yale, Thomas took a job as assistant attorney general working in Missouri and, after a brief stint as an attorney for the Monsanto Corporation, returned to government as a congressional aide to Republican Missouri Senator John Danforth. Despite misgivings about accepting a "black" post in government, in 1981 Thomas accepted the post as head of the Office of Civil Rights in the Department of Education, using the posi-

[12] Henry Abraham, *The Judicial Process* (New York: Oxford University Press, 1962), p. 58.
[13] John R. Schmidhauser, *The Supreme Court* (New York: Holt Rinehart and Winston, 1960), p. 59.

TABLE 4–5 Backgrounds of Supreme Court Justices

All U.S. Supreme Court Justices, 1789 to Present	Number of Justices (Total = 109)
Occupation before Appointment	
Private legal practice	25
State judgeship	22
Federal judgeship	27
U.S. attorney general	7
Deputy or assistant U.S. attorney general	2
U.S. solicitor general	2
U.S. senator	6
U.S. representative	2
State governor	3
Federal executive posts	10
Other	3
Religious Background	
Protestant	85
Roman Catholic	9
Jewish	7
Unitarian	7
No religious affiliation	1
Age on Appointment	
Under 40	4
41–50	30
51–60	59
61–70	15
Political Party Affiliation	
Federalist (to 1835)	13
Democrat-Republican (to 1828)	7
Whig (to 1861)	2
Democrat	45
Republican	42
Sex	
Male	107
Female	2
Race	
Caucasian	107
Other	2

Sources: Congressional Quarterly, *Congressional Quarterly's Guide to the U.S. Supreme Court* (Washington, D.C.: Congressional Quarterly, 1979); and *Congressional Quarterly's Guide to Government*, Spring 1983 (Washington, D.C., 1982). Updated to 2001 by author.

tion to speak out on self-reliance, self-discipline, and the value of education. In 1982, he was named chairman of the Equal Employment Opportunity Commission (EEOC), where he successfully eliminated much of that agency's financial mismanagement and aggressively pursued individual cases of discrimination. At the same time, he spoke out against racial "quotas" and imposed minority hiring goals only on employers with proven records of discrimination. In 1989, President Bush nominated him to the U.S. Court of Appeals and he was easily confirmed by the Senate.

In tapping Thomas for the Supreme Court, the Bush White House reasoned that the liberal groups who had blocked the earlier nomination of conservative Robert Bork would be reluctant to launch personal attacks on an African American. But during nationally televised hearings of the Senate Judiciary Committee, University of Oklahoma law professor Anita Hill, a former legal assistant to Thomas both at the Department of Education and later at the Equal Employment Opportunity Commission, contacted the staff of the Judiciary Committee with charges that Thomas had sexually harassed her in both jobs. Initially, Hill declined to make her charges public, but when Senator Joseph Biden, the committee chairman, refused to circulate anonymous charges, she agreed to be interviewed by the F.B.I. and went on to give a nationally televised press conference, elaborating on her charges against Thomas. Her bombshell became a media extravaganza and sent the Senate into an uproar.

The Judiciary Committee reopened its hearings, with televised emotional testimony from both Anita Hill and Clarence Thomas. Indeed, the confirmation process exploded into a sleazy soap opera, with lurid stories about pubic hairs, penis sizes, and pornographic films of women with animals. The only restraint was Chairman Biden's rule that no questions would be asked about either Clarence Thomas's or Anita Hill's sex life. But the damage was done anyway, not only to Clarence Thomas and Anita Hill, but to the Senate confirmation process and the Senate as an institution.

In the end, there was no objective way to determine who was telling the truth. Too often the truth in Washington is determined by opinion polls. An astonishing 86 percent of the general public said they had watched the televised hearings. A majority of blacks as well as whites, and a majority of women as well as men, sided with Clarence Thomas.[14] The final Senate confirmation vote was 52 to 48, the closest vote in the history of Supreme Court confirmations.

Sandra Day O'Connor: In the Center of the Court. For nearly 200 years the U.S. Supreme Court was America's most exclusive male club. After 101 male justices, Sandra Day O'Connor was named to the Supreme Court by President Reagan in 1981. At the time of her appointment, O'Connor was a fifty-one-year-old state appellate court judge in Arizona. Justice O'Connor had no previous experience as a federal court judge, but she had the active support of Arizona's senior U.S. senator and Republican warhorse, Barry Goldwater. More important, she was a "she." Reagan was anxious to deflect attacks on his opposition to the Equal Rights Amendment and his failure to appoint many women in his own administration. As one Reagan aide put it: "This is

---

[14] Gallup Opinion Reports, October 15, 1991, p. 209.

Clarence Thomas
Bill Clinton

worth twenty-five assistant secretaries, maybe more!" Feminist groups were forced to support the appointment, even though O'Connor's record in Arizona was moderately conservative.

Sandra Day grew up on her family's large Arizona ranch, graduated from Stanford with honors, and then went on to Stanford Law School. She finished near the top of her class, along with Chief Justice of the Supreme Court William Rehnquist (who was first in the class). She married John Jay O'Connor, a Phoenix attorney, and raised three sons. She entered Arizona politics about the time her youngest son entered school. She was appointed to the Arizona State Senate in 1969 and was later elected twice to that body. She rose to majority leader in 1973. She left the Arizona legislature in 1975 to become a Phoenix trial judge. In 1979, she was appointed by a Democratic governor to the Arizona Court of Appeals. Work on this state intermediate court, however, does not involve major constitutional questions.

O'Connor had some business experience; she was formerly a director of the First National Bank of Arizona and Blue Cross/Blue Shield of Arizona. But until her appointment to the U.S. Supreme Court, she was an obscure state court judge. Her service as a Republican leader in the Arizona State Senate qualified her as a moderately conservative party loyalist. However, it appears that her professional and political friendships had more to do with bringing her to President Reagan's attention than her record as a jurist. She had known Justice William Rehnquist since her law school days. She had known former Chief Justice Warren Burger for a long time. And Barry Goldwater had been her mentor in Arizona Republican politics. When Reagan's political advisers told him during the presidential campaign that he was not doing well among women voters, the candidate responded by pledging to appoint a woman to the Supreme Court. Reagan's fulfillment of his campaign pledge was a politically popular decision.

In recent years Sandra Day O'Connor has emerged as the leader of a middle bloc of votes on the High Court, mediating between the liberal and conservative blocs. O'Connor has taken the lead in shaping Supreme Court policy on women's issues—including abortion. O'Connor strongly reaffirmed a woman's fundamental right to abortion, yet recognized a state's interest in protecting a "viable" fetus (a late-term fetus capable of surviving outside of the womb).[15] She has also taken the lead in deciding Supreme Court policy in the controversial area of affirmative action, arguing that laws that distinguish between individuals based on their race must be narrowly tailored to remedy specific injustices. "Racial classifications of any sort pose the risk of lasting harm to our society. They reinforce the belief, held by too many for too much of our history, that individuals should be judged by the color of their skin."[16]

---

[15] *Planned Parenthood* v. *Casey* (1992).
[16] *Shaw* v. *Reno* (1993).

THE MILITARY ESTABLISHMENT

In his farewell address to the nation in 1961, President Dwight D. Eisenhower warned of "an immense military establishment and a large arms industry." He observed: "In the councils of government, we must guard against the acquisition of unwarranted influence, whether sought or unsought, by the military-industrial complex."

The phrase *the military-industrial complex* caught on with many commentators over the years. It implied that a giant network of defense contractors—for example, Lockheed Aircraft, General Dynamics, Rockwell, McDonnell Douglas, Boeing, Litton, Hughes Tool, Grumman Aircraft—together with members of Congress in whose districts their plants were located, conspired with the generals in the Pentagon to create a powerful force in governmental and corporate circles. Indeed, radical social commentators held the military-industrial complex responsible for war and "imperialism."

But whatever the power of defense contractors and the military at the height of the Cold War, their influence today in governing circles is miniscule. Indeed, their goal today is to avoid complete dismantlement. Spending for national defense has declined precipitously from 10 percent of the GNP in the Eisenhower and Kennedy years to less than 3 percent today. Spending on Social Security, Medicare, and welfare, including Medicaid, exceeds 58 percent of the federal budget, compared to 16 percent for national defense.[17] There are 2 million civilian employees of the federal government, compared to only 1.4 million people in the armed forces. The long-term decline of U.S. defense spending suggests that the American military-industrial complex was *not* a very powerful conspiracy.

It seems clear in retrospect that C. Wright Mills placed too much importance on the military in his work, *The Power Elite.*[18] Mills was writing in the early 1950s when military prestige was high following victory in World War II. After the war, a few high-level military men were recruited to top corporate positions to add prestige to corporate boards. But this practice ended in the 1960s. The contrast between the political prestige of the military in the post–World War II years and in the post–Vietnam years is striking: The Supreme Allied Commander in Europe in World War II, Dwight D. Eisenhower, was elected President of the United States; the U.S. Commander in Vietnam, William Westmoreland, was defeated in his bid to become governor of South Carolina! Moreover, in contrast with corporate and governmental elites, military officers do *not* come from the upper or upper-middle class of society. Military officers are more likely to be recruited from lower- and

---

[17] *Budget of the United States Government 2001* gives this breakdown by function: Social Security: 23.2%; Medicare: 12.0%; Income Security: 14.2%; Medicaid: 9.1%.

[18] C. WRight Mills, *The Power Elite* (New York: Oxford, 1956).

low class Southerners

lower-middle-class backgrounds, and more likely to have rural and southern roots than are corporate or governmental elites.[19]

Colin Powell: Soldier-Statesman. When General Colin Powell was named chairman of the Joint Chiefs of Staff by President George Bush in 1989, he became the first African American and the youngest man in history to hold that post. During the Gulf War General Powell oversaw the largest military deployment of American troops since the Vietnam War. He is credited with developing and implementing a doctrine of maximum force that kept U.S. casualties to a minimum while Saddam Hussein's army was routed from Kuwait and destroyed. Powell had previously served as national security adviser to President Ronald Reagan, making him a principal military adviser to three Presidents.

Born in Harlem to Jamaican immigrant parents, Powell recounts his youth as proof that "it is possible to rise above conditions." After his graduation from Morris High School in the South Bronx, Powell's parents encouraged him to attend college, and he enrolled at City College of New York on an ROTC scholarship. He graduated with a degree in geology in 1958 at the top of his ROTC class and was commissioned a second lieutenant in the U.S. Army. Powell went to South Vietnam as a military adviser in 1962 and returned for a second tour in 1968. In Vietnam he was awarded two Purple Hearts for wounds suffered in combat, and a Bronze Star and the Legion of Merit for valor under fire.

Powell returned to the classroom in 1972 and earned a master's degree in business administration from George Washington University. In 1972 he was appointed to the prestigious White House Fellows Program and was assigned to the Office of Management and Budget, where he worked under Caspar Weinberger, who later became secretary of defense in the Reagan administration. Powell's career was on a fast track after this early White House duty. He served as a battalion commander in Korea, graduated from the National War College, served as military assistant to the deputy secretary of defense, and won promotion to general and command of the Second Brigade of the 101st Airborne Division.

In 1983 Powell was recalled to Washington by Defense Secretary Weinberger to become his senior military adviser. During the invasion of Grenada in October 1983, Powell was assigned the task of running interference for the military against meddling White House and National Security Council staff. Later Powell supported Secretary Weinberger in opposing arms sales to Iran; he was overruled by President Reagan, but his memo urging that Congress be notified of the arms transfers would later stand him in good stead with the Congress after the Iran-Contra scandal became public. In 1986 Powell eagerly accepted command of the U.S. Fifth Corps in Germany, declin-

[19] Morris Janowitz, *The Professional Soldier* (New York: Free Press, 1960), p. 378.

ing offers to stay on in Washington. But when President Reagan himself called and urged him to accept the post as national security adviser and reform the operations of the NSC staff, he agreed. Powell lent credibility to Reagan's promises to implement the recommendations of the Tower Commission, which had investigated the Iran-Contra affair.

President Bush chose General Powell in 1989 to be Chairman of the Joint Chiefs of Staff—the nation's highest military position. It was General Powell who helped convince the President that if military force were to be used to oust Saddam Hussein from Kuwait, it should be overwhelming and decisive force, not gradual limited escalation, as in Vietnam. Powell "ran interference" in Washington for the field commander, General Norman Schwarzkopf. Powell's televised briefings during the course of the war, together with those of General Schwarzkopf, assured the American people of the competence and effectiveness of the U.S. military. He summed up U.S. military strategy toward the Iraqi Army in Kuwait: "First we're going to cut it off. Then we're going to kill it." Under Powell's leadership, the U.S. military achieved a brilliant victory in the Gulf War with precious few casualties.

Powell retired from the Army in 1993, inspiring speculation that the popular general might enter the political arena. Throughout his military career, Powell avoided partisan affiliation. Registered as a political independent, Powell always considered himself a soldier first. Powell credits his success to those who "suffered and sacrificed to create the conditions and set the stage for me."[20]

Early in 1996, public opinion polls showed Powell leading all other candidates for president, including incumbent Bill Clinton. But Powell steadfastly refused to become a candidate. Rather, he founded an organization, Alliance for Youth, dedicated to helping disadvantaged youngsters. In the 2000 presidential election he endorsed George W. Bush, the son of his old Boss. He declined to join the Republican ticket as vice-president, but he accepted the position of Secretary of State.

SUMMARY

Governmental power is even more concentrated than corporate and financial power in America. All government expenditures now account for about 30 percent of the GDP, and *federal* expenditures account for nearly two-thirds of all government expenditures. America's booming economy of the 1990s actually grew faster than government expenditures, causing a modest decline in the size of government spending relative to the economy. Yet government regulations continue to multiply.

Governmental elites include both elected politicians and appointed

[20] Colin Powell, *My American Journey* (New York: Random House, 1995), p. 12.

executives, as well as the "fat cat" campaign contributors who keep them in office. The costs of running for public office rise with each election cycle. The result is that campaign contributors become ever more important and powerful in politics. The top contributors from the corporate, banking, and investment worlds are those listed among the largest and most powerful institutions in those sectors of society. Campaign contributions from labor unions give these institutions more power in politics than they currently enjoy in the economy itself.

While a significant number of top political leaders have inherited wealth and power, most have climbed the ladder from relative obscurity to political success. The Kennedys and Bushes inherited great wealth and power, but Ronald Reagan, Bill Clinton, and many others climbed to prominence from relatively modest backgrounds. Bill Clinton's biography contrasts notably from the biographies of members of the Bush family dynasty.

The politicians' principal talent is running for office; most appointed executives, on the other hand, have had some experience in running large public or private organizations. Running for office is not the same as running a government. Presidents must depend on "serious" people to run government. Skill in campaigning does not necessarily prepare individuals for the responsibility of governing. Key government executives must be recruited from industry, finance, the law, universities, and the bureaucracy itself. These serious people do not appear to differ much in background or education from Republican to Democratic administrations.

Congress seldom initiates programs, but rather it responds to the initiatives of the President, the executive departments, influential interest groups, and the mass media. Power *within* Congress is concentrated in the House and Senate leadership and in the chairperson and ranking minority members of the standing committees. Compared to other national elites, congressional leaders appear localistic. Their claim to national leadership must be safely hedged by attention to their local constituencies. Even national figures, such as Ted Kennedy and Hillary Rodham Clinton, must attend to their states' concerns. Most members of Congress are recruited from very modest, middle-class backgrounds.

The Supreme Court is the most elitist branch of government. Its nine members are not elected, and they serve life terms. They have the authority to void the acts of popularly elected Presidents and Congresses. It was the Supreme Court, rather than the President or Congress, that took the lead in eliminating segregation from public life, ensuring voter equality in representation, limiting the powers of police, and declaring abortion to be a fundamental right of women. Although most Justices have been upper class in social origin, their appointment has generally been related to their political activities rather than to their experience in the law.

5

The Media Moguls

Great power derives from the control of information. Media power is the power to decide what Americans will see, hear, and read about their world. Media power lies in creating issues, publicizing them, dramatizing them, getting people to talk about them, and forcing corporate and government officials to confront them. Media inattention creates nondecisions. It allows conditions in society that might otherwise concern people to be ignored. "TV is the Great Legitimator. TV confers reality. Nothing happens in America, practically everyone seems to agree, until it happens on television."[1]

AGENDA SETTING: DECIDING WHAT WILL BE DECIDED

The mass media, particularly television, set the agenda for public discussion. They determine what we think about and talk about. Political journalist Theodore White asserts:

> The power of the press in America is a primordial one. It sets the agenda of public discussion; and this sweeping political power is unrestrained by any law. It determines what people will talk about and think about—an authority that in other nations is reserved for tyrants, priests, parties, and mandarins.[2]

[1] William A. Henry, "News as Entertainment" in *What's News,* ed. Elie Abel (San Francisco, CA: Institute for Contemporary Studies, 1981), p. 134.

[2] Theodore White, *The Making of the President, 1972* (New York: Bantam, 1973), p. 327.

As children, Americans spend more time in front of television sets than in school. As adults, Americans spend half of their leisure time watching television. In the average home, the television set is on seven hours a day. More than two thirds of Americans report that they get all or most of their "news" from television. More important, television is the "most believable" medium of communication (see Figure 5–1).

The power of television derives not only from its large audiences but also from its ability to communicate *emotions* as well as *information*. Television's power is found in its visuals—angry faces in a rioting mob, police beating an African American motorist, wounded soldiers being unloaded from a helicopter—scenes that convey an emotional message. Moreover, television focuses on the faces of individuals as well as on their words, portraying honesty or deception, humility or arrogance, compassion or indifference, humor or meanness, and a host of other personal characteristics. Media-skilled elites understand that *what* one says may not be as important as *how* one says it. Television tells Americans what to *feel* as well as what to think about.

FIGURE 5–1   Sources and Believability of the News
Questions: First, I'd like to ask you where you usually get most of your news about what's going on in the world today—from the newspapers, or radio, or television, or magazines, or talking to people, or where?

If you got conflicting or different reports of the same news story from radio, television, the magazines, and the newspapers, which of the four versions would you be most inclined to believe—the one on radio or television or magazines or newspapers?

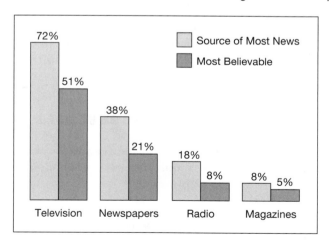

Note: Percentages (for sources of news) add up to 125 percent due to multiple responses. For trend line on these questions, see Harold W. Stanley and Richard G. Niemi, *Vital Statistics on American Politics, 1999–2000* (Washington, DC: Congressional Quarterly Press 1999). Between 1962 and 1964, television passed newspapers as the most believable medium.

The media elite—television and newspaper executives, reporters, editors, anchors, and producers—do not see themselves as neutral "observers" of American politics but rather as active "participants." They not only report events but also discover events to report, assign them political meaning, and predict their consequences. They seek to challenge government officials, debate political candidates, and define the problems of society. They see their profession as a "sacred trust" and themselves as the true voice of the people in public affairs.

Top executives in the news media, the "media moguls," do not doubt their own power. A generation ago they credited themselves with the success of the civil rights movement. The dramatic televised images of the nonviolent civil rights demonstrators of the early 1960s being attacked by police with night-sticks, cattle prods, and vicious dogs helped to awaken the nation and its political leadership to the injustices of segregation. Later, the television networks credited themselves with "decisively changing America's opinion of the Vietnam War," and forcing Lyndon Johnson out of the presidency.

Television news, together with the Washington press corps, also lays claim, of course, to the expulsion of Richard Nixon from the presidency. *The Washington Post* conducted the "investigative reporting" that produced a continuous flow of embarrassing and incriminating information about the President and his chief advisers. But it was the television networks that maintained the continuous nightly attack on the White House for nearly two years and kept Watergate in the public eye. Richard Nixon's approval rating in public opinion polls dropped from an all-time high of 68 percent in January 1973 following the Vietnam Peace Agreement to a low of 24 percent less than one year later.

Yet publicly the leadership of the mass media claim that they do no more than "mirror" reality. Although the "mirror" argument contradicts many of their more candid claims to having righted many of America's wrongs (segregation, Vietnam, Watergate), the leadership of the television networks still claim that television "is a mirror of society."

Of course, the mirror analogy is nonsense. Newspeople decide what the news will be, how it will be presented, and how it will be interpreted. Newspeople have the power to create some national issues and ignore others, elevate obscure people to national prominence, reward politicians they favor, and punish those they disfavor.

THE CONCENTRATION OF MEDIA POWER

Despite the multiplication of channels of communication in recent years, media power remains concentrated in the leading television networks (ABC, CBS, NBC, FOX, CNN), the nation's influential national newspapers (*Wash-*

ington Post, New York Times, Wall Street Journal, and *USA Today*), and the broad-circulation news magazines (*Time, Newsweek, U.S. News & World Report*). It is true that the national network evening news shows (*NBC Nightly News, ABC World News Tonight, CBS Evening News*) have lost viewership in recent years (down from a combined average of 40 million viewers in 1980 to 28 million today). But viewership of cable CNN and its headline companion HNN is rising, and viewership of local television news has remained strong. Moreover, television news magazines, notably CBS's *60 Minutes* and ABC's *20/20,* are regularly listed among the most popular shows on television. And television tabloids, such as *Hard Copy* and *Inside Edition,* are also gaining viewers.

The most influential New York and Washington newspapers are not so much instruments of mass communication as they are vehicles for *interelite* communication. It is especially important for top government officials to be familiar with both news stories and opinion columns that appear each day in the *Washington Post, New York Times, Wall Street Journal,* and *USA Today.* About 1,800 separate newspapers are published daily throughout the nation and read by approximately 70 percent of the adult population. But many of the news stories and virtually all of the opinion columns dealing with national affairs that appear in local newspapers throughout the country are taken from the national press.

News magazines have a somewhat broader readership than the New York and Washington press. *Time* is the nation's leading weekly news magazine, with a circulation of more than 4 million, followed by *Newsweek* and *U.S. News & World Report.* But the masses are more concerned with human interest stories, television and entertainment "news," travel, and tending their gardens— *Modern Maturity, Readers Digest, TV Guide, National Geographic,* and *Better Homes and Gardens* far exceed all news magazines in circulation.

Media megamergers in recent years have created corporate empires that spread across multiple media—television, film, print, music, and the Internet. These global conglomerates combine television broadcasting and cable programming, movie production and distribution, magazine and book publication, music recording, sports and recreation, and now Internet access and e-commerce. The seven multinational corporations listed in Table 5–1 dominate world media and cultural markets.

General Electric, Sony, and Seagram were originally industrial corporations; they bought into the media world. General Electric (GE appliances, aircraft engines, industrial products) is the largest of these corporations, but its ownership of media brings in only about 5 percent of its corporate revenue. Sony (a Japanese electronics multinational) receives only 30 percent of its corporate revenue from media operations. Seagram (a Canadian distillery) now receives more revenue from media enterprises than from its whiskey sales. Walt Disney, Viacom, and NewsCorp (Fox) are true media conglomerates.

The largest empire of all, AOL-Time Warner Inc., spreads itself beyond

TABLE 5–1   The Media Empires

1   AOL-Time Warner
Television: HBO, TNT, TBS, CNN, CNNSI, CNNFN, Cinemax, Time Warner Cable
Motion Pictures: Warner Brothers, New Line Cinema, Castle Rock, Looney Tunes
Magazines: Time, People, Sports Illustrated, Fortune, plus twenty-eight other speciality magazines
Books: Warner Books, Little, Brown Publishing, Book-of-the-Month Club
Music: Warner Brothers Records, Atlantic Records, Elektra
Sports and Entertainment: Atlanta Braves, Atlanta Hawks, World Championship Wrestling
Internet: AOL, Netscape, CompuServe

2   Walt Disney
Television: ABC-TV, plus ten stations; ESPN, ESPN-2, Disney Channel, A&E, E!, Lifetime
Motion Pictures: Walt Disney Pictures, Miramax, Touchstone
Music: Walt Disney Records, Mammoth
Sports and Recreation: Disney theme parks in Florida, California, France, Japan; cruise line; Anaheim Angels, Mighty Ducks

3   Viacom
Television: CBS, plus thirty-four TV stations: MTV, TNN, Nickelodeon, Showtime, VH1, NicK-At-Nite
Motion Pictures: Paramount Pictures, Spelling, Viacom
Books: Simon & Schuster, Scribner, Free Press
Music: Famous Music Publishing
Sports and Recreation: Blockbuster Video, SportsLine, plus five Paramount parks

4   NewsCorp (Fox)
Television: Fox Network plus fifteen TV stations; Fox News, Fox Sports, Fox Family Channel
Motion Pictures: 20th Century Fox, Searhlight
Books: HarperCollins
Music: Mushroom Records
Sports and Recreation: Los Angeles Dodgers

5   Seagram
Television: USA Network
Motion Pictures: Universal Pictures
Music: MCA, Geffen, Def Jam, Motown
Sports and Recreation: Universal Studios theme parks in California and Florida

6   Sony
Television: Game Show Network
Motion Pictures: Columbia Pictures, Sony Pictures, Tri Star
Music: Columbia Records, Epic Records, Nashville Records
Sports and Recreation: Sony Theaters

7   General Electric
Television: NBC Network plus thirteen TV stations; CNBC, MSNBC

television, cable, motion pictures, magazines, books, sports, and entertainment, into cyberspace. Time Warner was already a merged corporate conglomerate, the largest true media empire, *before* its merger with the nation's largest Internet provider, America Online. Time, Inc., originally a news magazine publisher (*Time, People, Sports Illustrated, Fortune,* etc) had merged with Warner Communications, originally a motion picture production company, in 1989. Then Time Warner merged with Ted Turner-owned CNN, Turner Broadcasting, and the Atlanta Braves, in 1996. One of the biggest mergers in American corporate history was announced in early 2000: the two giants of their respective industries—Time Warner, the media conglomerate, and America Online, with 22 million Internet subscribers—combined to form a new colossus. The combined stock market value of AOL and Time Warner is greater than that of any other corporation in America.

AOL is one of the few profit-making firms on the Internet. With over 20 million subscribers, it has the largest customer base. Its energetic young CEO, Stephen Case, had served short terms in the corporate ranks of Procter & Gamble, Pizza Hut, and Pepsico before jumping into a start-up computer firm, Quantum Control. Case quickly became "a serious geek," and in 1992 founded his own America OnLine and rocketed into cyberspace. In contrast, Time Warner was a well-established, prestigious media giant when it agreed to the merger with AOL-Time Warner's chairman, Gerald M. Levin, was once a partner in the prestigious New York law firm of Simpson Thacher and Bartlett (see Chapter 7) who specialized in media affairs, becoming CEO of HBO and eventually its parent, Time Warner. He was well connected politically as a member of the Business roundtable, the Council on Foreign Relations, and the Tri-lateral Commission. But both Case and Levin must deal with the unpredictable Ted Turner, who retains vice-chairmanship of AOL Time Warner as a result of the earlier merger between Turner Broadcasting and Time Warner.

Walt Disney has a large and prestigious Board of Directors (including actor Sidney Poitier) but the charismatic Michael Eisner dominates this vast media empire. Eisner came up through the rough and tumble ranks of programming at CBS, then went to Hollywood as CEO of Paramount Pictures and made a surprise switch to Walt Disney in 1984.

Viacom is closely held by the Redstone family and its patriarch, Sumner M. Redstone. Redstone served in the Army in World War II, received his bachelor's and law degrees from Harvard, and was a partner in a Washington law firm before getting into the entertainment industry. He took over Viacom in 1986 and began a series of corporate acquisitions in motion pictures (Paramount), publishing (Simon & Schuster), and finally in a surprise coup, CBS television. His son and daughter serve on the relatively small Board of Directors, apparently keeping Viacom decisions largely within the family.

TED TURNER: MAVERICK MEDIA MOGUL

Media power is *less* concentrated today than a decade ago, owing to the development of satellite and cable technology that adds greater variety of communication channels. Today over 65 percent of TV households are connected to cable, diluting the power of the older established networks—ABC, CBS, and NBC—and providing diverse news and entertainment broadcasting, from C-SPAN coverage of Congress to MTV and the Cartoon Network. Perhaps no single individual is more responsible for the development of diversity in television communication than the flamboyant tycoon Ted Turner. Once ridiculed by established media elites as "the Mouth of the South," Turner changed the course of television news broadcasting with the creation of his twenty-four-hour news network, CNN.

Reportedly a mischievous child with a difficult upbringing, Turner was sent to the Georgia Military Academy before entering Brown University. He was expelled for various infractions and served a brief tour with the U.S. Coast Guard before entering the family's billboard advertising company in Atlanta. When the business floundered and his father committed suicide, young Ted took over and began building his empire. He used the restored profits from the billboard company to buy television stations and invest in the new satellite technology. With FCC deregulation of satellite broadcasting in 1975, Turner was well positioned to challenge the major networks. Turner's Atlanta-based WTBS was the first "superstation" beaming its programs via satellite throughout the nation. He purchased the Atlanta Braves and the Atlanta Hawks to help feed his programming as well as his mountainous ego. In 1988 Turner purchased the MGM film library, including the classic *Gone with the Wind*, to add to offerings shown on WTBS and his entertainment network, TNT.

But Turner's greatest achievement was the creation of CNN in 1981, despite near-unanimous predictions of financial disaster. Turner borrowed heavily to establish CNN and nursed it financially for many years before it became profitable. The requirement to fill twenty-four hours with news, interviews, and commentary means that CNN offers more "raw" news than any other network. News on CNN is less burdened with editing, "interpretation," and context than on ABC, CBS, or NBC. And CNN recruits some conservative commentators (for example, on *Crossfire*) in order to spark controversy. The Gulf War cemented CNN as the nation's leading source of fast-breaking news. Only CNN had live satellite coverage as bombs began to fall on Baghdad on the night of January 16, 1991. CNN would later come under criticism for broadcasts of enemy propaganda by its correspondent, Peter Arnett, but CNN established itself as a serious rival to the established news organizations. Today CNN International is shown in hotels around the world.

As Turner transformed his empire, Turner Broadcasting, Inc., into a major media corporation, he increasingly recruited professional executives and producers to manage affairs. In order to finance his purchase of MGM in 1986, he diluted some of this authority by giving some cable systems operators seats on his board of directors. Despite his success in capitalism, Turner's personal politics are decidedly left of center; his marriage to "progressive activist" Jane Fonda (now estranged from Turner) no doubt reinforced his often expressed cynicism toward American institutions. But Turner wisely refrained from direct interference in programming.

The merger of Time Warner and AOL further diluted Turner's media power, reportedly to his dissatisfaction. He remains Vice-Chairman of the AOL-Time Warner Board of Directors and the largest individual shareholder in the corporation. Over the last twenty years he has amused himself by acquiring huge tracts of land throughout the United States. He is today the nation's single largest private landowner.

KATHERINE GRAHAM: THE MOST POWERFUL WOMAN IN AMERICA

For many years, Katherine Graham, the owner and publisher of the *Washington Post* and *Newsweek* magazine, was once recognized as the most powerful woman in America. Her leadership of the *Post*, which did more than any other publication to expose the Watergate scandal and force the resignation of President Richard Nixon, established Graham as one of the most powerful figures in Washington. The *Washington Post* is the capital's most influential newspaper, and it vies with the *New York Times* as the world's most influential newspaper. These are the papers read by all segments of the nation's elite, and both papers feed stories to the television networks and wire services.

Graham inherited her position from her father and husband, but when she became president of the Washington Post Company in 1963, she demonstrated her own capacity to manage great institutional power. She was the daughter of a wealthy New York banker, Eugene Meyer. Like many elites, her education was in the fashionable private preparatory schools; she also attended Vassar College and the University of Chicago. In 1933 her father bought the *Washington Post* for less than $1 million. Katherine Meyer worked summers on her father's paper, and then took a job as a reporter with the *San Francisco News*. After one year as a reporter, she joined the editorial staff of the *Washington Post*.

In 1940, she married Philip L. Graham, a Harvard Law School graduate with a clerkship under Supreme Court Justice Felix Frankfurter. After service in World War II, Philip Graham was made publisher of the *Washington Post* by his father-in-law. Meyer later sold the paper to the Grahams for one dollar. The Washington Post Company proceeded to purchase other competitive papers in the nation's capital; it also bought *Newsweek* magazine from the Vincent Astor Foundation, as well as five television stations and several pulp and paper companies.

In 1963, Philip Graham committed suicide, and Katherine Graham took control of the *Washington Post–Newsweek* enterprises. By the early 1970s the *Washington Post* was challenging the *New York Times* as the nation's most powerful newspaper. Graham relied heavily on her executive editor, Benjamin Bradlee, who was directly responsible for the Watergate "investigative reporting" of Bob Woodward and Carl Bernstein that led to President Nixon's downfall. But reportedly Graham herself made the key decisions.

Indeed, the Washington Post Company's domination of the Washington scene gives it great power over federal officials and agencies. As columnist Kevin Phillips observes:

> We might note the quasi-governmental role played by the Washington Post Company. The Post Company has a five-level presence in Washington—a newspaper (the *Washington Post*), a radio station (WTOP), a television station (WTOP-TV), a news magazine (*Newsweek*), and a major news service (L.A. Times–Washington Post). Not only does the Washington Post Company play an unmatched role as a federal government information system—from the White House to Congress to the bureaucracy and back—it serves as a cue card for the network news, and it plays a huge role in determining how the American government communicates to the American people.[3]

Graham was also a trustee of the John F. Kennedy School of Government of Harvard University, George Washington University, the University of Chicago, and the Urban Institute. She was a member of the Council on Foreign Relations.

In 1991 Katherine Graham turned over operating responsibility for the Washington Post Company to her son, Donald E. Graham. Donald graduated from Harvard in 1966, served in the Army for two years, and then spent over twenty years in various Washington Post management positions before his mother named him president and chief executive officer and later chairman of the board.

The current board includes corporate and banking ties (e.g., J.P. Morgan, Coca-Cola, Johnson & Johnson), a tie to the top law firm Cravath, Swaine & Moore (see Chapter 6), and the presence of Wall Street's most feared and admired investor, Warren Buffett (see Table 5–2).

Katherine Graham died following an accidental fall in 2001 at age 84. Her Washington funeral, broadcast on all major media outlets, brought together elites from virtually every sector of American society.

---

[3] Kevin Phillips, "Busting the Media Trusts," *Harpers* (July, 1977), p. 30.

TABLE 5–2   Inside the Washington Post Boardroom

Inside Directors

Donald E. Graham, Chairman & CEO
Katherine Graham,* Chairman Ex Com
Diana M. Daniels, Vice-President
Beverly R. Keil, Vice-President
John B. Morse, Vice-President

Outside (Public Interest) Directors

Ralph E. Gomory
   President, Sloan Foundation; Director of Ashland Oil, Bank of New York
William J. Ruane
   Chairman, West Philadelphia Corp. (inner city development); Roman Catholic priest

Outside (Corporate) Directors

Richard D. Simmons
   President, International Herald Tribune: Director of J.P. Morgan, Union Pacific
George J. Gillespie III
   Senior Partner, Cravath, Swaine & Moore
Donald E. Keogh
   President & CEO, Coca-Cola Co.
George W. Wilson
   President, Newspapers of New England
James E. Burke
   Former Chairman, Johnson & Johnson
Warren E. Buffett
   Chairman, Berkshire Hathaway (investments); Director of Saloman, Inc., Coca-Cola,
   Gillette

*Died 2001.

THE CELEBRITY NEWSMAKERS

Each night about 28 million Americans watch one of three men: Dan Rather, Peter Jennings, or Tom Brokaw. No other individuals—not presidents, movie stars, or popes—have had such extensive contact with so many people. These network celebrities are recognized and heard by more people than anyone else on the planet. The networks demand that an anchor be the network's premier journalist, principal showman, top editor, star, symbol of news excellence, and single most important living logo.

Anchors, then, are both celebrities and newspeople. They are chosen for their mass appeal, but they must also bring journalistic expertise to their jobs. The anchors help select from thousands of hours of videotapes and hundreds of separate stories that will be squeezed into the twenty-two minutes of nightly network news (eight minutes are reserved for commercials). Each minute represents approximately 160 spoken words; the total number of words on the entire newscast is less than found on a single newspaper page. These inherent restrictions of the medium give great power to the anchors and their executive producers through their selection of what Americans will see and hear about the world each night.

All three network anchors share liberal and reformist social values and political beliefs.

Dan Rather, who deliberately projects an image of emotional intensity, has created both strong attachments and heated animosities among his audiences. He is most despised by conservatives because of his undisguised and passionate liberal views. Rather worked his way up through the ranks of CBS news following graduation from Sam Houston State College. He was a reporter and news director for the CBS affiliate station in Houston, then chief of the CBS London Bureau, and later Vietnam correspondent. He came to national prominence in 1966 as a CBS White House correspondent and took over the anchor position from Walter Cronkite in 1981.

The Canadian-born Peter Jennings projects an image of thoughtful, urbane sophistication. He is widely traveled (his father was a journalist), but his formal education ended in the tenth grade. ABC's *World News Tonight with Peter Jennings* devotes slightly more time to international news than do its rival news shows.

Tom Brokaw offers a calm, unemotional delivery with occasional touches of wry humor. Brokaw graduated from the University of South Dakota and started his career at an Omaha television station. He anchored local news in Atlanta and Los Angeles before moving up to the post of NBC White House correspondent in 1973. He hosted the NBC *Today* show from 1976 to 1982, and his show biz and talk-show-host experience has served him well as anchor of the *NBC Nightly News* since then. He is less ideological than Rather or Jennings and can appear relaxed and friendly with Republicans as well as Democrats.

The ratings race among the anchors is very close. Indeed, the closeness of those ratings may be driving the shows toward even more sensational themes, violent confrontations, and dramatic hype. Although all current shows have expert commentators, they are used less often; and it is now almost mandatory to end the show with a crowd-pleasing human interest story.

BAD NEWS AND GOOD PROFITS

The economic interests of the media elite—the need to capture and hold audience attention—creates a bias toward "hype" in the selection, presentation, and interpretation of news. The media must attract and hold large audiences so that they may be sold to advertisers. On an average night, nearly 100 million people will watch television. Advertisers must pay $100,000 to $500,000 for a single fifteen- or thirty-second prime-time spot on any of the major networks. Advertisers pay the networks on the basis of ratings, compiled by independent services, the most popular of which is the A.C. Nielson Company. By placing electronic boxes in a national sample of television homes, Nielson calculates the proportion of all "TV households" that watch a program (the "rating"), as well as the proportion of TV households with their sets turned on that watch a specific program (the "share").

Bad news makes good profits. Bad news attracts larger audiences than good news. So television news displays a pervasive bias toward the negative in American life—in politics, government, business, the military, schools, and everywhere else. Bad news stories on television outnumber good news stories by at least three to one.[4] All presidential candidates receive more bad coverage than good.

The network's concentration on scandal, abuse, and corruption in government has not always produced the desired liberal, reformist notions in the minds of the masses of viewers. Contrary to the expectations of the media elite, their focus on political wrongdoing has produced feelings of general distrust and cynicism toward government and "the system." These feelings have been labeled "television malaise"—a combination of social distrust, political cynicism, feelings of powerlessness, and disaffection from parties and politics which seems to stem from television's emphasis on the negative aspects of American life.[5] The long-run effects of this elite behavior may be self-defeating in terms of elite interest in maintaining a stable political system.

LIBERAL BIAS IN THE NEWS

When TV newscasters insist that they are impartial, objective, and unbiased, they may sincerely believe that they are, because in the world in which they live—the New York and Washington world of newspeople, writers, intellectuals, artists—the established liberal point of view is so uniformly voiced. TV news executives can be genuinely shocked and affronted when they are charged with slanting their coverage toward liberal concerns. But the media elite—the executives, producers, reporters, editors, and anchors—are

---

[4] See Ben J. Wattenberg, *The Good News Is the Bad News Is Wrong* (New York: Simon & Schuster, 1984).

[5] Michael Robinson, "Public Affairs Television and the Growth of Political Malaise," *American Political Science Review,* 70 (June 1976), 409–32; and "Television and American Politics," *The Public Interest* (Summer 1977), pp. 3–39.

decidedly "liberal" and "left-leaning" in their political views. Political scientist Doris A. Graber writes about the politics of the media: "economic and social liberalism prevails, as does a preference for an internationalist foreign policy, caution about military intervention, and suspicion about the ethics of established large institutions, particularly government."[6] One study of news executives reported that 63 percent described themselves as "left-leaning," only 27 percent as "middle-of-the-road," and 10 percent as "right-leaning." Newsmakers describe themselves as either "independent" (45 percent) or Democratic (44 percent); very few (9 percent) admit to being Republican.[7]

The older, established television networks—ABC, CBS, and NBC—present nearly identical liberal "packages" of news each evening. They have been described as "rivals in conformity."[8] Liberal views also dominate at CNN (once described by Republicans as "Clinton's News Network"), although the need to broadcast 24 hours of news each day often leads to the presentation of "raw" (unadulterated) news on this network. And the need to fill so much time obliges CNN to broadcast many debate and commentary shows—shows that often present an adversarial format with both liberal and conservative voices. Only recently have moderate to conservative views been expressed on cable MSNBC and Fox news. The nation's prestigious press—the *New York Times* and the *Washington Post*—are decidedly liberal. However, the equally prestigious *Wall Street Journal* is moderate to conservative. In the nation's capital, the conservative newspaper the *Washington Times* is trying to challenge the *Washington Post*.

The liberal bias of the media elite contrasts with the moderately conservative views of business leaders (see Table 5–3). Most of the media elite enjoyed socially privileged upbringings. Fewer than one in five came from working-class families. Few of them are outright socialists; they overwhelmingly reject the idea that major corporations should be taken over by the government. Most reject rigid egalitarianism and support the idea that people with more ability should be paid more money. Most believe that free enterprise is fair. However, the media elite is strongly committed to the welfare state. They believe the government should reduce income differences between the rich and the poor, and nearly half believe that the government should guarantee jobs. They favor affirmative action and believe environmental problems are serious. They are liberals on social issues such as abortion and homosexuality.

[6] Doris A. Graber, *Mass Media and American Politics* (Washington, D.C.: Congressional Quarterly Press, 1980), p. 49.

[7] S. Robert Lichter, Stanley Rothman, and Linda S. Lichter, *The Media Elite* (New York: Hastings House, 1990), p. 47.

[8] Doris Graber, *Mass Media and American Politics*, p. 68.

TABLE 5–3 Liberal Values among Business, News, and Entertainment Leaders

	Percent of Leaders in Agreement		
	Business	News	Entertainment
Economic liberalism			
Government should redistribute income.	23	68	69
Government should guarantee jobs.	29	48	45
Big corporations should be publicly owned.	6	13	19
Private enterprise is fair.	89	70	69
People with more ability should earn more.	90	86	94
Reformism			
Structure of society causes alienation.	30	49	62
Institutions need overhaul.	28	32	48
Social liberalism			
Strong affirmative action for blacks is needed.	71	80	83
Women have the right to abortions.	80	90	97
Homosexuals should not teach in schools.	51	15	15
Homosexuality is wrong.	60	25	20
Adultery is wrong.	76	47	49

Sources: Robert Lichter and Stanley Rothman, "Media and Business Elites," *Public Opinion* (October–November 1981), pp. 42–46; Linda S. Lichter, S. Robert Lichter, and Stanley Rothman, "Hollywood and America: The Odd Couple," *Public Opinion* (December–January 1983), pp. 54–58; David Prindle, "Hollywood Liberalism," *Social Science Quarterly* (March, 1993), p. 121.

PRIME TIME: SOCIALIZING THE MASSES

Prime-time entertainment programming suggests to Americans how they ought to live and what values they ought to hold. Socialization—the learning, accepting, and approving of customs, values, and life styles—is an important function of the mass media. Network television entertainment is the most widely shared experience in the country. America's favorite TV shows are shown to over 50 million individual viewers in 20 million households. This is two-and-one-half times the average audience for network news. The network executives who decide what will be shown as entertainment have a tremendous impact on the values, aspirations, and life styles of Americans.

Top network executives and Hollywood producers are generally "coast oriented" in their values and life styles; that is, they reflect popular culture in New York and California. Almost all are from the big cities of the East and West coasts. Almost all are white males. A majority are Jewish. They are well-educated, extraordinarily well-paid, and independent or Democratic in their politics. They are *not* radicals or socialists. Almost all believe that "people with ability should earn more," and most support free enterprise and oppose government ownership of the economy. However, these television programmers are very critical of government and business; they believe strongly that society is unfair to women, blacks, and minorities; and they are socially very liberal in terms of their views on abortion, homosexuality, and adultery.

More important, perhaps, the programmers believe that they have a responsibility to change America's views to fit their own. They believe that television should "promote social reform." (Fully two thirds of the programmers interviewed agreed with this definition of their role in society.) "This is perhaps the single most striking finding in our study. According to television's creators, they are not in it just for the money. They also seek to move their audience toward their own vision of the good society."[9]

Much of our learning is subconscious. If these televised images are inaccurate, we end up with wrong impressions of American life. If television shows emphasize sex and violence, we come to believe that there is more sex and violence in America than is actually the case. For millions of Americans, television is a way of keeping in touch with their environment. Both entertainment and advertising provide model ways of life. People are shown products, services, and life styles that they are expected to desire and imitate.

Hollywood produces relatively few uplifting movies (e.g., *Forrest Gump*, *The Lion King*, the *Little Princess*) compared to the number of sex-obsessed, profanity-ridden, and excessively violent films (e.g., *Natural Born Killers*, *Pulp Fiction*, *Fight Club*). Television shows have become increasingly controversial; they glamorize unmarried motherhood and celebrate homosexual life styles. Records are released with lyrics that encourage cop-killing, rape, and suicide.

Media elites claim that their shows simply reflect the sex, vulgarity, and violence already present in our culture, that restraints on moviemakers would inhibit "creative oratory," and that censorship would violate "freedom of expression." They argue that politicians from Dan Quayle (who attacked *Murphy Brown* for glamorizing unmarried motherhood) to Bob Dole (who attacked Time-Warner for promoting "gangsta rap") and Tipper Gore (for advocating warning labels on records) are merely pandering for the votes of religious conservatives. And they contend that the popularity of their movies, television shows, and records (judged in terms of money received from million's of movie-goers, viewers, and listeners) prove that Americans are entertained by the current Hollywood output, regardless of what socially approved responses they give to pollsters. "Movies drenched in gore, gangsta rap, even outright pornography are not some sort of alien interstellar dust malevolently drifting down on us, but products actively sought out and beloved by millions."[10]

[9] Linda S. Lichter, S. Robert Lichter, and Stanley Rothman, "Hollywood and America: The Odd Couple," *Public Opinion* (December–January, 1983), p. 58.
[10] Quoting Katha Pollitt, *Time* June 12, 1995, pp. 33–36.

SUMMARY

The people who control the flow of information in America are among the most powerful in the nation. Television network broadcasting is the first form of truly *mass* communication; it carries a visual image with emotional content as well as information. Television news reaches virtually everyone, and for most Americans it is the major source of information about the world.

The power of mass media is primarily in agenda-setting—deciding what will be decided. The media determine what the masses talk about and what the elite must decide about. Political issues do not just "happen." The media decide what are issues, problems, even crises, which must be acted upon.

Control of the nation's news and entertainment is concentrated in a small number of media empires. These empires now combine television, motion pictures, magazines, books, music, sports and recreation, and the Internet—virtually all forms of mass communication. AOL-Time Warner is the nation's largest megamerged media conglomerate. Others include Walt Disney, Viacom, NewsCorp, Seagram, Sony, and General Electric. As in other sectors of the nation's elite, one finds both inheritors (Katherine Graham) and climbers (Ted Turner).

Despite multiplication of media channels, great power remains lodged in leading television networks—ABC, CBS, NBC, and CNN—together with the influential national press—the *New York Times,* the *Washington Post,* the *Wall Street Journal*—and the broad-circulation news magazines—*Time, Newsweek,* and *U.S. News and World Report.* Their power arises from their ability to set the agenda for both public discussion, and perhaps more importantly, inter-elite communication. It is especially important for Washington decision-makers to be familiar with news stories and opinion columns that appear each day in the nation's leading newspapers.

The mass media must attract large audiences to sell to advertisers. The principal source of bias in the news originates from the need to capture large audiences with drama, action, and confrontation. The result is an emphasis on *un*favorable stories about prominent people and business and government. However, media attention to scandal, abuse, violence, and corruption has not always produced liberal reformist values. Many scholars believe it has produced "television malaise"—distrust, cynicism, and disaffection from public affairs caused by negative reporting on American life. This reporting may also be contributing to the public's decline in confidence in the media.

The media elite is the most liberal segment of the nation's elite. While this elite supports the free enterprise system and reward based on merit, it favors government intervention to reduce income differences and to aid women, blacks, and minorities. News executives claim only to "mirror" reality, yet at the same time they take credit for civil rights laws, ending the Vietnam War, and expelling Richard Nixon from the White House. Prime-time programming executives are even more liberal in their views, and they acknowledge that their role is to "reform" society.

The entertainment industry plays an important role in socializing the masses of Americans as to how they should live and what values they ought to hold. Prime-time television entertainment as well as the motion picture industry generally reflect liberal values, but their messages are often obscured by their need to attract audiences with sex and violence.

6

The Civic Establishment

dedicated to truth, liberty & pub interest

In an advanced, complex society, there are many specialized institutions and organizations that exercise power. In addition to economic organizations (corporations, banks, insurance companies, and investment houses), governmental bureaucracies, television networks, and media organizations, there are other, less visible institutions that also provide bases of power in American society. An operational definition of a national elite must include individuals who occupy positions of power in influential law firms, major philanthropic foundations, recognized national cultural and civic organizations, and prestigious private universities. We shall refer to these institutions collectively as the "civic establishment."

CIVIC EST

THE AMERICAN "ESTABLISHMENT"

Is there a unifying "Establishment" in this nation, separate from business and government, which seeks to use its power, prestige, and wealth to further its own vision of America? The notion of an Establishment—with its old school ties, inherited wealth, upper-class life style, position, and privilege—flourishes even in a democratic society. Harvard historian Mark Silk and his brother, *New York Times* columnist Leonard Silk, write:

> Although the origins of the Establishment are ecclesiastical and aristocratic, in America it is firmly joined to both democratic and capitalist institutions. But its

ambitions go beyond: it seeks to protect and advance social, moral, and aesthetic values that transcend the interests of any single person, economic group, or political constituency or organization; it affects to be a harmonizer, an arbiter, a wise instructor of the nation—and particularly of its political and business leaders.[1]

This Establishment traces its roots, and even its name, to the established church in early Massachusetts. The nation's earliest democrats sought to ensure that there would be "no establishment of religion" by writing those words into the First Amendment of the Constitution. But in the early years the First Amendment applied only to the national government and not to the states; Massachusetts supported the established Congregationalist church well into the nineteenth century. Harvard College was the center of established religion, even after the more rigid Calvinists abandoned it in favor of more orthodox instruction at newer Yale College. This early schism in the established church was partly due to the greater openness, humanism, and tolerance of dissent at Harvard, traits which are supposed to characterize the Establishment even today.[2]

The Establishment today is said to "inhabit" the nation's most influential institutions. The Establishment is not an institution itself but rather a "collective entity" or "third force" (the other two being business and government) which links together various institutions in separate segments of society. The Establishment is concerned with maintaining a public ethos—a civic morality emphasizing tolerance, public-regardingness, and responsibility for the welfare of the masses.

CIVIC EST
responsi-
bilities

According to Silk and Silk the Establishment "inhabits" the following institutions:

Harvard University

New York Times

Ford Foundation

Brookings Institution

Council on Foreign Relations

Committee for Economic Development

Not every person associated with these institutions is a member of the Establishment. And there are other institutions which also possess Establishment connections:

---

[1] Leonard Silk and Mark Silk, *The American Establishment* (New York: Basic Books, 1980), p. 325.

[2] According to the Silks, Harvard represented a middle religious ground between the Calvinists at Yale and the Enlightenment Deists of the Virginia planters, notably Thomas Jefferson. Only six of the fourteen faculty members at Harvard in 1831 were Unitarians; the faculty even included three Roman Catholics and a Quaker. See Silk and Silk, ibid., p. 13.

Yale University

Princeton University

Columbia University

University of Chicago

Stanford University

Carnegie Endowment for International Peace

RAND Corporation

Twentieth Century Fund

Russell Sage Foundation

Century Club

Metropolitan Museum of Art

Museum of Modern Art

Metropolitan Opera

But these institutions do not define the Establishment. Instead, the Establishment is defined as "a national force, outside government, dedicated to truth, liberty, and however defined, the broad public interest."[3]

Our own notion of a civic establishment is similar yet somewhat broader than the Establishment described by Silk and Silk. Our definition includes the nation's most prestigious New York and Washington law firms; influential power-brokers ("fixers") in Washington; the nation's billion dollar foundations, including Ford, Rockefeller, Mellon, and Carnegie; the leading policy-planning organizations; and the private universities with billion dollar endowments. We acknowledge that the definition of a civic establishment involves many subjective judgments. We shall try to defend these judgments, but we recognize that equally valid defenses of alternative judgments might be made.

THE "SUPERLAWYERS"

As modern societies grow in size and complexity, the need for rules and regulations increases geometrically, and so does the power of people whose profession is to interpret those rules and regulations. As early as 1832, deTocqueville felt that the legal profession in this country would become the "new aristocracy" of the Republic. C. Wright Mills asserts that lawyers are indeed a key segment of the nation's aristocracy of power:

> The inner core of the power elite also includes men of the higher legal and financial type from the great law factories and investment firms who are profes-

---

[3] Silk and Silk, ibid, p. 20.

sional go-betweens of economic, political, and military affairs, and who thus act to unify the power elite.[4]

The predominance of lawyers among political elites has already been noted. Within the corporate elite—presidents and directors of the nation's largest industries, banks, utilities, and insurance companies—over 15 percent are lawyers. But neither the politician-lawyer nor the businessperson-lawyer really stands at the top of the legal profession. The "superlawyers" are the senior partners of the nation's most highly esteemed law firms. These are the firms that represent clients such as General Motors (King & Spalding), Exxon Mobil (Davis, Polk, Wardwell), Ford Motor (O'Melveny & Meyers), General Electric (Dewey, Balantine), IBM (Cravath, Swaine & Moore), Citigroup (Skadden, Arps), AT&T (Akin, Gump, Strauss, Hauer & Feld), Philip Morris (Arnold & Porter), not only in the courts but also before Congress and the federal regulatory agencies. Of course, the nation's largest corporate and financial institutions have their own legal departments; but attorneys in these departments, known as "house counsels," usually handle more routine matters. When the stakes are high, the great corporations turn to the superlawyers.

Identification of the nation's "top" law firms is necessarily a subjective task. Lists were developed by writers in the 1970s[5] and in the 1980s[6] (the statistical analyses in this book were performed with these earlier lists). Most of the firms identified in earlier years remain among the most powerful today. The *National Law Journal* now regularly lists the firms with the largest revenue as well as the firms most often mentioned as representatives of the nation's largest corporations.[7] The listings in Table 6–1 were compiled from a variety of sources and represents our best estimate of the nation's legal elite. The senior partners of these firms are our superlawyers.

The names of the firms themselves, of course, do not always identify the senior partners. Firms often retain the names of deceased founders, and most large firms have so many senior partners (twenty or thirty is not uncommon) that it would be impossible to put all their names in the title of the firm. Then, too, some firms change names upon the resignation of partners.

The senior partners of the nation's top law firms generally feel an obligation to public service. According to superlawyer Arthur Dean, the experience of serving in such a firm provides "an exceptional opportunity to acquire a liberal education in modern government and society. Such partnerships are likely in the future, as they have in the past, to prepare and offer for public

---

[4] C. Wright Mills, *The Power Elite* (New York: Oxford, 1956), p. 289.

[5] Joseph G. Goulden, *The Superlawyers* (New York: Dell, 1971).

[6] James B. Stewart, *The Partners: Inside America's Most Powerful Law Firms* (New York: Simon & Schuster, 1983).

[7] *National Law Journal,* June 21, 2000. www.law.com.

TABLE 6–1   The Nation's Top Law Firms

Highest Revenues

1	Skadden, Arps, Slate, Meagher & Flom	New York
2	Baker & McKenzie	International
3	Jones, Day, Reavis & Pogue	National
4	Latham & Watking	Los Angeles
5	Shearman & Sterling	New York
6	Mayer, Brown & Platt	Chicago
7	Davis Polk & Wardwell	New York
8	Sullivan & Cromwell	New York
9	Morgan, Lewis & Bocklus	National
10	Weil, Gotshal & Manges	New York
11	McDermott, Will & Emery	National
12	Simpson Thacher & Bartlett	New York
13	White & Case	International
14	Brobeck, Phleger & Harrison	San Francisco
15	Sidley & Austin	Chicago
16	Kirkland & Ellis	Chicago
17	Gibson, Dunn & Crutcher	Los Angeles
18	Gottlieb, Steen & Hamilton	New York
19	Wilson Sonsini Goodrich & Rosati	Palo Alto, California
20	Morrison & Foerster	San Francisco
21	Akin, Gump, Strauss, Hauer & Feld	National
22	O'Melveny & Myers	Los Angeles
23	Paul, Hastings, Janofsky & Walker	National
24	Vinson & Elkins	Houston
25	Cravath, Swaine & Moore	New York

Largest Number of Corporation's Represented

1	Skadden, Arps, Slate, Meagher & Flom	Washington
2	Howrey Simon Arnold & White	Washington
3	Jones, Day, Reavis & Pogue	National
4	Kirkland & Ellis	Chicago
5	Cravath, Swaine & Moore	New York
6	Davis Polk & Wardwell	New York
7	O'Melveny & Myers	Los Angeles
8	Sidley & Austin	Chicago
9	Akin, Gump, Strauss, Hauer & Feld	Washington
10	Mayer, Brown & Platt	Chicago
11	Wachtell, Lipton, Rosen & Katz	New York
12	King & Spalding	Atlanta
13	Baker & McKenzie	International
14	Gibson, Dunn & Crutcher	Los Angeles
15	Weil, Gotshal & Manges	National
16	Baker & Botts	Houston
17	Covington & Burling	New York
18	Latham & Watkins	Los Angeles
19	LeBoeuf, Lamb, Greene & MacRae	National
20	Morgan, Lewis & Bockius	National
21	Sullivan & Cromwell	New York

continued

TABLE 6–1   continued

Reputational Prestige (not ranked)	
Sullivan & Cromwell	New York
Milbank, Tweed, Hadley & McClay	New York
Dewey, Ballantine	New York
Wilkie Farr & Gallaher	New York
Cadwalader, Wickersham & Taft	New York
Cravath, Swaine & Moore	New York
Sherman & Stirling	New York
Davis, Polk & Wardwell	New York
Covington & Burling	Washington
Arnold & Porter	Washington
Clifford, Warke, Glass, McIlwain & Finney	Washington
Fried, Frank, Harris & Shriver	Washington
Wilmer, Cutler & Pickering	Washington
O'Melveny & Myers	Los Angeles
King & Spalding	Atlanta
Vinson & Elkins	Houston

Sources: See footnotes 5, 6, and 7.

service men exceptionally qualified to serve."[8] The arrogance of such an assertion has too much basis in fact to be dismissed as mere self-congratulation.

Superlawyers among the serious men who have been called upon over the years for governmental leadership include:

Dean Acheson.   Secretary of state under President Harry Truman (Covington & Burling)

John Foster Dulles.   Secretary of state under President Dwight Eisenhower (Sullivan & Cromwell)

Clark Clifford.   Secretary of defense under President Lyndon Johnson (Clifford, Warnke, Glass, McIlwain & Finney)

William P. Rogers.   Secretary of state under President Richard Nixon (Rodgers & Wells)

Cyrus Vance.   Secretary of state under President Jimmy Carter (Simpson, Thacher & Bartlett)

Warren Christopher.   Secretary of State under President Bill Clinton (O'Melveny & Myers)

James A. Baker III.   Secretary of State under George H. W. Bush (Baker & McKenzie)

In an even earlier era, the New York Wall Street law firms supplied presidential candidates:

[8] Quoted in Goulden, *The Superlawyers*, p. 36.

John W. Davis. Democratic party nominee for President of the United States, 1924 (Davis, Polk, Wardwell, Sunderland & Kiendl)

Wendell Willkie. Republican party nominee for President of the United States, 1940 (Willkie, Farr, Gallagher, Walton & Fitzgibbon)

Thomas E. Dewey. Republican party nominee for President of the United States, 1944 and 1948 (Dewey, Ballantine, Bushby, Palmer & Wood)

The typical path to the top of the legal profession starts with a Harvard, Yale, or Stanford law school degree, clerkship with a Supreme Court Justice, and then several years as an attorney with the Justice Department or a federal regulatory commission. Young government lawyers who are *successful* at defeating a top firm in a case are *more* likely to be offered lucrative junior partnerships than those who lose to big firms. Talented younger government lawyers are systematically recruited by the top firms.

THE "FIXERS": PEDDLING POWER FOR PROFIT

Washington is a city of "representatives"—agents, advocates, lawyers, lobbyists, and "fixers" who offer to influence government policy for a price. Washington representatives number in the thousands; their clients include individual corporations; professional and trade associations; communications, transportation, and utility companies; consumer and environmental groups; and foreign governments and corporations. As government *regulation* has grown, so also has the profitable business of defending clients from regulatory activity. As government *spending* has grown, so also has the lucrative profession of seeking out government grants and contracts. As government *power* has grown, so also have the profits of lawyers, lobbyists, consultants, and spokespersons, whose job it is to advance their clients' interests in Washington.

The fixers include the nation's prestigious law firms as well as lobbying firms and individual lobbyists. Their work includes legal counseling—representation before regulatory commissions or in civil or criminal proceedings—as well as legal advice on proposed laws and regulations and assistance in petitioning for special treatment under them. Their work also includes information and intelligence gathering—monitoring, analyzing, and informing their clients of current and future government activity. They may also provide public relations services—promoting a favorable climate of opinion for their clients. Their services usually include the various forms of direct lobbying—testifying before congressional committees and regulatory commissions; buttonholing Congress members, Cabinet officials, or White House staff; and trying to directly influence legislation or executive decisions. But perhaps most important of all, the Washington fixers provide their clients with *access* to the corridors and cocktail parties of power.

"Opening doors" is big business in Washington. To influence decision-makers, people must first acquire access to them. The Washington law firms, public relations agencies, and "consultants" all offer their insider connections along with their advice to their clients. Indeed, most of the top fixers are former government officials—former Congress members, Cabinet secretaries, White House aides, and the like—who "know their way around." The personal prestige and background of the fixer helps to open doors, to "just get a chance to talk" with top officials.

These are the services offered by notable Washington fixers such as Joseph A. Califano, of the Washington office of Dewey, Ballantine. Califano's clients reportedly include Bethlehem Steel, Bristol Myers, Chrysler, Walt Disney, Presidential Insurance, Seagrams, and Xerox. Califano also serves as a director of Chrysler, Primerica, Automatic Data Processing, and as a trustee of Urban Institute, New York University, Georgetown University, and the 20th Century Fund. He was secretary of Health Education and Welfare under President Jimmy Carter and special assistant to the President under Lyndon Johnson.

In recent years Wall Street investment firms have also seen the wisdom of bringing Washington insiders into their fold. It helps in putting together big deals to have "big names to help you get through the door." Consider the partners in the Carlyle Group, a Washington-based investment firm. In 1993 it added James Baker as a partner. Baker had been the most powerful appointed official in the Reagan and Bush administrations, serving first as secretary of the treasury, then chief of staff in the Reagan White House, and finally as secretary of state in the Bush administration. Baker's Washington and worldwide connections are unsurpassed. Baker was recruited to the Carlyle Group by its chairman, Frank Carlucci, former deputy CIA director who served briefly as secretary of defense in the Reagan administration. The Carlyle Group also includes Richard Darman, former budget director under President Bush. Carlucci acknowledges the value of good connections and powerful names in opening doors: "I'd be a fool to deny that having a number of high profile officeholders does provide Carlyle with certain advantages."[9]

Lobbying firms are obliged by law to report their total receipts as well as their political contributions. This makes it possible to rank the Washington lobbying firms by income (see Table 6–2). More than 100 lobbying firms in Washington earn at least $1 million representing heavyweight clients. Three of the firms at the top of the earnings list—Cassidy & Associates, Verner Liipfert, and Patton Boggs—regularly compete for the coveted reputation as "the most powerful firm in Washington." Patton Boggs leads in the number of clients, but Verner Liipfert boasts of having two former Senate majority leaders—Democrat George Mitchell and Republican Bob Dole—on its payroll. Some firms are weighted toward Democratic or Republican clients, as indicated by the percentage of their campaign contributions to each party.

[9] Quoted in *Time*, March 22, 1993, p. 39.

TABLE 6–2 Washington's Top Lobbying Firms (Ranked by Income)

		Percentage of Contributions to Parties	
		Democratic	Republican
1	Cassidy & Associates	63	37
2	Verner, Liipfert et al.	58	42
3	Patton Boggs LLP	74	26
4	Akin, Gump et al.	52	48
5	Preston, Gates et al.	44	55
6	Barbour, Griffith, & Rogers	0	100
7	Washington Counsel	46	54
8	Williams & Jensen	40	60
9	Baker, Donelson et al.	23	77
10	Hogan & Hartson	51	49
11	Pricewaterhouse Coopers	34	66
12	Van Scoyoc Associates	39	61
13	Timmons & Co.	50	50
14	Podesta.com	82	18
15	Alcalde & Fay	79	21
16	Arnold & Porter	63	37
17	Dutko Group	72	28
18	Black, Kelly et al.	33	67
19	Capitol Associates	61	39
20	Meyer, Brown, & Platt	66	34
21	Boland & Madigan Inc.	1	99
22	Griffin, Johnson et al.	99	1
23	McDermott, Will, & Emery	44	56
24	Arter & Hadden	24	76
25	Wexler Group	48	52

Source: Center for Responsive Politics.

THE FOUNDATIONS

The power of the nation's largest foundations derives from their financial support of projects in social problems, arts, and humanities. Actually, the foundations spend far less for research and development than does the federal bureaucracy. But the principal research components of the federal bureaucracy—the National Science Foundation, the U.S. Public Health Service—channel most of their funds into the physical, biological, and medical sciences. Thus, it has been the role of the nation's largest foundations to support and direct innovations in the social, intellectual, and cultural life of the nation.

The major foundations are in the forefront of national policy-making. They channel corporate and personal wealth into the policy-making process, providing both financial support and direction for university research and the activities of various policy-planning groups (see Chapter 8). Foundations are tax-exempt; contributions to foundations may be deducted from federal corporate and individual income taxes, *and* the foundations themselves are not subject to federal income taxation.

Foundations can be created by corporations or by individuals. These corporations or individuals can name themselves and their friends as directors or trustees of the foundations they create. Large blocs of corporate stock or large amounts of personal wealth can be donated as tax-exempt contributions to the foundations. The foundations can receive interest, dividends, profit shares, and capital gains from these assets without paying any taxes on them. The directors or trustees, of course, are not allowed to use foundation income or assets for their personal expenses, as they would their own taxable income. Otherwise, however, they have great latitude in directing the use of foundation monies—to underwrite research, investigate social problems, create or assist universities, establish "think tanks," endow museums, theaters, operas, symphonies, and so on.

According to *The Foundation Directory*, there were 10,445 foundations large enough to deserve recognition and listing in 2000; these are the foundations with at least $2 million in assets or $200,000 in yearly distributions. (There are tens of thousands of other smaller foundations and trusts, some established as tax dodges by affluent citizens and therefore not having any appreciable effect on public policy except to reduce tax collections.) These foundations controlled $304 billion in assets.[10] But as in other sectors of society, these foundation assets are concentrated in a small number of large foundations. The 38 largest, billion-dollar foundations control nearly half of all foundation assets in the nation (see Table 6–3).

Historically, the largest and most powerful foundations have been those established by the nation's leading families—Ford, Rockefeller, Carnegie, Mellon, Pew, Duke, Lilly, Danforth. Over the years, however, some foundations—for example, the Ford Foundation and the Carnegie Corporation—have become independent of their original family ties. Independence occurs when the foundation's own investments prosper and new infusions of family money are not required. A number of foundations limit their contributions to specific fields: The Johnson Foundation, for example, sponsors research in health care, and the Lilly Endowment supports advances in education and religion. In contrast, the Ford and Rockefeller foundations deliberately focus on a wide range of key national policy areas.

The trustees of the major foundations are drawn primarily from the corporate, banking, and investment worlds. However, a significant number are also drawn from the leadership of universities, civil rights organizations, and consumer and environmental movements. The chairman of the Board of Trustees of the Ford Foundation, for example, is Henry B. Schacht, former chairman of the board of Cummins Engine and a director of AT&T, CBS, and Chase Manhattan Bank. He is also a trustee of the Brookings Institution and

---

[10] *The Foundation Directory*, 1999 ed. (New York: Russell Sage Foundation, 2000).

TABLE 6–3   The Billion Dollar Foundations

Rank	Name	State
1	Lilly Endowment Inc.	Indiana
2	The Ford Foundation	New York
3	The David and Lucile Packard Foundation	California
4	W.K. Kellogg Foundation	Michigan
5	J. Paul Getty Trust	California
6	The Robert Wood Johnson Foundation	New Jersey
7	The Pew Charitable Trusts	Pennsylvania
8	John D. and Catherine T. MacArthur Foundation	Illinois
9	Robert W. Woodruff Foundation, Inc.	Georgia
10	The Rockefeller Foundation	New York
11	The Andrew W. Mellon Foundation	New York
12	The Annenberg Foundation	Pennsylvania
13	The Starr Foundation	New York
14	The Kresge Foundation	Michigan
15	The Duke Endowment	North Carolina
16	Charles Stewart Mott Foundation	Michigan
17	The Harry and Jeanette Weinberg Foundation, Inc.	Maryland
18	The William and Flora Hewlett Foundation	California
19	The California Endowment	California
20	The McKnight Foundation	Minnesota
21	Ewing Marion Kauffman Foundation	Missouri
22	The New York Community Trust	New York
23	Richard King Mellon Foundation	Pennsylvania
24	Robert R. McCarmick Tribune Foundation	Illinois
25	Carnegie Corporation of New York	New York
26	W. M. Keck Foundation	California
27	Houston Endowment, Inc.	Texas
28	The Annie E. Casey Foundation	Maryland
29	Doris Duke Charitable Foundation	New York
30	The Cleveland Foundation	Ohio
31	The Brown Foundation, Inc.	Texas
32	Joseph B. Whitehead Foundation	Georgia
33	Donald W. Reynolds Foundation	Oklahoma
34	John S. and James L. Knight Foundation	Florida
35	Alfred P. Sloan Foundation	New York
36	The California Wellness Foundation	California
37	The James Irvine Foundation	California
38	The William Penn Foundation California	Pennsylvania

Source: The Foundation Directory 1999.

Yale University. The Ford Foundation board also includes the veteran civil rights leader Vernon E. Jordan, Jr., who once served as executive director of the United Negro College Fund as well as the National Urban League. Jordan has also served as a director of American Express, Union Carbide, Corning Glass, Dow Jones and Company, Revlon, and Xerox Corp. (As a close friend of Bill and Hillary Clinton, his name was frequently mentioned in press reports of White House scandals.) The current chairman of the Board of Trustees of the Rockefeller Foundation is Alice Stone Ilchman, former president of Sarah Lawrence College, a director of Tri-Continental Corp., New York Telephone Co. (Verizon), Seligman Group (investments), and a member of the Council on Foreign Relations. The Rockefeller board also includes celebrity actor and political activist Alan Alda.

THE POLICY-PLANNING ORGANIZATIONS

CENTRAL IN POLICY MAKING PROCESS

Among the nation's many policy-planning organizations and "think tanks," we shall focus particular attention on the power of the Council on Foreign Relations, the Trilateral Commission, the Committee for Economic Development, the Business Roundtable, the Brookings Institution, the American Enterprise Institute, and the Heritage Foundation. These organizations are central coordinating mechanisms in national policy-making. They bring together people from the corporate and financial worlds, the universities, the media, the law firms, and the government to develop policies and programs for submission to Congress, the president, and the nation. Here we provide a general description of these organizations and their leadership; in Chapter 8 we shall examine their role in the policy-making process in greater detail.

The Council on Foreign Relations. The most influential policy-planning group in foreign affairs is the Council on Foreign Relations. The origins of the CFR go back to the Versailles Treaty in 1919 ending World War I. Some Americans, including Woodrow Wilson's key adviser, Edward M. House, believed that top leadership in the United States was not sufficiently informed about world affairs. The Council on Foreign Relations was founded in 1921 and supported by grants from the Rockefeller and Carnegie foundations and later the Ford Foundation. Its early directors were internationally minded Wall Street corporation lawyers such as Elihu Root (who was secretary of state), John W. Davis (1924 Democratic presidential nominee), and Paul Cravath (founder of the famous law firm of Cravath, Swaine & Moore), as well as Herbert Hoover (later to become President), Yale University president Charles Seymour, Harvard professor Archibald Cary Coolidge, and Columbia professor James T. Shotwell.

elite consensus on foreign policy

The CFR is designed to build consensus among elites on foreign policy questions. It initiates new policy directions by first commissioning scholars to undertake investigations of foreign policy questions. Its studies are usually made with the financial support of foundations. Upon their completion, the CFR holds seminars and discussions among its members and between its members and top government officials.

CFR publishes the journal *Foreign Affairs*, considered throughout the world to be the unofficial mouthpiece of U.S. foreign policy. Few important initiatives in U.S. policy have not been first outlined in articles in this publication. It was in *Foreign Affairs* in 1947 that George F. Kennan, chief of the policy-planning staff of the State Department, writing under the pseudonym of "X," first announced U.S. intentions of "containing" Communist expansion in the world. Current CFR concerns, as reflected in the pages of *Foreign Affairs*, the *Annual Report*, and other public sources, are discussed in Chapter 8.

The CFR limits its membership to 3,400 individuals who are proposed by existing members and who meet "high admissions standards." There is a long waiting list of individuals seeking membership in this prestigious organization. Broadly categorized, the membership profile look like this:[11]

Business and banking executives	25%
Academic scholars and administrators	21
U.S. government officials	14
Foundation, nonprofit administrators	19
Journalists, media executives	11
Lawyers	9
Other	1

The CFR's list of former members includes every person of influence in foreign affairs from Elihu Root, Henry Stimson, John Foster Dulles, Dean Acheson, Robert Lovett, George F. Kennan, Averill Harriman, and Dean Rusk, to Henry Kissinger, Cyrus Vance, Alexander Haig, George Schultz, and former president George Bush. The CFR describes itself as "a unique forum for bringing together leaders from the academic, public, and private worlds."

For almost two decades the CFR chairman was David Rockefeller, then chairman of the board of Chase Manhattan Bank (see Chapter 7). The international investment activity of Chase and the foreign policy influence and expertise of CFR dovetailed neatly in the person of the chairman. Rockefeller became honorary chairman in 1985 and turned over the reins of power to Peter G. Peterson. The CFR board of directors has always been a compendium of power and prestige:

Peter G. Peterson. Chairman of the board of the CFR. Former chairman and chief executive officer of Lehman Brothers, Wall Street investment firm. Former chairman of Bell and Howell Co., and former secretary of commerce. A director of Minnesota Mining & Mfg., General Foods, and the Rockefeller Center; and a trustee of the Committee on Economic Development and the Museum of Modern Art.

Cyrus R. Vance. Director emeritus of CFR. Former secretary of state. Former chairman of the Rockefeller Foundation; senior partner in the prestigious Wall Street law firm of Simpson, Thacher & Bartlett.

---

[11] Council on Foreign Relations, *Annual Report*, 1993, p. 105.

Lewis V. Gerstner, Jr. Chairman and CEO of IBM and a director of Bristol-Myers Squibb. Former chairman and CEO of RJR-Nabisco. A member of the Business Roundtable, a trustee of the New York Public Library, and a regent of the Smithsonian Institution (see also "The Battle for IBM" in Chapter 2).

Carla A. Hills. Former U.S. Trade representative and former Secretary of Housing and Urban development. A director of IBM, Corning Glass, American Airlines, and Chevron.

Paul A. Volcker. Former chairman of the Federal Reserve Board.

Diane Sawyer. ABC News television journalist.

Paul A. Allaire. Chairman and CEO of Xerox. A director of Sara Lee, J.P. Morgan, Smith Kline Beecham, Lucent Technologies, and the Ford Foundation.

The Trilateral Commission. The global economy requires a global elite. The Trilateral Commission was created in 1973 "to foster closer cooperation among these principal democratic industrialized areas [Japan, Western Europe, and the United States] with shared leadership responsibilities in the wider international system."[12] The Commission was originally established by the Council on Foreign Relations chairman David Rockefeller with the support of the Council and the Rockefeller Foundation.

The Trilateral Commission proclaims itself to be a "nongovernmental organization." It boasts of drawing together "the highest level unofficial group possible." Its membership consists of over 300 "distinguished individuals" from each of the three regions. The work of the Commission generally involves teams of authors from the three regions working together for a year or more on draft reports which are then discussed at the annual meeting of the Commission and later published as the "Triangle Papers." In addition, each regional group within the Commission carries out some activities on their own.

The current North American Chairman of the Trilateral Commission is Paul A. Volcker, former chairman of the Board of Governors of the U.S. Federal Reserve System. (David Rockefeller currently holds the title of "Founder and Honorary Chairman.")

The Committee on Economic Development. The Committee on Economic Development (CED) describes itself as "an independent, nonpartisan organization of business and education leaders dedicated to policy research on the major economic and social issues of our time." Its Board of trustees is composed of more than 200 executives of major U.S. corporations together with a small contingent of university presidents. The trustees organize and oversee the work of many policy-specific committees as well as the organization's staff in New York—deciding what policy issues CED will address, review-

---

[12] Quotations from the Trilateral Commission, *About the Trilateral Commission* (1998).

ing the progress of its "policy projects," and approving official CED policy statements. Recently, the board has approved policy statements in support of welfare reform, limiting the regulatory authority of federal agencies, and tort reform—limiting corporate liability for defective products. The CED executive committee includes:

> **Frank P. Doyle.** Chairman of the Committee on Economic Development's Executive Committee. Former executive vice-president of General Electric.
>
> **Raymond V. Gilmartin.** Chairman and CEO of Merck & Co. A director of General Mills; a member of the Business Roundtable.
>
> **Charles E. Lee.** Chairman and CEO of GTE. A director of United Technologies, Procter & Gamble, and USX; a member of the Business Roundtable.
>
> **John H. Bryan.** Chairman and CEO of Sara Lee. A director of General Motors, Amoco, and First Chicago Bank; a trustee of the University of Chicago.

The Business Roundtable. The Business Roundtable was established in *head* 1972 to provide direct representation of the chief executive officers of the *CEOs* nation's 200 largest corporations in the policy process. Unlike other policy-planning groups, which emphasize policy formation and consensus-building, the Roundtable engages in direct lobbying on behalf of specific bills it wants passed by the Congress and supported by the President.

The Roundtable has formed task forces on a wide variety of policy *policy issues* issues—antitrust, energy, environment, inflation, government regulation, health, social security, taxation, welfare, and so on. These task forces submit their policy recommendations to a powerful policy committee. The strength of the organization is derived from the willingness of its member chiefs to appear *in person* in Washington. In 2000 its leadership included the following individuals:

> **Robert N. Burt.** Chairman of the Business Roundtable and Chairman and CEO of FMC. A director of Phelps Dodge and Warner Lambert.
>
> **Philip M. Condit.** Chairman and CEO of Boeing. A director of Nordstrom and Chairman of the Advisory Council of NASA.
>
> **Joseph T. Gorman.** Chairman and CEO of TRW. A director of Alcoa, Procter & Gamble, and a member of the Trilateral Commission.
>
> **John W. Snow.** Chairman and CEO of CSX. A director of Textron, Circuit City Stores, Johnson & Johnson. A trustee of Johns Hopkins University and former administrator of the U.S. National Highway Traffic Safety Administration.

The Brookings Institution. Over the years, the foremost policy-planning group in domestic affairs has been the Brookings Institution. Since its formation in 1921, it has overshadowed the American Enterprise Institution, the American Assembly, the Twentieth Century Fund, the Urban Institute, and all other policy-planning "think tanks." Brookings has been extremely influential in planning the war on poverty, welfare reform, national health care, defense programs, and taxation programs. The Brookings Institution is generally regarded as moderate-to-liberal in its policy orientation. The American Enterprise Institute (AEI) was reorganized in the 1970s to try to offset Brookings' influence by providing moderate-to-conservative advice on public policy. While the AEI enjoyed a resurgence in Washington in the Reagan administration, its long-term influence was no match for the well-established Brookings Institution (see Chapter 8).

The current Brookings Board of Trustees combines university people (Harvard, University of Chicago, University of Pennsylvania) with charitable foundation directors (Doris Duke Foundation, Heinze Family Philanthropies, Markle Foundation) and corporate and financial elites, including:

James A. Johnson.   Chairman of the Board of Trustees of the Brookings Institution. An investment banker and former CEO of Fannie Mae, and the former executive assistant to Vice-President Walter Mondale.

Zoe Baird.   President of the Markle Foundation, a former partner in O'Melveny & Myers, and President Clinton's unsuccessful nominee for Attorney General.

William A. Haseltine.   Chairman and CEO of Human Genome Sciences (codiscoverer of the human genetic code).

Warren Rudmond.   Former U.S. Senator from New Hampshire and cofounder of the Concorde Coalition (dedicated to national debt reduction). A partner in Paul, Weiss, Rifking, Wharton & Garrison; and a director of Raytheon, Dreyfus (investments), and Chubb.

Stephen M. Wolf.   Chairman and CEO of USAirways.

The "Honorary Trustees" indicate the historic influence of Brookings in national affairs:

Louis W. Cabot.   Honorary trustee and former chairman of the Brookings Institution. Chairman of the board of the Cabot Corporation. Served as director of Owens-Corning Fiberglass and New England Telephone, as chairman of the Federal Reserve Bank of Boston, and as a trustee of the Carnegie Corporation, M.I.T., and Northeastern University; a member of the Council on Foreign Relations. Ancestors discovered America.

Alden W. Clausen.   Former chairman and chief executive officer of the Bank of America; former president of the World Bank.

Vernon E. Jordan.   Partner in Akin Gump Strauss Hauer & Field and managing director of Lazard Freres (investments). Former president of the National Urban League. A director of American Express; Bankers Trust, Union Carbide, J.C. Penney, Xerox, Revlon, and Corning Glass.

Robert D. Hass.   Chairman of the Board of Levi Strauss & Co. A trustee of the

Ford Foundation, and a member of the Business Roundtable, the Council on Foreign Relations, and the Trilateral Commission.

Lloyd N. Cutler. Senior Partner, Wilmer, Cutler & Pickering. Former Counsel to the President (Jimmy Carter). A trustee of Yale University and the Metropolitan Opera.

If some names are growing repetitious by now, it is for good reason. Those who occupy top posts in the leading corporate, governmental, and mass media institutions are frequently the same individuals who direct the leading foundations, cultural organizations, and civic associations. Our purpose in "naming names," even when they become repetitive, is to suggest the frequent interlocking of top elites in different institutional sectors. In Chapter 7, we will examine interlocking in greater detail.

THE BILLION DOLLAR UNIVERSITIES

The growth of public higher education since World War II—the creation of vast state university, state college, and community college systems in every state in the nation—has diminished the influence of the prestigious private universities. There are now nearly 4,000 separate institutions of higher education in America, enrolling over 14 million students—nearly two-thirds of all recent high school graduates. Only about one-quarter of these students are enrolled in *private* colleges and universities. However, most state universities depend heavily upon annual appropriations by state legislatures. With a few notable exceptions, state universities have little control over their own revenues or assets. The thirty-four universities listed in Table 6–4 control over two-thirds of all endowment funds in higher education in the nation. These are the universities with $1 *billion* or more in total endowment funds. All but seven of these forty-one top ranked universities are private institutions. And, as we shall observe in Chapter 7, a disproportionate number of the nation's top leaders attended one or another of these universities.

Boards of regents for state universities are generally composed of individuals who would probably *not* be among the top institutional elites according to our definition in Chapter 1. Many of these regents hold directorships in smaller corporations, smaller banks, and smaller utility companies; they frequently have held state rather than national political office; their legal, civic, cultural, and foundation affiliations are with *state* institutions rather than with prestigious and powerful *national* institutions.

University presidents, particularly the presidents of the nation's top institutions, are frequently called upon to serve as trustees or directors of other institutions and to serve in high government posts. Most university presidents today have come up through the ranks of academic administration, suggesting that universities themselves may offer a channel for upward

TABLE 6–4   The Billion Dollar Universities—Universities with Endowments of $1 Billion or More

Rank	University	Endowment ($ Millions)
1	Harvard	$18,844
2	Yale	10,084
3	University of Texas*	10,013
4	Stanford	8,649
5	Princeton	8,398
6	M.I.T.	6,475
7	University of California*	5,639
8	Emory University	5,032
9	Columbia	4,263
10	Washington University	4,234
11	Texas A&M*	4,205
12	University of Chicago	3,828
13	University of Michigan*	3,468
14	Cornell	3,436
15	Rice	3,372
16	Northwestern	3,368
17	University of Pennsylvania	3,200
18	Notre Dame	3,089
19	Duke	2,663
20	Dartmouth	2,490
21	Vanderbilt	2,314
22	Southern California	2,152
23	Johns Hopkins	1,825
24	University of Virginia*	1,738
25	Case Western Reserve	1,550
26	University of Minnesota*	1,550
27	California Institute of Technology	1,535
28	Brown	1,416
29	Rockefeller	1,372
30	Williams College	1,357
31	Purdue	1,301
32	Ohio State*	1,294
33	Rochester	1,278
24	Wellesley	1,253
35	Pomona College	1,109
36	University of North Carolina*	1,105
37	University of Richmond	1,068
38	Baylor	1,044
39	Boston College	1,044
40	New York University	1,030
41	University of Pittsburgh*	1,018

* An asterisk indicates a state-supported institution.
Source: Chronicle of Higher Education, April 13, 2001.

mobility into the nation's elite. We must keep in mind, however, that presidents are hired and fired by the trustees, not by students or faculty.

SUMMARY

The *civic establishment* refers collectively to the nation's leading law firms, influential power brokers, major foundations, prestigious and well-endowed private universities, and influential policy-planning organizations.

Commentators have speculated about a unifying American "Establishment," separate from business and government, that "inhabits" influential private institutions. This Establishment is not an institution itself but rather a "third force" that links together various institutions in separate sectors of American society. The Establishment is believed to assist in maintaining a public ethos, emphasizing tolerance, civic responsibility, and public-regardingness.

At the top of the legal profession, the senior partners of the nation's best-known New York and Washington law firms exercise great power as legal representatives of the nation's largest corporations. These superlawyers are frequently called upon for governmental leadership, particularly when high-level, delicate negotiations are required. Most superlawyers have been educated at Ivy League law schools and served apprenticeships in governmental agencies before entering law firms.

Washington is awash in lobbyists, agents, and lawyers, whom we have labeled collectively as the "fixers." Washington's most influential lobbying firms do most of their work for the same corporations, banks, and investment firms identified earlier. They frequently employ former top governmental elites to assist in "opening doors" in the nation's capital.

The power of the nation's large foundations rests in their ability to channel corporate and personal wealth into the policy-making process. They do this by providing financial support and direction over university research and the activities of policy-oriented civic associations. There is great concentration of foundation assets. There is also a great deal of overlapping among the directorates of the leading foundations and corporate and financial institutions, the mass media, universities, policy-planning groups, and government.

The civic associations, particularly the leading policy-planning groups—the Council on Foreign Relations, the Trilateral Commission, the Committee on Economic Development, the Business Roundtable, and the Brookings Institution—play key roles in national policy-making. They bring together leaders at the top of various institutional sectors of society to formulate recommendations on major policy innovations. More will be said about the important role of policy-planning groups in Chapter 8. We have noted here that the directors of these groups are top leaders in industry, finance, government, the mass media, law, and the universities.

effect National policy-making

There may not be as much concentration of power in higher education as in other sectors of American life. The development of state universities since World War II has diminished the influence of the private, Ivy League–type universities. However, among *private* universities, a relative few institutions control over two-thirds of all private endowment funds.

7

The Structure
of Institutional Power

Power in America is organized into large institutions, private as well as public—corporations, banks, investment firms, governmental bureaucracies, media empires, law firms, universities, foundations, cultural and civic organizations. The nation's resources are concentrated in a relatively few large institutions, and control over these institutional resources is the major source of power in society. The people at the top of these institutions—those who are in a position to direct, manage, and guide institutional programs, policies, and activities—compose the nation's elite.

QUESTIONS IN ELITE RESEARCH

Our selection of positions of institutional power involved many subjective judgments, but it provides a starting place for a systematic inquiry into the character of America's elite structure. It allows us to begin investigating a number of important questions:

Hierarchy or Polyarchy?   Is there a convergence of power at the top of an institutional structure in America, with a single group of individuals—recruited primarily from industry and finance—who occupy top positions in corporations, education, government, foundations, civic and cultural affairs, and the military? Or are there separate institutional structures, with elites in each sector of society having little or no overlap in authority and many separate channels of recruitment? In short, is the structure of power in America a hierarchy or a polyarchy?

A Ruling Class or an Open Leadership System? Are there opportunities to rise to the top of the institutional structure of America for individuals from all classes, races, religions, and ethnic groups, through multiple career paths in different sectors of society? Or are opportunities for entry into top circles limited to white, Anglo-Saxon Protestant, upper- and upper-middle-class individuals whose careers are based primarily in industry and finance?

Conflict or Consensus among Elites? How much agreement exists among people at the top about the fundamental values and future directions of American society? Do America's top leaders agree on the *ends* of policies and programs and disagree merely on the *means* of achieving those ends? Or are there significant differences among American elites over the goals and purposes of our society? Are there significant fault lines in America's elite structure?

It is not really possible to provide definitive answers to these questions. The *systematic* study of the nation's institutional elite is still in an exploratory stage. Although a great deal has been written about "the power elite," much of it has been speculative, impressionistic, and polemical. Serious difficulties confront the social scientist who wishes to move away from anecdote and ideology to serious scientific research on national elites—research that "names names," attempts operational definitions, develops testable hypotheses, and produces some reliable information about national leadership.

CONVERGENCE OR SPECIALIZATION AT THE TOP?

Social scientists have differed over the extent of elite convergence. At least two varieties of leadership models can be identified in the literature on power.[1] A *hierarchical model* implies that a relatively small group of individuals exercises authority in a wide variety of institutions—forming what has been called a "power elite." In contrast, a *polyarchical model* implies that different groups of individuals exercise power in various sectors of society and acquire power in separate ways.

---

[1] This literature is voluminous, and any characterization of positions results in some oversimplification. For good summary statements of positions, see the works of Mills, Hunter, Kolko, and Dahl, cited elsewhere in chapter notes. See also Nelson Polsby, *Community Power and Political Theory,* 2nd ed. (New Haven: Yale University Press, 1980); David Ricci, *Community Power and Democratic Theory* (New York: Random House, 1971); and Robert J. Waste, ed., *Community Power: Directions for Future Research* (Beverly Hills, Calif.: Sage, 1986).

The hierarchical model derives from the familiar "elitist" literature on power. Sociologist C. Wright Mills argues that "the leading men in each of the three domains of power—the warlords, the corporation chieftains, and the political directorate—tend to come together to form the power elite of America."[2] According to Mills, leadership in America constitutes "an intricate set of overlapping cliques." And Floyd Hunter, in his study *Top Leadership, U.S.A.*, concludes: "Out of several hundred persons named from all sources, between one hundred and two hundred were consistently chosen as top leaders and considered by all informants to be of national policy-making stature."[3] The notion of interlocking directorates has widespread currency in the power elite literature. Gabriel Kolko writes that "interlocking directorates, whereby a director of one corporation also sits on the board of one or more other corporations, are a key device for concentrating corporate power. . . ."[4] The hierarchical model also implies that top leaders in all sectors of society—including government, education, civic and cultural affairs, and politics—are recruited primarily from business and finance.

In contrast, pluralist writers have implied a polyarchical leadership structure, with different sets of leaders in different sectors of society and little or no overlap, except perhaps by elected officials responsible to the general public. According to this view, leadership is exercised in large measure by "specialists" who limit their participation to a narrow range of societal decisions. *Segmental elites* These specialists are believed to be recruited through separate channels—not drawn exclusively from business and finance. Generally, pluralists have praised the dispersion of authority in American society. Robert A. Dahl writes: "The theory and practice of American pluralism tends to assume, as I see it, that the existence of multiple centers of power, none of which is wholly sovereign, will help (may indeed be necessary) to tame power, to secure the consent of all, and to settle conflicts peacefully."[5] *power is better when dispersed*

SOURCES OF ELITE COHESION *Background, directorates, experiences attitude & belief*

It is the responsibility of elitist scholars to demonstrate the cohesiveness of the nation's leadership, and to counter the pluralist argument that elites are plural, specialized, relatively independent, frequently competitive, and occasionally conflictual. Elite theorists postulate several different mechanisms which provide the necessary cohesion among the leaders of different institutions in American society.

[2] C. Wright Mills, *The Power Elite* (New York: Oxford University Press, 1956), p. 9.

[3] Floyd Hunter, *Top Leadership, U.S.A.* (Chapel Hill: University of North Carolina Press, 1959), p. 176.

[4] Gabriel Kolko, *Wealth and Power in America* (New York: Praeger, 1962), p. 57.

[5] Robert A. Dahl, *Pluralist Democracy in the United States* (Chicago: Rand McNally, 1967), p. 24.

Interlocking Directorates. Institutions are linked by a network of interlocking memberships, whereby the directors of various industrial corporations, banks, foundations, media empires, civic and cultural organizations sit on the governing boards of more than one institution. Banks and other financial institutions are often considered central to this network. Banks may function to mediate in intercorporate conflict since they usually have investments in many different segments of the economy.[6]

Institutional Experiences. In addition to *concurrent* interlocking where individuals hold more than one top institutional post at the same time, members of the elite may enjoy *sequential* interlocking, where individuals hold a number of leadership positions over their lifetime. This is especially important in securing cohesion between governmental and corporate elites. Government officials are usually expected to resign their corporate directorships when they assume a government post, but many top government leaders bring their corporate experience to government and return to corporate life after their government work.

Class Backgrounds, Education, Clubs, Kinship. Still another source of cohesion may be the shared social class backgrounds which transmit relatively uniform upper- and upper-middle-class values and aspirations to future elite members. These class values are transmitted through uniform educational experiences for a large proportion of elite members, including attendance at prestigious private prep schools and Ivy League universities. These social class and educational ties are frequently reinforced through marriage and family relations. Finally, elite cohesion is abetted through a network of private prestigious social clubs, which purposefully encourage interaction and solidarity within the elite.[7]

Shared Attitudes and Beliefs. The result of shared social class backgrounds, similar educational experiences, and numerous social, family, and business ties, is broad agreement on societal values. Elites agree on the goals and purposes of public policies; disagreement is limited to specific means for achieving these goals and purposes. Elite consensus includes support for the free enterprise system, limited government, and rewards based on individual

[6] See, for example, Beth Mintz and Michael Swartz, "Interlocking Directorates and Interest Group Formations," *American Sociological Review*, 46 (1981), 851–69; Ronald F. Burt, "A Structural Theory of Interlocking Corporate Directorates," *Social Networks*, 1 (1979), 415–35; Ronald S. Burt, et al., "Testing a Structural Theory of Corporate Cooptation: Intraorganizational Directorate Ties," *American Sociological Review*, 45 (1980), 821–41; Thomas Koenig, "Interlocking Corporate Directorates as a Social Network," *American Journal of Economics and Sociology*, 40 (1981), 37–50.

[7] See, for example, G. William Domhoff, *The Bohemian Grove and Other Retreats* (New York: Harper and Row, 1974); Gwen Moore and Richard D. Alba, "Class and Prestige Origins in the American Elite," in *Social Structure and Network Analysis*, eds. Peter V. Marsden and Nan Lin (Beverly Hills, Calif.: Sage, 1982).

merit; a devotion to personal liberty, due process of law, and equality of opportunity; opposition to discrimination; a desire to mitigate the worst effects of poverty and ill-health; an impulse to do good and instill middle-class values in all citizens; a desire to exercise influence in international affairs and spread Western cultural values throughout the world. The range of disagreement among elites is relatively narrow compared to this broad consensus on fundamental values.[8]

Private Policy-Planning Organizations. Planning, coordination, and consensus-building in national policy is achieved through a complex process which ensures that major policy directions are determined *before* the "proximate policy-makers"—Congress, the White House, administrative agencies, and so on—become directly involved. Central to this process are a small number of private policy-planning organizations. These organizations bring together leaders from corporate and financial institutions, universities, foundations, the mass media, the top law firms, and government, in order to set the agenda of national decision-making, direct research into policy questions, and most important, try to reach a consensus on the major policy directions for the nation.[9] In Chapter 8, "How Institutional Elites Make Public Policy," we describe the policy-planning process and the role of the private policy-planning organizations.

"INTERLOCKERS" AND "SPECIALISTS"

Our definition of institutional power identified 7,314 top institutional positions in 10 different sectors of society (see Chapter 1). Individuals in these positions control more than one-half of the nation's industrial and financial assets, over half of all the assets of private foundations, and two-thirds of the assets of private universities; they control the television networks, influential newspapers, and media empires; they control the most prestigious civic and cultural organizations; and they direct the activities of the executive, legislative, and judicial branches of the national government.

These 7,314 top positions were occupied by 5,778 individuals. In other words, there were fewer top individuals than top positions—indicating multiple holding of top positions by some individuals. Table 7–1 presents specific data on this phenomenon, which we shall call *interlocking*.

[8] See Richard Hofstadter, *The American Political Tradition* (New York: Knopf, 1948).

[9] See, for example, Thomas R. Dye, "Oligarchic Tendencies in National Policy-Making," *Journal of Politics*, 40 (May 1978), 309–31; G. William Domhoff, *The Powers That Be* (New York: Vintage, 1979); Michael Useem, "The Social Organization of the American Business Elite and Participation of Corporate Directors in the Governance of American Institutions," *American Sociological Review*, 44 (August 1979), 553–72.

TABLE 7–1 Interlocking and Specialization in Top Institutional Positions

	Number of Top Institutional Positions	Percent of Total Positions	Number of Individuals in Top Positions	Percent of Total Individuals
Total	7,314	100.0	5,778	100.0
Specialized	4,981	68.1	4,911	85.0
Interlocked	2,333	31.9	867	15.0

Approximately 15 percent of those we identified as the nation's elite held more than one top position at a time. These are our "interlockers." Most of them held only two top positions, but some held five, six, seven, or more! Eighty-five percent of the people at the top are "specialists"—individuals who hold only one top position. Many of these specialists hold other corporate directorships, governmental posts, or civic, cultural, or university positions, but not *top* positions as we have defined them. Thus, our specialists may assume a wide variety of lesser positions: directorships in corporations below the top 100; positions on governmental boards and commissions; trusteeships of less well-known colleges and foundations; and directorships of less influential civic and cultural organizations. We will also observe that over a lifetime, many specialists tend to hold a number of top positions serially, rather than concurrently.

About 32 percent of all top positions are interlocked with other top positions. The reason that 32 percent of the top positions are interlocked, but only 15 percent of the top individuals hold more than one position, is that some individuals are "multiple interlockers"—they hold three or more positions.

Multiple interlockers are only a small percentage of the total number of leaders we identified, but they are in a unique position to communicate and coordinate the activities of a variety of institutions.[10] Multiple interlockers have significant "connections" with corporations, banks, media, cultural organizations, universities, foundations, and civic associations. Virtually every major corporation in America is interlocked with a significant number of other corporations and financial institutions as well as civic, cultural, and educational institutions (see, for example, Figure 7–1).

Multiple interlocking encourages leaders to take a broader view of business and social problems. They cannot take narrow positions based upon the interests of a single firm, but instead they must consider the well-being of a wider range of American institutions. They come together not only in

[10] Maurice Zeitlin, "Corporate Ownership and Control," *American Journal of Sociology*, 79 (September 1974), 1073–119; Michael Patrick Allen, "Continuity and Change within the Core Corporate Elite," *Sociological Quarterly*, 19 (Autumn 1978), 510–21; Michael Useem, "The Inner Group of the American Capitalist Class," *Social Problems* 25 (June, 1978), 225–40.

FIGURE 7–1   Interlocking Directorates: Exxon Mobil

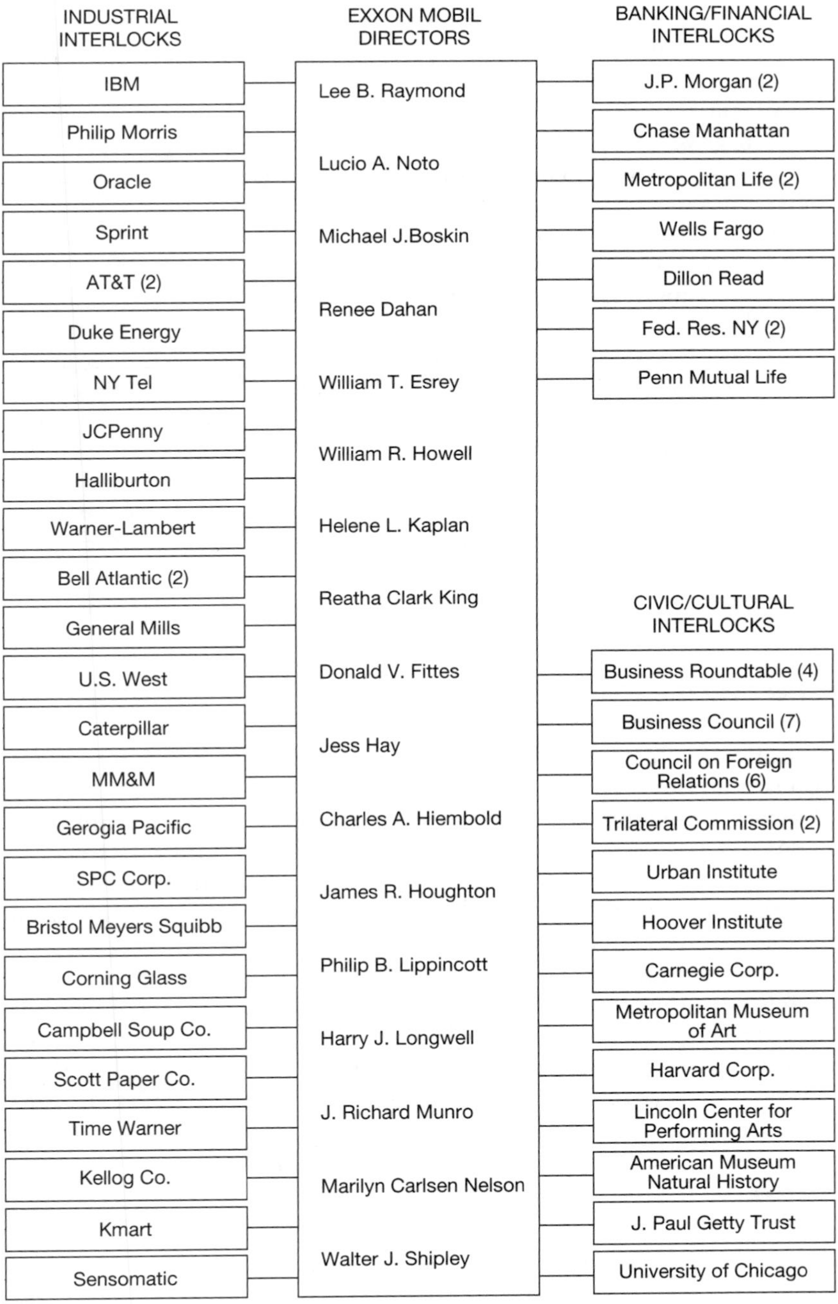

INDUSTRIAL INTERLOCKS	EXXON MOBIL DIRECTORS	BANKING/FINANCIAL INTERLOCKS
IBM	Lee B. Raymond	J.P. Morgan (2)
Philip Morris		Chase Manhattan
Oracle	Lucio A. Noto	Metropolitan Life (2)
Sprint	Michael J.Boskin	Wells Fargo
AT&T (2)		Dillon Read
Duke Energy	Renee Dahan	Fed. Res. NY (2)
NY Tel	William T. Esrey	Penn Mutual Life
JCPenny		
Halliburton	William R. Howell	
Warner-Lambert	Helene L. Kaplan	
Bell Atlantic (2)		
General Mills	Reatha Clark King	CIVIC/CULTURAL INTERLOCKS
U.S. West	Donald V. Fittes	Business Roundtable (4)
Caterpillar		Business Council (7)
MM&M	Jess Hay	Council on Foreign Relations (6)
Gerogia Pacific	Charles A. Hiembold	Trilateral Commission (2)
SPC Corp.		Urban Institute
Bristol Meyers Squibb	James R. Houghton	Hoover Institute
Corning Glass	Philip B. Lippincott	Carnegie Corp.
Campbell Soup Co.		Metropolitan Museum of Art
Scott Paper Co.	Harry J. Longwell	Harvard Corp.
Time Warner	J. Richard Munro	Lincoln Center for Performing Arts
Kellog Co.		American Museum Natural History
Kmart	Marilyn Carlsen Nelson	J. Paul Getty Trust
Sensomatic	Walter J. Shipley	University of Chicago

multiple corporate boardrooms but also at cultural and civic events, charitable endeavors, foundation meetings, and university trustee and alumni get-togethers. They are also members of the same exclusive *social clubs*, for example, the Links, Century, Knickerbocker, Burning Tree, Metropolitan, Pacific Union.

Multiple interlocking plays a major role in linking the corporate world with government, foundations, universities, cultural organizations, and civic associations. "The multiple corporate connections place inner group members in an exceptionally good position to help mobilize the resources of many firms on behalf of policies they favor—and institutions whose governance they assist—making inner group members preferable to other businessmen when appointments to positions of governance are decided."[11]

However, interlocking of directorates appears to be declining modestly over time. In 1970, we estimated from our own data that about 20 percent of all top leaders were interlockers. In 1980, our estimate was only 15 percent. The 1990s brought added responsibilities to the boardroom (see Chapter 2) and a resulting decline in the number of directorships an individual can comfortably handle. Leading business sources report a new reluctance on the part of corporate leaders to assume more than two corporate directorships at a time.[12] Thus, increasing proportions of top leaders are "specialists."

THE ROCKEFELLERS: END OF A DYNASTY?

Historically the greatest concentration of power in America centered on the Rockefeller empire—a network of industrial, financial, political, civic, and cultural institutions under the control of the Rockefeller family. Until recently this empire was actively directed by David Rockefeller. But David Rockefeller retired as chairman of the board of the core financial institution of the Rockefeller empire, Chase Manhattan Bank, in 1981. He gradually relinquished direct control over New York's Rockefeller Center and various Rockefeller investment holding companies, including Rockefeller Group Inc. and the Rockefeller Brothers Fund. Earlier he had set the Rockefeller Foundation on an independent course. Finally, in 1985 he gave up his chairmanship of the Council on Foreign Relations. No other member of the Rockefeller family, numbering nearly 100 today, has stepped forward to hold the empire

---

[11] Useem, "The Social Organization of the American Business Elite," p. 557.

[12] See "Board Games," *Time*, February 8, 1993, pp. 54–55; "The King Is Dead," *Fortune*, January 11, 1993, pp. 34–40; however, for evidence that interlocking among all corporations remained fairly constant from 1935 to 1970, see Michael Patrick Allen, "The Structure of Interorganizational Elite Corporation: Interlocking Corporate Directorates," *American Sociological Review*, 39 (June 1974), 393–406.

together. Nonetheless, the Rockefeller empire, as it evolved over the last century, remains our best illustration of convergence of power in America.

The Rockefeller family fortune was founded by John D. Rockefeller, originator of the Standard Oil Company. With his partners, H.M. Flagler and S.V. Harkness, Rockefeller created the company that controlled 90 percent of the nation's oil production by the 1880s. A series of antitrust cases, culminating in the Supreme Court in *U.S.* v. *Standard Oil* (1911), resulted in the forced dissolution of the company into several separate corporations: Exxon, formerly Standard Oil of New Jersey, Mobil (now recombined with Exxon to be America's largest industrial corporation), and other large oil companies. The Rockefeller family continues to hold a large bloc of stock in Exxon-Mobil. But gradually the center of Rockefeller power shifted to banking and finance.

The core financial institution of the Rockefeller family was Chase Manhattan Bank, which David Rockefeller supervised for nearly thirty years. However, the family was also interested in Citicorp, which was headed for many years by James Stillman Rockefeller, a cousin of David's.

The Rockefeller financial influence in corporate decision-making was felt in several ways: by giving or withholding loans to corporations, by placing representatives on corporate boards of directors, and by owning or controlling blocs of common stock of corporations. Chase Manhattan directors were interlocked with more than 100 major industrial corporations, banks, utilities, and insurance companies. These included giants such as Exxon, AT&T, ITT, Metropolitan Life, Equitable Life, and USX (United States Steel). In addition, Chase Manhattan owned or held in trust over 5 percent of the corporate stock of many other large companies, including Eastern Airlines, Pan American World Airways, Boeing, TWA, Mobil, and CBS. The rules of the Securities and Exchange Commission presume that 5 percent of a corporation's stock can give the holder dominant influence in the corporation.

The Rockefeller interest in foreign affairs was particularly strong. The oil companies, which were the industrial core of Rockefeller holdings, required constant attention to foreign sources of supply. In addition, Chase Manhattan was deeply involved in overseas banking and investment activities. The Rockefellers supplied many of the top foreign affairs personnel for the nation, including Secretaries of State John Foster Dulles, Dean Rusk, and Henry Kissinger. Dulles, secretary of state under President Eisenhower, was a senior partner in the Wall Street law firm of Sullivan & Cromwell, whose principal client for many years was the Standard Oil Company (Exxon). Dulles was also chairman of the trustees of the Rockefeller Foundation. Dean Rusk, secretary of state under Presidents Kennedy and Johnson, served seven years as president of the Rockefeller Foundation. John J. McCloy, a Chase Manhattan director, served as U.S. high commissioner for Germany during the postwar occupation; in 1962, he was chairman of the Coordinating Committee on the Cuban Missile Crisis. Henry Kissinger was personal adviser on foreign policy to Nelson Rockefeller before becoming national security adviser and secretary of state under President Richard Nixon. Cyrus Vance, secretary of state under President Carter, was a Wall Street lawyer and a director of the Rockefeller Foundation, as well as of Pan American World Airlines, Aetna Life Insurance, and IBM. Zbigniew Brzezinski, President Carter's national security adviser, was director of the Trilateral Commission—David Rockefeller's influential group of top leaders from industrialized nations of the world. David Rockefeller himself served as chairman of the influential Council on Foreign Relations, which has been responsible for many of the nation's most important foreign policy initiatives (see the section "The Council on Foreign Relations and the Trilateral Commission" in Chapter 8).

For many decades, the single most powerful private citizen in America was David Rockefeller—"the only man for whom the presidency of the United States would be a step down." David Rockefeller is the youngest of five sons of John D. Rockefeller, Jr., himself the only son of the founder of the Rockefeller empire, John D. Rockefeller. Despite the seniority of his brothers,[13] it was recognized that David was the serious and scholarly one. It was to David that the family wisely entrusted its wealth.

David was raised with his brothers at the Rockefeller's 3,500-acre Pocantico Hills estate, east of Tarrytown, New York. He attended nearby Lincoln School. As a child, he traveled about to Rockefeller holdings—the Seal Harbor, Maine, retreat, the Virgin Islands estate, the Venezuela ranch, the Grand Teton Mountains ranch—and collected beetles as a hobby. It soon became clear to David's father and grandfather that Nelson, Lawrence, and Winthrop were more interested in politics and pleasure than hard work, and that John D. III was content to pursue cultural interests. The elder Rockefellers wanted a businessman to care for the family fortune, and they were successful in motivating David in this direction.

David's undergraduate career at Harvard was undistinguished. But later he spent a year at the Harvard Graduate School of Business and a year at the London School of Economics. He married Margaret "Peggy" McGrath, whose father was a senior partner in the esteemed Wall Street law firm of Cadwalader, Wickersham & Taft. He enrolled at the Rockefeller-funded University of Chicago and earned a Ph.D. in economics in 1940. He returned to New York for a short stint in public service as an unpaid assistant to Mayor Fiorello La Guardia. In 1942 he enlisted in the Army as a private, went through Officers Training School, and served in North Africa and Europe as an intelligence officer. He was fluent in French, Spanish, and German.

After the war he began his banking career in his uncle Winthrop W. Aldrich's bank, Chase Manhattan. His first post was assistant manager of the

---

[13] John D. III (deceased), former chairman of the Rockefeller Foundation and the Lincoln Center for the Performing Arts; Nelson A. (deceased), former Vice-President of the United States and four-term governor of New York; Lawrence S., family dilettante in "venture capitalism" and "conservationist"; and Winthrop (deceased), former governor of Arkansas and cattle rancher.

foreign department; three years later he became vice-president and director of the bank's business in Latin America. When his uncle became ambassador to England in 1952, David became successively executive vice-president, vice-chairman of the board, and finally, president and chairman of the board.

Of course, David Rockefeller was active in civic and cultural affairs. He was chairman of the Museum of Modern Art, president of the Board of Overseas Study of Harvard University, a trustee of the Carnegie Endowment for International Peace, a trustee of the University of Chicago, a trustee of the John F. Kennedy Library, and so forth.

Above all, David Rockefeller was an internationalist. His active intervention in American foreign policy produced remarkable results. He was personally involved in Nixon's arrangement of détente with the USSR, the Strategic Arms Limitations Talks (SALT), and the "normalization" of U.S. relations with the mainland People's Republic of China. He was chairman of the board of the Council on Foreign Relations, and he formed the Trilateral Commission in 1972. Through the CFR, Rockefeller was instrumental in most of the nation's important foreign policy initiatives including the Paris Peace Agreement ending U.S. involvement in the Vietnam War.

Under David Rockefeller's direction, Chase Manhattan developed a reputation in the business world for "social responsibility," which included the active recruitment and promotion of blacks, women, and other minorities; the granting of a large number of loans to minority-owned business enterprises; and the making of loans to businesses and governments in unstable Third World countries. Indeed, this may be one reason why Chase Manhattan lost its number one position in banking and eventually merged with J.P. Morgan.

David Rockefeller exercised great power but always with *modesty*, of course, as one would expect of a man who has no reason to try to impress anyone. Indeed, he consistently understated his own power:

> I feel uncomfortable when you ask how I exert power. We accomplish things through cooperative action, which is quite different than exerting power in some mysterious and presumably evil way. I have no power in the sense that I can call anybody in the government and tell them what to do. Because of my position, I'm more apt to get through on the telephone than somebody else, but what happens to what I suggest depends on whether they feel this makes sense in terms of what they are already doing.[14]

Of course, what Rockefeller was really saying is that when David Rockefeller called, people answered their phone; when he asked them to serve on a committee, they were flattered to be asked; when he suggested that they do something, they did it.

---

[14] "Beyond Wealth, What?" *Forbes*, May 15, 1972, p. 250.

Yet it may be that all great family dynasties eventually splinter and disperse. Despite the best efforts of the founders, the passage of time and the multiplication of family inheritors, together with an erosion of the entrepreneurial spirit in generations born to great wealth, gradually dissolve family concentrations of wealth and power.[15]

ELITE RECRUITMENT: GETTING TO THE TOP

Social scientists have studied data on the social backgrounds of corporate and governmental leaders for many years. But there is still disagreement on the interpretation of the data. A "ruling class" school of thought stresses the fact that elites in America are drawn disproportionately from among wealthy, educated, prestigiously employed, socially prominent, "WASP" groups in society. Many of the elite have been educated at a few esteemed private prep schools and gone to Ivy League colleges and universities. They have joined the same private clubs, and their families have intermarried. Ruling-class social scientists infer that these similarities contribute to cohesion and consensus among the institutional leaders in America.

By contrast, pluralists describe an open leadership system that enables a significant number of individuals from the middle and lower classes to rise to the top. High social background, or wealth, or WASPishness *itself* does not provide access to top leadership positions. Instead, top institutional posts go to individuals who possess outstanding skills of leadership, information, and knowledge, and the ability to organize and communicate. Admittedly, opportunities to acquire such qualities for top leadership are unequally distributed among classes. But lower-class origin, the pluralists believe, is not an insurmountable barrier to high position.

Pluralists also argue that social background, educational experience, and social group membership are poor predictors of decision-making behavior. Members of the social elite often hold very different views about policy questions. Thus, pluralists argue that the class homogeneity among top leaders that is reported in many social background studies is meaningless, since the class background/decision-making behavior linkage is weak.

Classical elitist writers such as Mosca acknowledge that some "circulation of elites" is essential for the stability of a political system. The opportunity for the brightest among the lower classes to rise to the top siphons off potentially revolutionary leadership, and the elite system is actually strengthened when talented and ambitious individuals enter top positions. The recruitment of some non-upper-class individuals to elite positions may be essential to society, because these individuals bring new and different perspectives to societal

[15] For an argument to the contrary, see Michael Patrick Allen, *The Founding Fortunes* (New York: Dutton, 1988).

problems.[16] Thus, we would expect to find some recruitment of non-upper-class individuals to elite positions even in an essentially hierarchical society. The question remains, how much opportunity exists in America for middle- and lower-class individuals to climb to the top?

What do we know about the people who occupy top institutional positions in American society? Over the years studies have consistently shown that top institutional leaders are *atypical* of the American public.[17] They are recruited from the well-educated, prestigiously employed, older, affluent, urban, white, Anglo-Saxon, upper- and upper-middle-class male populations of the nation. We had expected our top institutional elites to conform to the pattern, and we were not at all disappointed.

> *Age:* The average age of all the corporate leaders identified in our study is sixty. Leaders in foundations, law, education, and civic and cultural organizations are slightly older—average age sixty-two. Top positions in the governmental sector are filled by slightly younger people—average age fifty-six.

> *Sex:* The feminine sector of the population is seriously underrepresented at the top of America's institutional structure. Male dominance in top positions is nearly complete in the corporate world. But even in government, women hold less than 20 percent of the key posts. Only in cultural affairs, education, and foundations are women found in significant numbers among the top position-holders.

> *Ethnicity:* WASPs are preeminent in America's institutional structure. Our own data do not include ethnic identification, but the work of sociologists Richard D. Alba and Gwen Moore confirm the disproportionate representation of WASPs in high positions in business and government.[18] Their studies revealed that WASPs (who made up only 22.9 percent of all persons born before 1932) made up 57.3 percent of top business leaders and 53.4 percent of Congress. ("Other Protestants" increase these figures to 79.4 percent for business and 72.4 percent for Congress.) However, ethnics have made some inroads: 37 percent of union leaders are Irish Catholics, and 25.8 percent of mass media leaders are Jews. A WASP background, they conclude, is an "incremental advantage" in achieving elite status.

[16] See Suzanne Keller, *Beyond the Ruling Class: Strategic Elites in Modern Society* (New York: Random House, 1968), p. 172.

[17] Among the early studies, see Donald R. Matthews, *The Social Background of Political Decision-Makers* (New York: Doubleday, 1954); David T. Stanley, Dean E. Mann, and Jameson W. Doig, *Men Who Govern* (Washington: Brookings Institution, 1967); Morris Janowitz, *The Professional Soldier* (New York: Free Press, 1960); and Lloyd Warner and James C. Abegglen, *Big Business Leaders in America* (New York: Harper & Row, 1955).

[18] Richard D. Alba and Gwen Moore, "Ethnicity in the American Elite," *American Sociological Review*, 47 (June 1982).

Education: Nearly all our top leaders are college-educated, and more than half hold advanced degrees. Some 25.8 percent hold law degrees, and 31.1 percent hold advanced academic or professional degrees. (These are earned degrees only; there are a host of honorary degrees that were not counted.) Governmental leaders are somewhat more likely to hold advanced degrees than corporate leaders. What is even more impressive is the fact that 54 percent of the corporate leaders and 42 percent of the governmental leaders are graduates of twelve heavily endowed, prestigious "name" private universities—Harvard, Yale, Chicago, Stanford, Columbia, M.I.T., Cornell, Northwestern, Princeton, Johns Hopkins, Pennsylvania, and Dartmouth. Elites in America are notably Ivy League.[19]

Urban: Most of our top leaders were urban dwellers. Governmental leaders (notably members of Congress) are somewhat more likely to be drawn from rural areas than are leaders in business, finance, and law, but less than one third of the key government posts in our study were found to be filled by individuals from rural areas.

Preppy: Elites are notably "preppy." At least 10 percent of the corporate leaders and 6 percent of the governmental leaders attended one of only thirty-three prestigious private prep schools before entering college.[20] (Actually, the proportion of "preppies" among top leaders may be double these figures—up to 20 percent for corporate leaders and 10 percent for government leaders. The reason for suggesting these higher figures is that less than half of known preppies report their prep school affiliation to *Who's Who in America.* Thus, their prep school backgrounds would be overlooked in our biographical search.) It is astonishing to realize that these proportions of top leaders went to only thirty-three prep schools, since these schools educate an infinitesimal proportion of the nation's population. As *The Official Preppy Handbook* explains: "There are preparatory schools and then there are Prep Schools, those institutions that bless you with a certain luster along with your diploma."[21] Among the Eastern Establishment, the phrase "old school ties" refers to prep schools, not to colleges or universities. It is considered more prestigious to have attended Groton,

---

[19] Our figures are confirmed in a separate study of over 55,000 top executives by Standard & Poor's Corporation, showing that half received degrees from these twelve universities. See *Chronicle of Higher Education,* September 29, 1980, p. 1.

[20] Andover, Buckley, Cate, Catlin, Choate, Cranbrook, Country Day, Deerfield, Episcopal, Exeter, Gilman, Groton, Hill, Hotchkiss, Kingswood, Kent, Lakeside, Lawrenceville, Lincoln, Loomis, Middlesex, Milton, St. Andrew's, St. Christopher's, St. George's, St. Mark's, St. Paul's, Shattuck, Taft, Thatcher, Webb, Westminster, Woodberry Forest. Listing courtesy of G. William Domhoff.

[21] Lisa Birnbach, ed., *The Official Preppy Handbook* (New York: Workman, 1980), p. 50.

Hotchkiss, Phillips Exeter, Loomis, Phillips at Andover, or Choate, than to have attended Harvard, Yale, Princeton, or Columbia.

Social Clubs: The overwhelming majority of those who hold top positions in America belong to one or more social clubs. Indeed, over one-third of the people at the top belong to just a very few prestigious private clubs, such as the Links and the Knickerbocker in New York, and the Metropolitan, Cosmos, and Burning Tree in Washington.[22] The importance of these clubs in developing elite consensus and cohesion is a subject of a great deal of speculation. E. Digby Baltzell writes: "At the upper class level in America . . . the club lies at the very core of the social organization of the access to power and authority."[23] Ferdinand Lundberg says: "The private clubs are the most 'in' thing about the . . . elite. These clubs constitute the societal control centers of the elite."[24] Perhaps the most persuasive case for the importance of such private social clubs is set forth by sociologist G. William Domhoff:

> The Bohemian Grove [a luxury retreat on 2,700 acres of giant redwoods maintained by the Bohemian Club of San Francisco], as well as other watering holes and social clubs, are relevant to the problem of class cohesiveness in two ways. First, the very fact that rich men from all over the country gather in such close circumstances as the Bohemian Grove is evidence of the existence of a socially cohesive upper class. It demonstrates that many of these men do know each other, that they have face-to-face communications, and that they are a social network. In this sense we are looking at [clubs] as a *result* of social processes that lead to class cohesion. But such institutions also can be viewed as facilitators of social ties. Once formed, these groups became another avenue by which the cohesiveness of the upper class is maintained.[25]

It is our judgment, however, that club membership is a result of top position-holding in the institutional structure of society rather than an important independent source of power. An individual is selected for club membership *after* acquiring an important position in society; position and power do not come as a result of club memberships. Personal interaction, consensus-building, and friendship networks all develop in the club milieu, but the clubs merely help facilitate processes that occur anyway.

---

[22] Based on a *Wall Street Journal*–Gallup Poll survey of chief executives of 1,300 large U.S. companies. *Wall Street Journal*, August 19, 1980, p. 31.

[23] E. Digby Baltzell, *The Protestant Establishment* (New York: Random House, 1964), p. 354.

[24] Ferdinand Lundberg, *The Rich and the Super-Rich* (New York: Bantam Books, 1968), p. 339.

[25] G. William Domhoff, *The Bohemian Grove and Other Retreats* (New York: Harper & Row, 1974), p. 88.

[handwritten margin note: corp elites more UC than gov]

These social background characteristics suggest a slight tendency for corporate elites to be more "upper class" in origin than government elites. Among governmental leaders there are slightly fewer Ivy Leaguers. Moreover, there is a slight tendency for governmental leaders to have had more advanced professional education.

CLASS: A TOUCHY SUBJECT

All known societies have some system of ranking individuals along a superiority-inferiority scale. Yet in America, the ideological assertion "All men are created equal" is so pervasive that people are reluctant to even acknowledge the existence of social classes. Most Americans describe themselves as "middle class"; nearly nine out of ten will choose "middle class" when they are asked in surveys to choose between this term and either upper class or lower class.[26] Sociologists use measures of occupation, income, and education to assess class position and to study social classes.

America's upper classes avoid using the term *class* altogether. Upper-class members will discuss class in subtle terms ("all of us," "old families")[27]; lower-class members will discuss class in terms of humor and derision ("snobs," "fat cats," "fancy pants"). The middle class prefers to avoid the topic altogether. The lower classes believe class is defined by the amount of money a person has; the middle class grants that money has something to do with it but thinks that education and occupation are more important; the upper class thinks that taste, values, style, and behavior define class, regardless of money or education or occupation.[28]

The ambiguities about class in America make it difficult to assess the role of class in elite composition. We must avoid the circularity of saying "the power elite is the upper class" and then defining the upper class as "the power elite." We have already defined our elite as individuals who occupy the top positions in the institutional structure of society. Certainly these people are granted high status and accorded great deference by virtue of the institutional positions they occupy. But their institutional status cannot itself be synonymous with upper social class; upper social class must have some independent meaning if it is to have any meaning at all.

---

[26] See *The American Enterprise* (May–June, 1993), pp. 82–83, reporting National Opinion Research Center data on class identifications.

[27] Susan A. Ostrander, "Upper-Class Women," in *Power Structure Research*, ed. G. William Domhoff (Beverly Hills, Calif.: Sage, 1980), pp. 78–79; see also Ostrander, *Women of the Upper Class* (Philadelphia: Temple University Press, 1984).

[28] Paul Fussell, *Class: A Guide Through the American Status System* (New York: Summit Books, 1983).

One of the few class analysts to recognize this distinction between class and power is sociologist G. William Domhoff:

> The upper class as a whole does not rule. Instead class rule is manifested through the activities of a wide variety of organizations and institutions. . . . Leaders within the upper class join with high-level employees in the organizations they control to make up what will be called the *power elite*. This power elite is the leadership group of the upper class as a whole, but it is not the same thing as the upper class. It is the members of the power elite who take part in the processes that maintain the class structure.[29]

[handwritten margin notes: DOMHOFF / UC not / Power / Elite / but / rather leadership group / of the UC]

To demonstrate upper-class "dominance" of the elite, Domhoff employs several upper-class "indicators": (1) listing in the *Social Register*, (2) attendance at a private prestigious preparatory school; or (3) membership in a private prestigious club. But Domhoff fails to acknowledge that listing in the *Social Register* and membership in a prestigious club usually come to an individual *after* he or she has attained high institutional position. In other words, one may attain these indicators of upper social class as a result of climbing the institutional ladder from a middle-class background. We certainly cannot contend that the upper class "dominates" the elite, if it turns out that elite membership is what determined upper-class status.

The only way to avoid circularity in studying the class composition of an elite group is to focus on social *origins*. Are top institutional positions largely limited to the sons and daughters of upper-class families? Our own estimate is that approximately *30 percent* of our total institutional elite are upper class in social origin. This estimate derives from a sample of our elite for whom we endeavored to learn their parents' class circumstances. We attributed *upper-class social origin* on the basis of the following: (1) attendance at a private prestigious preparatory school; (2) parent is an officer or a director of a major corporation, bank, insurance company, or utility; (3) parent is a high government official or general in the military; (4) parent is an attorney in a top law firm, a newspaper owner or director, or a university president or trustee of a university, foundation, or major civic or cultural association.

[handwritten margin note: 30% UC]

Certainly individuals with upper-class family origins are disproportionately represented in institutional leadership positions. (Far less than 1 percent of the general population would meet our definition of upper-class origin.) But we cannot conclude that the upper class "dominates" on the basis of our estimate of 30 percent upper-class origins. On the contrary, 70 percent of our institutional elite appeared to be middle class in family origin; their parents were able to send them to college, but there is no indication that their parents ever achieved high institutional position.

[handwritten margin note: 70% MC]

---

[29] G. William Domhoff, *Who Rules America Now?* (Englewood Cliffs, N.J.: Prentice Hall, 1983), p. 2.

AFRICAN AMERICANS AT THE TOP

There are very few African Americans in positions of power in corporate America. While it is true that many Fortune 500 corporations include one or more African Americans on their boards of directors, none are found as chairman or chief executive officer. Edward W. Jones, Jr., a black business consultant and former AT&T executive, argues that "colorism"—"a predisposition to act in a certain manner because of a person's skin color"—is the major obstacle to black advancement to top corporate positions. He distinguishes "colorism" from "racism," which he defines as overt bigotry and hatred. "All people possess stereotypes, which act like shorthand to avoid mental overload. . . . a decision about a promotion is a subjective thing. For blacks, colorism adds an extra layer of subjectivity."[30]

Nonetheless, a number of African Americans exercise considerable influence in corporate and financial circles. Among the most notable:

> ***William T. Coleman.*** Former secretary of transportation under President Gerald Ford. Senior partner, O'Melveny & Myers, Washington. Attended the University of Pennsylvania and Harvard Law School. Chairman of the board of the NAACP Legal Defense and Education Fund. Served as a director of IBM, Chase Manhattan, Pepsico, American Can, Pan American World Airways, Philadelphia Electric. A trustee of the Brookings Institution; a member of the Council on Foreign Relations and the Trilateral Commission; and a trustee of Harvard University.
>
> ***Andrew F. Brimmer.*** Independent financial consultant. Served as a director of BankAmerica, International Harvester, United Airlines, Du Pont, BellSouth, Gannett Newspapers, Mercedes Benz, and Navistar International. A graduate of the University of Washington with a Ph.D. (economics) from Harvard. He taught at the Wharton School of the University of Pennsylvania and moved on to be assistant secretary of commerce and later a member of the Federal Reserve Board. He now heads Brimmer and Company, an independent financial and managerial consulting firm. He is a member of the Council on Foreign Relations and the Trilateral Commission, and he is a trustee of Atlanta University, Tuskegee Institute, the Urban League, and the Ford Foundation.
>
> ***Vernon E. Jordan, Jr.*** Former president of the National Urban League. A graduate of DePauw University and Howard University Law School. He began his career in civil rights affairs as the Georgia field secretary of the NAACP in the early 1960s, and later became director of the Vote Education Project of the Southern Regional Council, leading black voter registration drives in the south. He served briefly as executive director of the United Negro College Fund before becoming head of the National Urban League in 1972. In recent years he has accepted directorships of Bankers Trust of New York, American Express, Celanese Corporation, J.C. Penney Co., Union Carbide, Corning Glass, Dow Jones & Co., Revlon, RJR-Nabisco, Ryder Systems, Sara Lee, and the Xerox Corporation. He is also a trustee of the Rockefeller Foundation and the Brookings Institution.

---

[30] See Edward W. Jones, Jr., "Black Managers: The Dream Deferred," *Harvard Business Review* (May–June, 1986), 84–93.

Franklin A. Thomas. President of the Ford Foundation. Former president of the Bedford Stuyvesant Restoration Corporation in New York. He received his B.A. and law degree from Columbia University, and served as deputy police commissioner under New York's Mayor John Lindsay. Served as a director of Citicorp, AT&T, Aluminum Co. of America, CBS, Cummins Engine, and New York Life Insurance. He is also a trustee of the Lincoln Center for the Performing Arts, the Urban Institute, and Columbia University.

Clifton R. Wharton, Jr. Chairman and CEO of TIAA-CREF (insurance) and former chancellor of the State University of New York. Educated at the private prestigious Boston Latin School and later Harvard and Johns Hopkins; he received his Ph.D. (economics) from the University of Chicago. Former president of Michigan State University. Served as a director of Ford Motors, Burroughs Corp., Equitable Life, and the New York Stock Exchange. A trustee and later chairman of the board of the Rockefeller Foundation. A director of the Carnegie Corporation and the Council on Foreign Relations.

Patricia Roberts Harris. Former Secretary of Health, Education, and Welfare in the Carter administration. The daughter of a railroad dining-car waiter and a graduate of Howard University (B.A., 1945). Received a law degree from George Washington University in 1960. She began her career as a YWCA director in Chicago and later as executive director of Delta Sigma Theta, a national black sorority. She was a delegate to the Democratic National Convention in 1964, and seconded the nomination of Lyndon Johnson; President Johnson appointed her ambassador to Luxembourg (1965–67). She became a law partner of Sargent Shriver (Kennedy brother-in-law) and a prominent Washington attorney. She served as a director of IBM, Chase Manhattan, and Scott Paper Co. She was a member of the Council on Foreign Relations.

Samuel R. Pierce. Former Secretary of Housing and Urban Development in the Reagan administration. Pierce was a senior partner in the New York law firm of Fowler, Jaffin, Pierce & Kneel and a governor of the American Stock Exchange. Pierce received his law degree from Cornell in 1949 and began his long career as an assistant district attorney in New York. He was named an assistant U.S. attorney under President Eisenhower and later assistant to the undersecretary of labor. He was a Ford Foundation fellow at Yale for a year, and a New York City judge. Under Nixon, he was general counsel for the U.S. Department of the Treasury (1970–73). He served as a director of General Electric, Prudential Insurance, First National Boston Corp., International Paper, and U.S. Industries.

African Americans have been more successful in achieving prominence in governmental circles than in the corporate and financial worlds. Every recent presidential administration has included African Americans in the Cabinet. However, none achieved a top cabinet position (usually defined as Secretary of State, Defense, or Treasury, or Attorney General) until Colin Powell was named Secretary of State by President George Bush (see "The Military Establishment" in Chapter 4).

Ron Brown was the first African American to become chairman of a major political party. A long-time Washington lobbyist and insider, Brown navigated the Democratic party to victory with Bill Clinton in 1992. Brown grew up in Harlem. Both of his parents were college graduates, and his father managed the Theresa Hotel next door to the Apollo Theater. Brown was exposed to the upper strata of black society in New York, including many of the famous entertainers that played the Apollo. He attended a prestigious New York preparatory school and went on to graduate from Middlebury College in Vermont. At Middlebury, brown was the only black student in the freshman class. He was popular among his classmates and was invited to join a then all-white fraternity. When the national organization prohibited Brown's membership, his fraternity brothers renounced their national affiliation. The college stood by Brown and barred all race-exclusive fraternities from campus. Brown subsequently served as a trustee of Middlebury College. Brown earned a law degree at St. John's University and became a Washington lobbyist for the National Urban League. Later he worked as a campaign manager for Senator Edward Kennedy and became Kennedy's staff director. In 1988 he managed Jesse Jackson's presidential campaign. Subsequently, Brown joined the Washington lawyer-lobbying firm of Patton, Boggs. Michael Dukakis helped Brown become Democratic National Chairman after Brown brought the Jackson Democrats back into the party and avoided a serious racial split. As national chairman, Brown proved to be an impressive fund-raiser. Following Clinton's victory in 1992, Brown's reward was being appointed to the Clinton Cabinet as Secretary of Commerce, the first African American ever to hold that post.

WOMEN AT THE TOP

The nation's institutional elite remains predominantly male. Overall, only about 10 percent of top institutional leaders—presidents, directors, and trustees of the nation's largest industrial corporations, banks, insurance companies, media empires, foundations, universities, civic and cultural organizations, and partners in the nation's leading law firms and investment houses—are women.

Most corporate boardrooms continue to resemble male clubs. Few of the nation's largest corporations have more than two or three women on their boards of directors. The Exxon-Mobil board, for example, includes three women on its seventeen-member board, including:

> **Helene Kaplan.** A senior partner in the heavyweight law firm of Skadden Arps (see Chapter 6). A director of May Department Stores, Metropolitan Life, Chase Manhattan, and Bell Atlantic. Chairman of the Board of the Carnegie Corporation and a trustee of the Guggenheim Foundation, the J. Paul Getty Trust, and the American Museum of Natural History.

Only two woman served as Chairman and CEO of a top 100 corporation in 2001:

> **Carleton "Carly" S. Fiorina.** Chairman and Chief Executive Officer, Hewlett-Packard. B.A. (medieval history and philosophy) Stanford University; M.B.A. Uni-

versity of Maryland; M.S. MIT. Fiorina rose through the ranks of AT&T and Lucent Technologies before transferring to Hewlett-Packard, where she became chairman and CEO in 1999.

Anne Mulcahy. President and Chief Executive Officer, Xerox. B.A. (English) Marymont College. Mulcahy came up through the ranks of Xerox beginning as a sales representative. Over twenty-five years she rose to increasingly responsible positions including senior vice-president and president. She is a member of the Board of Directors of Fuji, Target, Axel Johnson, Catalyst, and Fannie Mae.

Most of the women serving on corporate boards are *outside* directors; few are inside manager-directors. However, some women appear to be moving into high officer-director posts in leading corporations, including: Debby Hopkins, chief financial officer, Lucent Technologies; Karen Kater, president, Pfizer; Betsy Holden, Kraft Foods. Other women have risen to power in firms primarily serving women customers, including: Martha Stewart, CEO, Martha Stewart Living: Andrea Jung, CEO, Avon Products; and Oprah Winfrey, chairman and CEO, Harpo Entertainment.

Women have been somewhat more successful in the *mass media* than in industry or banking. We estimate that women hold about 15 percent of the officer and director posts in the leading media corporations. And for nearly twenty years, Katherine Graham served as chairman of the board of the Washington Post Company (see "Katherine Graham: the Most Powerful Woman in America" in Chapter 5).

The nation's leading private *universities* have begun to appoint more women to their governing boards of trustees. Today about 25 percent of the governing trustees of the nation's leading private universities are women. Eight of Harvard's thirty trustees are women. All of the leading universities have at least one woman trustee. And women are frequently encountered on the governing boards of trustees of leading *foundations*. The Ford and Rockefeller foundations each have five women trustees, and the Carnegie Corporation has six women trustees on its sixteen-member board. Some women, of course, have long served as foundation trustees because of their family associations: Mary Ethel Pew, Pew Memorial Trust; Doris Duke, Duke Endowment; Harriet Bush Melin, Bush Foundation; Mary Moody Northern, Moody Foundation; Josephine Hartford Bryce, Hartford Foundation; Mary Ann Mott Meynet, Mott Foundation; Ida Calloway, Calloway Foundation; Drue M. Heinz, Heinz Endowment.

Women have made greater inroads in *government* than in the corporate world. Women's major gains in government have occurred in both Republican and Democratic administrations. Women were sell represented in the Reagan, Bush, and Clinton administrations, and they are well represented in the George W. Bush cabinet (see Table 7–2). Currently there are thirteen women serving in the U.S. Senate (3 Republicans, 10 Democrats) and 59 (18 Republicans, 41 Democrats) in the House of Representatives.

TABLE 7–2   Prominent Women in the Cabinet

Reagan-Bush Administrations

    Margaret Heckler. Secretary of Health and Human Services. Catholic College, Boston College law degree; fourteen years a Republican congresswoman from Massachusetts.

    Elizabeth Hanford Dole. Secretary of Transportation. Duke University and Harvard Law School; Commissioner, Federal Trade Commission; later assistant to President Reagan.

    Jeanne Kirkpatrick. UN ambassador. Barnard College, Columbia University, Ph.D. Political science; Georgetown University professor.

    Carla Anderson Hills. Cabinet-level post as U.S. trade representative. She had formerly served as secretary of Housing and Urban Development in the Ford administration. She was a prominent Washington lawyer and a director of IBM, Corning Glass, American Airlines, Chevron, and the Signal Corporation. She was a member of the Council on Foreign Relations and the Trilateral Commission; she was once a trustee of the Brookings Institution but later became an adviser to the American Enterprise Institute. She was also chairman of the board of trustees of the Urban Institute. She earned her bachelors at Stanford and her law degree at Yale.

Clinton Administration

    Janet Reno. Attorney General. B.A. in chemistry from Cornell and law degree from Harvard Law School. She worked in private law practice and served briefly as staff director for the judiciary committee of the Florida House of Representatives, before becoming assistant state attorney in Miami in 1973. She was initially appointed state attorney in 1978 and subsequently elected and reelected to that post.

    Donna E. Shalala. Secretary of Health and Human Services. Ph.D. in political science at Syracuse University, served in the Peace Corps in Iran, and taught at City University of New York and Columbia University, before going to Washington in the Carter administration as assistant secretary of Housing and Urban Development. Following Reagan's victory she was a successful candidate for president of Hunter College, part of the City University of New York; she was appointed chancellor of the University of Wisconsin in 1988. She was a governor of the American Stock Exchange; a member of the Council on Foreign Relations and the Trilateral Commission; and a trustee of the Brookings Institution.

    Hazel R. O'Leary. Secretary of Energy. B.A. from Fisk University and law degree from Rutgers University. Served briefly in state and county government legal posts in New Jersey. She went to Washington, first to serve in the Federal Energy Administration in the Ford administration, and later the department of energy in the Carter administration. From 1981 to 1989 her Washington-based O'Leary Associates lobbied state and federal agencies on energy issues. She was recruited to a high management post in Northern States Power Company, became executive vice-president in 1990, and won promotion to president just prior to her appointment as secretary of energy by President Clinton.

Continued

Madeleine Korbel Albright. Secretary of State. B.A. form Wellesley College and Ph.D. from Columbia University in international relations. Legislative assistant to U.S. Senator Edward Muskie (D-ME). Georgetown University professor of international relations. U.S. Ambassador to the United Nations, 1995–97, before appointment as Secretary of State.

Bush Administration

Elaine Chao. Secretary of Labor. B.A. Mount Holyoke, M.B.A. Harvard University. CEO of the Peace Corp and later president of the United Way. A director of Bank of America, Northwest Airlines, Clorox, HCA, and Dole Foods. Married to U.S. Senator Mitch McConnell (R-KY).

Gale Norton. Secretary of Interior. B.A. and law degrees, University of Denver. An attorney for the Mountain States Legal Foundation (opposition to public land and environmental regulations). Assistant Secretary of the Interior in the Reagan Administration. Attorney general of Colorado (1991–99).

Ann Veneman. Secretary of Agriculture. B.A. University of California-Davis, M.A. and law degrees, University of California-Berkeley. Deputy Secretary of Agriculture in the Reagan and Bush administrations. Secretary of the California Department of Food and Agriculture. A director of the Calgene Co., which was bought out by Monsanto and later merged with Pharmacia, a leader in genetically engineered foods.

Condoleeza Rice. National Security Adviser. B.A. University of Denver, M.A. University of Notre Dame, Ph.D. University of Denver in international relations. Professor of international relations at Stanford University and associate at the Hoover Institute; later Provost of Stanford University. A director of Chevron, Charles Schwab, and Transamerica.

Women leaders, like their male counterparts, are disproportionately upper class in social origin. More than half of the nation's women leaders attended prestigious private colleges. About one quarter of them attended one of the "Seven Sisters": Vassar, Radcliffe, Smith, Wellesley, Barnard, Bryn Mawr, or Mt. Holyoke. Another one quarter attended one of the traditional prestigious private universities: Harvard, Yale, Chicago, Stanford, Columbia, Cornell, Northwestern, Princeton, Johns Hopkins, or Pennsylvania.

The educational level of top women leaders is very high; nearly half possess earned masters or doctorate degrees, and an additional quarter possess law degrees. (Honorary degrees were not counted.) Thus, a total of 71 percent of the women leaders earned advanced degrees; the comparable figure for male leaders is 55.8 percent. This strongly suggests that women need more education than men to compete effectively for top posts.

Despite the impressive progress of women in leadership positions in the last two decades, women still still are underrepresented in elite circles. Serious explanations are not easy to develop. Blatant sexism—dirty jokes, references to "girls," or overt hostility toward women—is seldom encountered in high corporate and banking circles. The barriers women confront are very subtle and often not recognized by men. Women frequently fail to get "fast-track" assignments or especially sensitive posts. Yet these are the jobs that lead to the top. The reasons are difficult to pinpoint. One observer remarked, "At senior management levels competence is assumed. What you're looking for is someone who fits, someone who gets along, someone you trust. Now that's subtle stuff. How does a group of men feel that a woman is going to fit? I think it's very hard."[31] A woman bank executive says, "The men just don't feel comfortable."

There are many other explanations, and all of them are controversial. Men are reluctant to openly criticize a woman, and therefore women executives do not receive constructive feedback. Government affirmative-action efforts are directed primarily at entry-level positions rather than senior management posts. Women choose staff assignments rather than fast-track, operating-head assignments; they are cautious and unaggressive in corporate politics. Women have lower expectations about peak earnings and positions, and these expectations become self-fulfilling. Women bear children, and even during relatively short maternity absences they fall behind their male counterparts. Women are less likely to want to change locations than men, and immobile executives are worth less to a corporation than mobile ones. Women executives in sensitive positions come under even more pressure than men in similar posts; women executives believe that they get much more scrutiny than men and must work harder to succeed.

Cross-national elite studies confirm these patterns of women in elite positions. Results of a systematic study of institutional elites in the United States, West Germany, and Australia by sociologist Gwen Moore indicate that (1) few women have achieved elite positions in major national institutions; (2) women elites are concentrated in the political and the voluntary association sectors; (3) women elites have fewer inter-sectoral ties; (4) marriage and parenthood is less common among women elites than their male counterparts; (5) most women elites are recruited from very high-status social backgrounds; and (6) women elite participation, while still very low, has increased significantly over the last two decades.[32]

ELITE FACTIONALISM: COWBOYS AND YANKEES

Elite factionalism occurs along a number of fault lines. One of the more important factional divisions occurs between the newly rich, entrepreneurial Southern and Western "cowboys" and the established, managerial Eastern

31 Susan Fraker, "Why Women Aren't Getting to the Top," *Fortune*, April 16, 1984, p. 40.

32 Gwen Moore, "Women in Elite Positions," *Sociological Forum*, Vol. 3 (December, 1988), 566–85.

"yankees." This factionalism transcends partisan squabbling among Democrats and Republicans, or traditional riffs between Congress and the President, or petty strife among organized interest groups. The conflicts between cowboys and yankees derives from differences in their sources of wealth and the relative newness of the elite status of the cowboys.

New opportunities to acquire wealth and power develop as a result of technological changes and adjustments in the economy. Many of the cowboys acquired their wealth in independent oil drilling operations, the aerospace industry, computer technology and business machines, real estate development (particularly in the "Sunbelt" from southern California and Arizona through Texas to Florida), discount drugs and merchandising, fast foods, and low-cost insurance. By contrast, yankees include the descendants of the great entrepreneurial families of the Industrial Revolution (the familiar Rockefellers, Fords, Mellons, du Ponts, Kennedys, Harrimans, and so forth). Other yankees have been recruited through established corporate institutions, New York and Washington law firms, Eastern banking and investment firms, well-known foundations, and Ivy League universities.

The cowboys do not fully share in the liberal social welfarism of the dominant Eastern Establishment. The cowboys are "self-made" individuals who have acquired wealth and power in an intense competitive struggle that continues to shape their outlook on life. Their upward mobility, their individualism, and their competitive spirit shape their view of society and the way they perceive their elite responsibilities. In contrast, the yankees have either inherited great wealth or have attached themselves to established institutions of great wealth, power, and prestige. The yankees are socialized, sometimes from earliest childhood, in the responsibilities of wealth and power. They are secure in their upper-class membership, highly principled in their relationships with others, and public-regarding in their exercise of elite responsibilities.

The cowboys are newly risen from the masses—many had very humble beginnings. But it is their experience in *rising* from the masses that shapes their philosophy, rather than their mass origins. As we would expect, they are less public-regarding and social welfare-oriented than the yankees, and they tend to think of solutions to social problems in individualistic terms—they place primary responsibility for solving life's problems on the individual. Cowboys believe that they "made it" themselves through initiative and hard work and advise anyone who wants to get more out of life to follow the same path. They do not feel guilty about poverty. Their wealth and position was not given to them—they earned it themselves and they have no apologies for what they have accomplished in life.

The personal wealth of the cowboys places many of them at the top of lists of America's wealthiest individuals (see Table 3–6). But their wealth is not yet institutionalized in the fashion of the great Establishment families—the Rockefellers, the Mellons, the du Ponts. The billionaire cowboys do *not* con-

trol the nation's largest corporations, banks, insurance companies, foundations, and policy-planning organizations. Nonetheless, they represent a potential challenge to the Establishment as they consolidate and institutionalize
their wealth over time.

The Bechtels.   Representative of the swashbuckling style of the true
Sunbelt cowboys is the father and son construction team that heads the Bechtel Corporation. Steven D. Bechtel and his son Steven D. Bechtel, Jr. control
a little-known, family-held corporate colossus, which is the *world's* largest construction company. The senior Bechtel never obtained a college degree, but
he acquired engineering know-how as a builder of the Hoover Dam. Bechtel
conceived of and built the San Francisco Bay Area Rapid Transit, and he and
his son built the Washington, D.C., METRO subway system.

Steven D. Bechtel, Jr. received an engineering degree from Purdue University in 1946 after service in the U.S. Marine Corps during World War II. He
worked in many positions in the Bechtel Corporation before replacing his
father as chairman.

The Bechtel Corporation has built an entire industrial city—Jubayl in
Saudi Arabia; a copper industry including mines, railroads, and smelters in
Indonesia; and the world's largest hydroelectric system in Ontario, Canada.
Bechtel was fired as the contractor for the Trans-Alaska pipeline when cost
overruns first occurred; but the final price of $8 billion turned out to be eight
times higher than the original estimate, and it seems in retrospect that Bechtel would have done a more cost-effective job if it had been allowed to complete the work. The Bechtel Corporation remains family-owned and, therefore,
refuses to divulge to the SEC or other prying bureaucracies its real worth.

The Bechtels have recruited established leaders to direct their far-flung
enterprises. Before he became secretary of state, George Shultz was serving as
president of the Bechtel Corporation. Before he became secretary of defense,
Casper Weinberger was serving as vice-president of Bechtel. Both men had
gone to Bechtel after serving in President Nixon's Cabinet, and both men
have excellent Eastern Establishment connections. So even though the Bechtels themselves remain independent, their personal wealth and the colossal
size of their privately owned corporation allow them to hire the top leadership
in the nation.

The Hunts.   The late billionaire H.L. Hunt was once asked by reporters
whether he was worried about his son's extravagance (Lamar Hunt had lost
over $1 million in one year as the owner of the new American League football
team, the Kansas City Chiefs). "Certainly it worries me," replied the legendary
oil magnate. "At that rate he'll be broke in 250 years."

The senior Hunt began drilling for oil in Smackover, Arkansas, in 1920.
His very first well (which he won in a poker game) produced a gusher. By

1937, the independent Hunt Oil Company of Dallas, Texas, was worth millions, and at his death in 1974, H.L. Hunt was believed to be one of the richest men in America. His sons, Nelson Bunker, William Herbert, and Lamar, have continued to amass vast personal wealth. "Bunky" Hunt, who regularly refuses interviews and declines publicity, admitted to a congressional committee that he was probably worth over a billion dollars, but he added, "A billion dollars isn't what it used to be." He refused to say exactly how much he was worth: "Senator, it's been my experience that anyone who knows how much they're worth, ain't worth very much."

Operating out of the First National Bank of Dallas, the Hunts manage a vast array of businesses, including the Hunt Energy Corporation and Placid Oil; 3.5 million acres of real estate, including prime downtown Dallas properties; 100,000 head of cattle; and 700 thoroughbred horses. But in 1979, Bunky Hunt and his brother William Herbert decided on an even more ambitious scheme—to corner the world market in silver.

The Hunts began to buy silver at $6 an ounce. Their purchases were so vast that they decided to buy a leading Wall Street investment firm, Bache Halsey Stuart Shields, to facilitate their operations. When silver jumped to $11 an ounce, they contacted their oil-rich Arab friends and recommended more heavy buying. By early 1980, the Hunts had forced the price of silver to $50 an ounce, and their holdings were worth an estimated $7.5 billion. However, much of their holdings were in the form of "futures contracts"—guarantees to pay a set price for silver at a certain date in the future. Rising interest rates in the United States attracted many investors away from silver (and gold) and into high-interest-paying bank certificates and money market funds. Increasingly the Hunts were called upon to pay cash for the unpaid portions of their futures contracts. Finally, on March 27, 1980, "Silver Thursday," the Hunts and their Bache brokers were unable to meet their debts. Panic ensued on Wall Street, as well as in the Federal Reserve System, the U.S. Treasury, and the Commodities Future Trading Commission. The price of silver tumbled. Bache was barely saved from bankruptcy, and many investors lost millions. A $1.1 billion loan was made to the Hunts to keep them from dumping their silver on the market and further depressing the price. Their scheme to corner the silver market failed.

The wealth of the Hunts and many other cowboys is unstable; it is not tied to large institutions. At one time Bunky Hunt was the world's wealthiest man, worth an estimated $16 billion. Today, much of the Hunt empire and its assets are tied up in bankruptcy court. Other Texas oilmen have also fallen: Clint Murchison, Jr., was forced to sell the Dallas Cowboys and later to file bankruptcy; John Connally, former Texas governor, secretary of the treasury, and oil and real estate entrepreneur, was also forced into bankruptcy. The problems of these new-wealth cowboys have been attributed to declining worldwide oil prices and deflation in land and real estate values.

The Bass Brothers. The original Bass fortune was created in typical cowboy fashion. Sid Richardson was a Texas oil wildcatter who had worked the fields for many years before finding his gusher. He borrowed, traded, and financed oil leases, and bought out the New York Central railroad, winning and losing fortunes over his lifetime. He backed winners in politics, including former Texas Governor John B. Connally and President Lyndon B. Johnson. He never married, but he took in his only nephew, Perry Bass, as a partner. When Sid Richardson died in 1959, he left his Texas oil wells to Perry Bass's four sons.

Over time the four Bass brothers amassed a vast empire in oil and gas (Texaco, Northwest Energy, Consolidated Oil and Gas, Charter Co.); high tech (GTECH, Prime Computers); real estate (downtown Ft. Worth; Americana Hotels; Pier 39, San Francisco; Punta Gorda, Florida); clothing (Munsingwear, Nike); fast foods (Church's Fried Chicken); manufacturing (LTC, Fairchild, Champion Parts, Allis Chalmers); banking (InterFirst); and entertainment (Walt Disney). And their personally owned oil wells kept flowing.

The rapid expansion of the Bass fortune is generally attributed to the skills of the oldest Bass brother—Sid Richardson Bass, named after the family's founder. All of the brothers—Sid, Edward, Robert, and Lee—were schooled at Andover and Yale. Sid Richardson Bass is also a Stanford M.B.A., a trustee of the Yale Corporation, a trustee of New York's Museum of Modern Art, and head of Bass Brothers Enterprises, the umbrella group for the many Bass companies and corporations.

The Basses may not have invented "greenmail," but they have been one of its leading practitioners. "Greenmail" is the profit made by a corporate raider who begins buying up a company's stock, threatens a takeover and ouster of the current management, and then sells his stock back to the worried management at a large profit. The Basses were involved in major threats to the management of Texaco and Walt Disney Productions. The Basses have adopted Ft. Worth as their family project, turning the "cowtown" with its stockyards and familiar scents into a complex of gleaming new towers with fashionable shops and restaurants. The Basses are deeply involved in Texas politics through their Good Government Fund and the Bass Brothers Political Action Committee. They support both Democrats (former U.S. Senator Lloyd Bentsen, former Speaker of the House Jim Wright) and Republicans (U.S. Senator Phil Gramm).

To date, the Bass family has displayed considerable unity, even though each brother is associated with different projects. In Ft. Worth they are described simply as "the boys."

H. Ross Perot: Challenging the Establishment? No one better fits the cowboy image than the diminutive billionaire tycoon H. Ross Perot. He has spent most of his lifetime, as well as substantial outlays from his massive fortune, in various challenges to the nation's corporate and political establishment. In the 1992 presidential election, Perot financed his own campaign against "politics as usual" and garnered the largest independent vote since Teddy Roosevelt in 1912. He basks in his celebrity status, paying for his own television time when not appearing on talk shows. He founded his own political party, the Reform Party.

Ross Perot is the son of a Texarkana horse trader and cotton broker who taught his offspring the value of hard work at an early age. Young Ross was not a standout scholar or athlete in high school but worked at breaking horses and selling newspapers. He escaped Texarkana Junior College through drive and self-discipline and won an appointment to the U.S. Naval Academy. Upon graduation, he served four years of active duty in the Navy, although he admits that he was disenchanted with military life. His petition for early release from active duty was rejected; he claims to have had a dispute with his commanding officer over the use of the crew's social fund to redecorate the captain's cabin. He sold computers for IBM in Dallas and quickly became a high-volume salesman. But he soon became disenchanted with IBM's emphasis on selling hardware, believing instead that customers wanted software especially designed for their own business. Acting on his own insight, he quit IBM and formed his own software company, Electronic Data System Inc., on his thirty-second birthday in 1962. But his big break came three years later when Congress passed the Medicare and Medicaid programs as part of President Lyndon Johnson's "Great Society." EDS soon became the leading subcontractor providing computer software to process Medicare and Medicaid claims in Texas, California, and other states. In 1968 EDS went public with the Wall Street sale of its stock, and Perot became a billionaire.

EDS fluctuated violently on the stock market, first rising from $17 a share to $162 and then crashing back to $29. At one point in his career, Perot had the dubious distinction of being the only man ever to *lose* $1 billion. Annoyed at these stock market fluctuations, he purchased du Pont Walston Inc., one of the largest brokerage firms on the New York Stock Exchange. But Perot failed as an investment broker; du Pont Walston collapsed, and Perot temporarily disappeared from the list of wealthiest Americans. But EDS gradually recovered, and Perot's interests in oil, gas, and real estate prospered. In 1984 he sold EDS to General Motors for $2.5 billion and a seat on the GM board.

Perot hoped to use his GM post to reform corporate America, to bring to the nation's largest industrial corporation the same initiative, energy, and competitiveness that drove the cowboy entrepreneur. But GM's established management was not ready for Perot; his public attacks on GM's "archaic" management style were not appreciated in the boardroom. GM Chairman Roger Smith won approval from the board to buy out Perot. Perot left GM, reportedly bitter and vengeful.

Perot's swashbuckling style was not limited to business. In 1979 Perot solved his own Iranian hostage crisis by flying to Iran, breaking some of his employees out of jail, and smuggling them to the Turkish border. The exploit inspired a book and TV miniseries, *On the Wings of Angels*. Perot also undertook to reform the Texas school system; he forced Texans to reevaluate traditional priorities by successfully sponsoring a law to require high school football players to pass courses. Perot acquired a taste for secret, covert operations and a penchant for conspiracy theories. He became an active force in the Vietnam POW-MIA movement, believing that a widespread conspiracy existed to suppress information about living Americans who were left behind in the jungle.

When Perot first announced on *Larry King Live* in 1992 that he intended to run for president, he was not taken very seriously in Washington. But he quickly motivated tens of thousands of supporters in a grass-roots effort, "United We Stand," that succeeded in placing his name on the ballot in all fifty states. He used his own money, nearly $100 million, to build a nationwide organization. Early in the campaign his poll numbers mushroomed to 35 percent, higher than any independent candidate's support in the history of modern polling. His twangy Texas quotes activated audiences. His political support came mostly from the center of the political spectrum—people who identified themselves as independent rather than as Democrats or Republicans. But "Perot mania" faded when he abruptly withdrew from the race in July immediately before the Democratic Party convention. His withdrawal gave Bill Clinton a giant leap in the polls. Perot reentered the race in September, participated in the first three-way presidential television debates, and won 19 percent of the popular vote in the general election, the highest percentage won by a third party candidate since Teddy Roosevelt in 1912. But Perot's voters were spread across the nation and therefore he failed to win a single electoral vote.

The temperamental tycoon proceeded to turn his independent "United We Stand" organization into a political party—the Reform Party. The Party not only enjoyed ballot access in all of the states in 1996, but because of Perot's 1992 vote showing, the Reform Party qualified for federal campaign matching funds. However, Perot's popular support in 1996 languished at only 5 percent of likely voters. He was excluded from the presidential debates; he accepted taxpayer-funded presidential campaign money this time; and in his television appearances, including *Larry King Live*, he often appeared prickly, irritating, and autocratic. On Election Day he won fewer than half of the votes (9 percent) that he had garnered four years earlier, and again failed to win any state's electoral votes.

The Reform Party imploded at a raucous midsummer 2000 convention with rival factions almost coming to blows over control of the microphone. Firebrand conservative commentator Pat Buchanan appeared to control a majority of the delegates. But Perot followers, as well as Minnesota Governor Jesse Ventura, viewed Buchanan's candidacy as a hostile takeover of the Reform Party. They walked out of the convention hall and nominated their own candidate, John Hagelin, a Ph.D. in physics and a devotee of transcendental meditation. The Federal Elections Commission recognized Buchanan as the official nominee and awarded him the $12.6 million due to the Reform Party based on Perot's vote total in 1996. But Buchanan's right-wing rhetoric attracted less than one percent of the voters. Ralph Nader outpolled the combative commentator and the Reform Party was left in a shambles, its future in doubt.

THE NEW TYCOONS

Established corporate management has long professed a concern for the public interest and a devotion to the "corporate conscience." Indeed, the Business Roundtable issued a formal *Statement on Corporate Responsibility,* which asserted that "the long-term viability of the business sector is linked to its responsibility to the society of which it is a part."[33] It quotes its own former chairman and the former chairman of General Electric, Reginald Jones:

> A corporation's responsibilities include how the whole business is conducted every day. It must be a thoughtful institution which rises above the bottom line to consider the impact of all of its actions on all, from stockholders to the society at large. *Its business activity must make social sense just as its social activities must make business sense.*[34]

But these sentiments are encountered more often among established corporate managers than among self-made entrepreneurs. They are sentiments more likely to be expressed by yankees in New York corporate boardrooms than by cowboys lunching at the Dallas Petroleum Club. New tycoons, whether they make their home in Manhattan or Houston, are more likely to believe that they best serve society by serving their own economic interests. They share with a few "classical" economists—most notably Nobel Prize–winner Milton Friedman—the belief that entrepreneurs best serve the nation by pursuing profit, increasing productivity, and striving for optimum efficiency.

Donald Trump. Perhaps no one better exemplifies the energy, vision, and daring of America's new generation of self-made tycoons than Donald Trump. The most celebrated real estate baron of our time, Donald Trump literally changed the face of our world—from Manhattan's dazzling Trump Tower and Grand Hyatt to the glitzy casinos of Atlantic City. And Trump's rise to wealth and power at a very young age testifies to the extraordinary opportunities in America.

Donald Trump started with a mere $50 million—a stake derived from his

---

[33] Business Roundtable, *Statement on Corporate Responsibility,* New York, October 1981.
[34] Ibid., p. 14. Italics in original.

father's modest yet successful New York building and real estate business. He turned this stake into $1 billion before reaching age thirty. "I gave Donald free rein," said his father. "He has great vision and everything he touches seems to turn to gold. Donald is the smartest person I know."[35]

Young Donald attended private schools in New York City and graduated from New York Military Academy as an honor cadet. As a boy he reportedly hung around his father's construction sites. He started college at Fordham University in New York, but at his father's urging, transferred to the Wharton School at the University of Pennsylvania. Bored with classes, he renovated property in his spare time, worked in his father's office during summers, and absorbed the real estate business. At twenty-two, with his Wharton School degree in hand, he was ready to rebuild New York City. He convinced his father to remortgage apartment buildings to generate cash for expansion; Donald Trump wanted to leave the "outer boroughs"—Queens, the Bronx, Brooklyn—to invade Manhattan.

Trump had already developed a reputation as the boy wonder of New York real estate when the opportunity arose to become a true real estate mogul. In 1974 New York City was on the verge of bankruptcy, and one of the nation's oldest corporate institutions—the Penn Central railroad—was already bankrupt. Other Manhattan real estate owners were liquidating their holdings or lying low waiting for more promising times. Then Donald Trump appeared, in his early trademark burgundy-colored suits and matching shoes, his initials "DLT" on his shirts, cuff links, and chauffeur-driven Cadillac limousines, offering to buy Penn Central's Manhattan properties. These he purchased for Depression-era prices, and he proceeded to develop, in a deal with the Hyatt Corporation, his first major hotel, the Grand Hyatt. Trump was twenty-eight years old when he negotiated these deals and then pushed a major tax abatement for his new buildings through City Hall. Construction of the magnificent Trump Tower in Manhattan quickly followed, and then Trump turned his sights on Atlantic City. The voters of New Jersey passed a referendum permitting casino gambling in the dilapidated old resort city. Trump moved in quickly, obtained the necessary casino license from the state, and built the dazzling casino-hotel Harrah's. He purchased Resorts International, retained its Taj Mahal property in Atlantic City, and sold its remaining casinos to game-show mogul Merv Griffin. In one of his first failures, he created the USFL to challenge the NFL for the allegiance of the nation's professional football fans; his team, the New Jersey Generals, prospered but the league floundered.

Typical of many new wealth entrepreneurs, Trump does not hide his assets. Indeed he believes that using his own name on a property increases its value. Currently Trump owns the following: in Manhattan, the Trump Tower, the Trump Plaza, and the Trump Parc Hotel; in Atlantic City, casinos Trump

---

[35] Jerome Tuccille, *Trump* (New York: Jove, 1985), p. 57.

Plaza and Trump's Castle and the new Taj Mahal; in Palm Beach Florida, Trump Towers and the Mar-a-Lago private mansion, golf course, and beach; as well as the Trump Princess, reportedly the world's greatest private yacht, a ghostwritten book *Trump: The Art of the Deal*, and even a bicycle race—the "Tour de Trump."

Trump has demonstrated that the entrepreneurial spirit can prevail over the bureaucratic mindset in government. Trump is politically shrewd and media smart. He regularly succeeds in overcoming the obstacles to development thrown up by armies of bureaucrats in New York City, New York State, and New Jersey. His empire is largely private, operating under a maze of corporate enterprises, most of which bear his own name.

Bill Gates. Harvard University's most famous dropout, Bill Gates, is the modern day version of the nineteenth-century tycoons who dominated entire industries—John D. Rockefeller in oil, Andrew Carnegie in steel, Henry Ford in automobiles. Born in 1955, the offspring of a prominent attorney in Seattle, young Bill was always at the head of his class, especially in math and science. As a self-admitted computer nerd at private Lakeside Prep, Bill and his buddy Paul Allen, and a small group of followers, regularly skipped classes to work in the school's computer room. They became so good at hacking into systems, they were actually hired by a Seattle firm to find weaknesses in its own system. Gates describes himself as a "hard-core" computer nerd: "I mean it was day and night."

Bill went off to Harvard University in 1973, but his friends, Paul Allen and Steve Ballmer, convinced him to drop out and to form a small firm, eventually to become Microsoft, to write programs for the emerging market in personal computers. Initially the company struggled, but in 1980 IBM asked Gates to provide an operating system for its first personal computer. Gates purchased a system called QDOS ("Quick and Dirty Operating System") for $50,000, revised and renamed it MS-DOS, and licensed it to IBM. Microsoft continued to develop software systems, including the popular Microsoft Word, and when the company finally went public in 1986, Gates became an instant billionaire. The next year the first version of Windows was introduced; by 1993 one million copies of Windows were being sold each month. Virtually every computer maker (except Apple) incorporated Windows 95 into its operating software. In 1995 Microsoft also produced the Internet Explorer (IE) browser. Microsoft required computer manufacturers to install the IE browser icon on its Windows.

Bill Gates had always disdained politics. He initially forbade the Microsoft Corporation from making campaign finance contributions. This naivety nearly cost him his fortune. In 1995 the Clinton Justice Department, under the supervision of Attorney General Janet Reno, initiated an antitrust case against Microsoft, charging that their requirement that Windows carry the IE browser was "coercive, unfair, and anticompetitive." Other browser sellers, including Netscape, applauded when Microsoft was forced to enter into a "consent agreement" to discontinue its policy of requiring manufacturers to include IE on the Windows opening page. But virtually all computer manufacturers continue to incorporate the Windows IE browser icon. The Justice Department renewed its case, claiming that Microsoft had violated the consent decree.

By 2000, Bill Gates had learned his political lesson. Microsoft became one of the nation's largest political campaign contributors (see Chapter 4, "The Fat Cat Contributors"). Gates was uncooperative in his appearance before Congress. He denounced the Justice Department and argued that Microsoft's "power" was merely a product of its success in developing innovative, cheap, and popular products. A federal District Court, nonetheless, ordered the "break up" of Microsoft. The case is subject to endless appeals, and a new Bush Justice Department under Attorney General John Ashcroft may not continue to pursue Microsoft.

SUMMARY

Several key questions confront research on America's elite structure. Is institutional power structured hierarchically, with a single group of individuals recruited primarily through business and finance, at the top? Or is it polyarchial, with separate institutional elites functioning in separate sectors of society and recruited from a variety of backgrounds? Are there opportunities to rise to elite positions from relatively modest social backgrounds, or are elite positions largely reserved for the offspring of the nation's upper classes? Is interaction among elites primarily consensual or are there serious conflicts over the goals and purposes of society?

Our institutional approach to power in america indicates considerable concentration of resources in industry, banking, finance, government, the media, foundations, and civic organizations. However, our definition of the leadership of these organizations results in the identification of over 7,300 top positions occupied by about 5,800 individuals. This is a tiny proportion of the nation's 285 million people, but it is a larger number of elites than that reported by earlier researchers.

The nation's leading institutions are linked together by a network of interlocking directorates. However, only about 15 percent of our elites are "interlockers," persons occupying more than one top position simultaneously. We believe that these multiple interlockers play an important role in unifying the nation's elite.

Elites are drawn disproportionately from America's upper classes. They are recruited from the well-educated, prestigiously employed, older, affluent, urban, white, Anglo-Saxon, upper- and upper-middle-class male population of the nation. However, there is considerable upward mobility in American society—opportunity for individuals from relatively modest backgrounds to enter elite circles. Indeed, we estimate that 70 percent of our top elites climbed the ladder of success. Yet the nation's institutional elite remains predominantly male, and only a very few African Americans are found at the top.

Factionalism among America's elite occurs along several fault lines. First of all, newly rich, entrepreneurial Southern and Western "cowboys" do not fully share in the liberal social welfare liberalism of the dominant, Eastern "yankee" establishment. The yankees are recruited from established corporate institutions, New York and Washington law firms, Eastern banking and investment firms, older established foundations, and Ivy League universities. The cowboys are self-made, upwardly mobile, and competitive in outlook.

New technologies, including revolutions in electronics and communications and the continuing expansion of the American economy, create continuing opportunities for the emergence of "new tycoons." Their style is often more independent than that of established institutional elites.

Factionalism also occurs, of course, along traditional liberal and conservative dimensions. (Liberal-conservative factionalism is discussed in more detail in the next chapter.)

However, elite factionalism results only in differences over the *means* of achieving generally agreed-upon *ends*—economic growth, global free enterprise, the protection of private property, and a stable money supply.

8

How Institutional Elites
Make Public Policy

POLICY AS ELITE PREFERENCE

Are the major directions of public policy in America determined by a relatively small group of like-minded individuals interacting among themselves and reflecting their own values and preferences in policy-making? Or are the major directions of American policy a product of competition, bargaining, and compromise among a large number of diverse groups in society? Does public policy reflect the demands of "the people" as demonstrated in elections, opinion polls, and interest-group activity? Or are the views of "the people" easily influenced by communications flowing downward from elites?

The elitist model of the policy process would portray policy as the preferences and values of the dominant elite. According to elitist political theory, public policy does not reflect demands of "the people," but rather the interests, sentiments, and values of the very few who participate in the policy-making process. Changes or innovations in public policy come about when elites redefine their own interests or modify their own values. Of course, elite policy need not be oppressive or exploitative of the masses. Elites may be very public-regarding, and the welfare of the masses may be an important consideration in elite decision-making. Yet the central feature of the model is that the *elites* make policy, not the masses. The elite model views the masses as largely passive, apathetic, and ill-informed about policy. Public opinion is easily manipulated by the elite-dominated mass media, so that communication between elites and masses flows *downward*. The "proximate policy-makers"—

the President, Congress, the courts, and bureaucracy—knowingly or unknowingly respond primarily to the opinions of elites.

No serious scholar today claims that the masses make policy—that each individual can participate directly in all of the decisions that shape his or her life. The ideal of the New England town meeting where the citizenry convenes periodically as a legislature to make decisions for the whole community is irrelevant in today's large, complex industrial society. Pure democracy is, and always has been, a romantic fiction. Social scientists acknowledge that all societies, even democratic societies, are governed by elites.

However the pluralist model of the policy process portrays public policy as the product of competition, bargaining, and compromise among many diverse *groups* in society. Few individuals can participate directly in policy-making, but they can join groups that will press their demands upon government. Interest groups are viewed as the principal actors in the policy-making process—the essential bridges between individuals and government. Public policy at any time reflects an equilibrium of the relative influence of interest groups.

The individual can play an indirect role in policy-making by voting, joining interest groups, and working in political parties. Parties themselves are viewed as coalitions of groups: the Democratic party, a coalition of labor, ethnic groups, blacks, Catholics, central-city residents, black intellectuals, and southerners; the Republican party, a coalition of middle-class, white-collar workers, rural and small-town residents, suburbanites, and Protestants. According to this model, mass demands flow *upward* through the interest groups, parties, and elections to the proximate policy-makers.

AN OLIGARCHICAL MODEL OF NATIONAL POLICY-MAKING

Any model of the policy-making process is an oversimplification. The very purpose of a model is to order and simplify our thinking about the complexities of the real world. Yet too much simplification can lead to inaccuracies in our thinking about reality. Some models are too simplistic to be helpful; others are too complex. A model is required that *simplifies*, yet at the same time *identifies*, the really significant aspects of the policy process.

Let us try to set forth a model of the policy-making process derived from the literature on national elites—an "oligarchical model of the national policy-making process." Our model will be an abstraction from reality—not every major policy decision will conform to our model. But we think the processes described by the model will strike many knowledgeable readers as familiar, that the model indeed actually describes the way in which a great many national policies are decided, and that the model at least deserves consideration by students of the policy-making process.

Our "oligarchical model" of national public policy-making is presented in Figure 8–1. The model assumes that the initial resources for research,

FIGURE 8–1 The Policy Process: The View from the Top

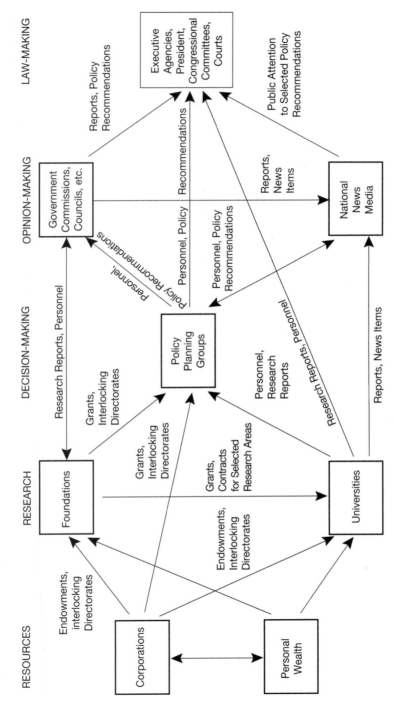

study, planning, and formulation of national policy are derived from corporate and personal wealth. This wealth is channeled into foundations, universities, and policy-planning groups in the form of endowments, grants, and contracts. Moreover, corporate presidents, directors, and top wealth-holders also sit on the governing boards of the foundations, universities, and policy-planning groups to oversee the spending of their funds. In short, corporate and personal wealth provides both the financial resources and the overall direction of policy research, planning, and development.

The foundations are essential linkages between wealth and the intellectual community. The foundations provide the initial "seed money" to identify social problems, to determine national priorities, and to investigate new policy directions. At a later period in the policy-making process, massive government research funds will be spent to fill in the details in areas already explored by these initial studies.

Universities necessarily respond to the policy interests of foundations, although of course they also try to convince foundations of new and promising policy directions. Nonetheless, research proposals originating from universities that do *not* fit the previously defined "emphasis" of foundation interests are usually lost in the shuffle of papers. While university intellectuals working independently occasionally have an impact on the policy-making process, on the whole, intellectuals respond to policy directions set by the foundations, corporations, and government agencies that underwrite the costs of research.

The *policy-planning groups* are the central coordinating points in the policy-making process. They bring together people at the top of the corporate and financial institutions, the universities, the foundations, the mass media, the powerful law firms, the top intellectuals, and influential figures in the government. They review the relevant university- and foundation-supported research on topics of interest, and more important, they try to reach a consensus about what action should be taken on national problems under study. Their goal is to develop *action recommendations*—explicit policies or programs designed to resolve or ameliorate national problems. At the same time, they endeavor to build consensus among corporate, financial, media, civic, intellectual, and government leaders around major policy directions.

Certain policy-planning groups—notably the Council on Foreign Relations, the Business Roundtable, the Committee for Economic Development, the Brookings Institution, the American Enterprise Institute, and the Heritage Foundation—are influential in a wide range of key policy areas. Other policy-planning groups—the Population Council (world population control), Resources for the Future (environmental concerns), and the Urban Institute (urban problems), for example—specialize in certain policy issues.

Corporate representatives—company presidents, directors, or other high officials—sit on the boards of trustees of the foundations, universities, and policy-planning groups. The personnel interlocking between corporation boards, university trustees, foundation boards, and policy-planning boards is extensive (see Chapter 6).

Policy recommendations of the key policy-planning groups are then distributed to the mass media, federal executive agencies, and the Congress. The mass media play a vital role in preparing public opinion for policy change. The media define the "problem" as a problem and thus set the agenda for policy-making. They also encourage political personalities to assume new policy stances by allocating valuable network broadcast time to those who will speak out in favor of new policy directions.

The White House staff, congressional committee staffs, and top executive administrators usually maintain close contact with policy-planning groups. Frequently, before the results of government-sponsored research are available, federal executive agencies, with the assistance of policy-planning groups, will prepare legislation for Congress to implement policy decisions. Particular versions of bills will pass between executive agencies, the White House, policy-planning groups, and the professional staffs of the congressional committees that eventually will consider the bills. The groundwork is laid for making policy into law. Soon the work of the people at the top will be reflected in the actions of the "proximate policy-makers."

THE COUNCIL ON FOREIGN RELATIONS
AND THE TRILATERAL COMMISSION

The center of our oligarchic model of national policy-making in the fields of foreign affairs, national security, and international trade is occupied by the Council on Foreign Relations and its multinational arm, the Trilateral Commission. In Chapter 6 we described the top leadership of the CFR, including its many interlocking directorships with leading corporations, banks, and investment firms. Now let us describe the role of the CFR and the Trilateral Commission in the policy-making process.

The Council on Foreign Relations. Political scientist Lester Milbraith once observed that the influence of the CFR throughout government is so pervasive that it is difficult to distinguish the CFR from government programs: "The Council on Foreign Relations, while not financed by government, works so closely with it that it is difficult to distinguish Council actions stimulated by government from autonomous actions."[1] Of course, the CFR denies that it exercises any control over U.S. foreign policy. Indeed its by-laws declare that "The Council shall not take any position on questions of foreign policy and no person is authorized to speak or purport to speak for the Council on such matters."[2] But policy initiation and consensus building do not require the CFR to officially adopt policy positions.

---

[1] Lester Milbraith, "Interest Groups in Foreign Policy," in *Domestic Sources of Foreign Policy,* ed. James Rosenau (New York: Free Press, 1967), p. 247.

[2] Council on Foreign Relations, *Annual Report,* 1992, p. 174.

CFR meetings are secret. The remarks of government officials who speak at CFR meetings are held in confidence. A CFR rule states:

> Full freedom of expression is encouraged at Council meetings. Participants are assured that they may speak openly, as it is the tradition of the Council that others will not later attribute their statements to them in public media or forums or knowingly transmit them to persons who will. All participants are expected to honor that commitment.[3]

The history of CFR policy accomplishments is dazzling. It developed the Kellogg Peace Pact in the 1920s, stiffened U.S. opposition to Japanese Pacific expansion in the 1930s, and designed major portions of the United Nations' charter. It devised the "containment" policy to halt Soviet expansion in Europe after World War II and guided U.S. policy toward the Soviet Union during the long Cold War. It laid the groundwork for the NATO agreement and devised the Marshall Plan for European recovery. In the Kennedy and Johnson administrations, the Council took the lead in formulating U.S. policy in Southeast Asia—including both the initial decision to intervene militarily in Vietnam and the later decision to withdraw. Council members in the Kennedy-Johnson administration included Secretary of State Dean Rusk, National Security Adviser McGeorge Bundy, Assistant Secretary of State for Far Eastern Affairs William P. Bundy, CIA Director John McCone, and Undersecretary of State George Ball.

The Council consensus up to November 1967 was clearly in support of the U.S. military commitment to South Vietnam. Following the Tonkin Gulf Resolution and the introduction of U.S. ground combat troops in February 1965, President Lyndon Johnson created a private, informal group of CFR advisers, with the assistance of CFR chairman John J. McCloy, which later became known as the "Senior Advisory Group on Vietnam." The group was not an official governmental body, and it included more private elites than public officeholders. Twelve of the fourteen members of the Senior Advisory Group were CFR members; only Johnson's close personal friend Abe Fortas and General Omar Bradley were *not* CFR members. As the war continued unabated through 1967, the Council, at the urging of George Ball, recruited Professor Hans Morganthau of the University of Chicago to conduct a new private study, "A Reexamination of American Foreign Policy." Following the Tet offensive in February 1968, President Johnson called a special meeting of his Senior Advisory Group. The Group, all CFR members, met for two days, March 25 and 26, during which time key members Douglas Dillon, Cyrus Vance, Arthur Dean, Dean Acheson, and McGeorge Bundy switched from "hawks" to "doves." They presented their new consensus to end the war to the President. Five days later, on March 31, 1968, President Johnson announced a de-escalation of the war and his personal decision to retire from public office.

---

[3] Council on Foreign Relations, *Annual Report,* 1982, p. 188.

At this point, the CFR, which was doubtlessly relieved that Johnson and his immediate advisers were left as the scapegoats of the Vietnam disaster, immediately launched a new group, the "Vietnam Settlement Group," headed by investment banker Robert V. Roosa and Wall Street lawyer Cyrus Vance. The group devised a peace proposal allowing for the return of prisoners and a stand-still ceasefire, with the Viet Cong and Saigon dividing the territory under their respective controls. Secretary of State Kissinger avoided directly attributing U.S. policy to the CFR plan, but the plan itself eventually became the basis of the January 1973 Paris Peace Agreement.

Following Vietnam, the CFR, under David Rockefeller's tenure as chairman, began its "1980s Project." Money from the Ford, Lilly, Mellon, and Rockefeller foundations provided the necessary resources. The project officially began in 1975 and lasted until 1980, and it included an international campaign on behalf of "human rights"; an effort to restrict international arms sales; and a study of "North-South global relations"—relations between richer and poorer countries. Upon taking office in 1977, the Carter administration set all of these policies in motion. It restricted international arms sales; it encouraged private and World Bank loans to less developed countries; and, most important, it initiated a worldwide "human rights" campaign in which U.S. trade and aid were curtailed in countries that did not live up to human rights standards. Not only did the Carter administration adopt the CFR program in full, but it also brought CFR members into the government to administer these programs, including Cyrus Vance (secretary of state), Harold Brown (secretary of defense), Walter Mondale (Vice-President), Zbigniew Brzezinski (national security adviser), W. Michael Blumenthal (secretary of the treasury), Sol Linowitz (negotiator of the Panama Canal Treaty), Andrew Young (U.N. ambassador), and Paul Warnke (negotiator of the SALT II Agreement).

But the CFR itself, still under Rockefeller's direction, gradually became aware of the crumbling foreign and military policies of the United States during the Carter administration. In 1980, the CFR issued a stern report citing "sharp anguish over Americans held hostage by international outlaws" (Iran) and "the brutal invasion of a strategic nation" (Afghanistan by the Soviet Union).[4] It described U.S. defenses as "a troubling question." More important, the CFR announced the end of the "1980s Project," with its concern for "human rights," and initiated a new study program on U.S.–Soviet relations. Even before Carter left office, leading CFR members had decided that the "human rights" policy was crippling U.S. relations with its allies but was not affecting policies in Communist countries. Moreover, the CFR recognized "the relentless Soviet military buildup and extension of power by invasion, opportunism, and proxy," and recommended that the U.S–Soviet relationship

---

[4] Council on Foreign Relations, *Annual Report,* 1978–80, p. 11.

"occupy center stage in the coming decade."[5] Thus, elite support for a harder line in foreign policy and a rebuilding of America's defenses had been developed through the CFR even before Ronald Reagan took office.

The CFR announced its new hard line toward the Soviet Union in a 1981 report, *The Soviet Challenge: A Policy Framework for the 1980s*. It recommended a comprehensive, long-term military buildup by the United States, and it even argued that arms control should no longer be the "centerpiece" of U.S. policy toward the Soviets. It also recommended that the United States be prepared to use force in unstable areas of the world such as the Persian Gulf.

The Reagan administration, like those that preceded it, relied heavily on CFR advice. However, because of some conservative objections to the "internationalism" of the Council on Foreign Relations, CFR members on the Reagan team did not publicize their membership. Indeed, during the 1980 campaign, CFR and Trilateral Commission member George Bush was forced to resign from both organizations to deflect right-wing attacks that he was part of the CFR "conspiracy" to subvert U.S. interests to an "international government." Nonetheless, Reagan's Secretary of State George P. Shultz, Defense Secretary Casper Weinberger, Treasury Secretary Donald Regan, and CIA Director William Casey were CFR members.

When David Rockefeller stepped down as CFR chairman in 1985, his place was taken by Peter G. Peterson, chairman of the board of the Wall Street investment firm of Lehman Brothers Kuhn Loeb and a director of RCA, General Foods, Minnesota Mining & Manufacturing, Black and Decker, and Cities Services.

The CFR strongly supported the new thaw in U.S.–Soviet relations "spurred by the atmosphere of *glasnost*, the summit, and the Intermediate-range Nuclear Force treaty."[6] It welcomed a number of high Soviet officials to its meetings. NBC anchorman Tom Brokaw introduced Soviet Information Chief Gennadi Gerasimov, and arms negotiator Paul C. Warnke introduced chief Soviet negotiator Victor Karpov.

The Council credited itself with the success of America's Cold War containment policy that was first outlined by CFR member George Kennan in his 1947 article in *Foreign Affairs*. The collapse of the Soviet Union in 1989 and the ouster of communist governments from Eastern European nations appeared to confirm the wisdom of the CFR in guiding Cold War policy over four dangerous decades.

But the end of the Cold War caused the CFR "to formulate a new organizing principle for American activities overseas in place of the East-West paradigm of the Cold War."[7] Above all, the Council sought to keep the United States actively involved in international politics; that is, to avoid post-Cold-War

---

[5] Ibid., p. 12.

[6] Council on Foreign Relations, *Annual Report*, 1988, p. 22.

[7] Council on Foreign Relations, *Annual Report*, 1992, p. 14.

isolationism and "xenophobia." Its members supported U.S. aid to Russia and other former Soviet republics, and an active U.S. role in maintaining ethnic peace in the republics of the former Yugoslavia. CFR publications urged U.S. and NATO involvement in Bosnia (and later Kosovo) well before Presidents Bush and Clinton sent troops to the region.

The CFR has long supported an active U.S. role in the Middle East. It has been mindful of the traditional U.S. commitment to the safety and security of Israel. But the CFR's close connections and interlocking leadership with America's oil industry has continuously guided CFR recommendations and U.S. policy in the region. Council members voiced approval of President Bush's actions in the Gulf War to defend pro-Western oil-producing regimes in the region, including not only Kuwait, but also Saudi Arabia, Oman, Qatar, and other oil-rich emirates.

In honor of the Council's seventy-fifth anniversary, a major new fund-raising campaign, headed by David Rockefeller and former Wall Street investment banker Douglas Dillon, was initiated by the Council to give itself "the means to reach abroad in a far more comprehensive way . . . as the United States begins to share more fully in its international responsibilities."[8] The CFR acknowledges that it is "rethinking national security"—developing policies to cope with the growing availability throughout the world of biological, chemical, and nuclear weapons. But the CFR's principal efforts today appear to be in support of the development of a truly global economy. In these efforts the CFR relies heavily on its international arm, the Trilateral Commission.

The Trilateral Commission. A *global* economic elite has been forming in the Trilateral Commission since its establishment by David Rockefeller in 1973. In explaining why the Trilateral Commission was created, Rockefeller, in typically condescending elitist language states:

> Governments don't have time to think about the broader longer-range issues. It seemed to make sense to persuade a group of private, qualified citizens to get together to identify the key issues affecting the world and possible solutions.[9]

The Trilateral Commission has played a major role in virtually every important international agreement involving the industrialized democracies over the past three decades. The first contribution of the commission was the initiation of regular economic summit meetings between the heads of the Western European nations, the United States, and Japan. These economic summits, with the support of national elites and the Trilateral Commission, in turn, advanced the global economy through the World Trade Organization and the General Agreement on Tariffs and Trade, the World Bank, and the

---

[8] Ibid., p. 12.
[9] *Newsweek*, March 24, 1980, p. 38.

International Monetary Fund (see "Institutionalizing the Global Economy" in Chapter 2).

Membership on the Trilateral Commission is currently limited to the following: North American group, 100; European group, 150; Japanese group, 85. The current chairman of the North American group is Paul A. Volcker, former chairman of the Board of Governors of the Federal Reserve System. David Rockefeller is recognized as the founder and honorary chairman of the Commission itself. An executive committee includes 36 top corporate and financial elites from all three groups of nations. The annual meeting of the Commission rotates among the three regions. Members are teamed together to develop projects and reports (referred to as "Triangle Papers") that set forth policy recommendations for the approval of the full Commission. The titles of some recent Triangle Papers indicate the current policy concerns of this emerging global elite: "Advancing, Common Purposes in the Middle East," "Managing the International System over the Next Ten Years," "Globalization and Trilateral Labor Markets," "Maintaining Energy Security in a Global Context."[10]

Mass opposition to the globalism of the Trilateral Commission has been sporadic and ineffective. Mass demonstrations at the meeting of the WTO in Seattle in 1999 caused some embarrassment to the host committee (chaired by Microsoft CEO Bill Gates and Boeing CEO Philip Condit). But they failed to halt or even slow the inexorable movement toward globalization. The opposition includes elements of organized labor, human rights groups, and environmental activists.

THE BUSINESS ROUNDTABLE AND THE COMMITTEE ON ECONOMIC DEVELOPMENT

Corporate America has always been well represented in Washington. For many years, the U.S. Chamber of Commerce, the National Association of Manufacturers, the Business Council, and hundreds of industry associations such as the powerful American Petroleum Institute, have represented business in traditional pluralist interest-group fashion. But during World War II and later during the Cold War, American corporate and financial elites decided they needed to come together and form superorganizations for national policy planning.

The Business Roundtable.   The Business Roundtable was established in 1972 "in the belief that business executives should take an increased role in the continuing debates about public policy." The organization is composed of the chief executives of the 200 largest corporations in America and is financed

---

[10] See "The Trilateral Commission at 25," published by The Trilateral Commission, 1998.

through corporate membership fees. Former Du Pont chairman Irving Shapiro summarized the purposes of the Roundtable: "We wanted to demonstrate that there are sensible human beings running big companies, people who think beyond their own interests."[11]

The real impetus for the formation of the Business Roundtable, however, was the worsening inflation of the 1970s, a series of oil crises and resulting public criticism of the oil companies, and the growing consumer and environmental movements that threatened big business with costly regulations. The Roundtable came together from three existing business organizations: (1) the "March Group" of chief executive officers of large corporations, led by John Harper of Alcoa and Fred Borch of General Electric, which was fighting the creation of a federal consumer protection agency; (2) the Construction Users Anti-Inflation Roundtable, headed by Roger Blough of U.S. Steel, which was devoted to combating rising construction costs, especially the cost of labor; and (3) the Labor Law Study Committee, which was fighting changes in labor laws which permit common-site picketing.

Why did business create this superorganization? The Business Roundtable itself says:

> The answer is that business leaders believed there was a need that was not being filled, and they invented the Roundtable to fill it. They wanted an organization in which the chief executive officers of leading enterprises would get together, study issues, try to come to a consensus, develop positions and advocate those positions. The executives who created the Roundtable believed that the U.S. economy would be healthier, there would be less unwarranted intrusion by government into business affairs, and the interests of the public would be better served if there were more cooperation and less antagonism. It was decided that one way business could be a more constructive force, and have more impact on government policymaking, was to bring the chief executives directly into the picture. The Roundtable therefore was formed with two major goals:
>
> —to enable chief executives from different corporations to work together to analyze specific issues affecting the economy and business, and
>
> —to present government and the public with knowledgeable, timely information, and with practical, positive suggestions for action.[12]

In brief, traditional interest-group representation was inadequate for the nation's top corporate leadership. It wished to come together *itself* to decide upon public policy.

The power of the Business Roundtable stems in part from its "firm rule" that a corporate chief executive officer cannot send a substitute to its meetings. Indeed, Roundtable chief executives are called upon to directly lobby the Congress. Congress members are impressed when Edward B. Rust, chair-

---

[11] *Time*, April 13, 1981, p. 76.

[12] Business Roundtable public statement, "What the Roundtable Is," dated January 1988—201 Park Avenue, New York, New York 10166.

man and CEO of State Farm Insurance, appears before the House Committee on Education and strongly endorses annual testing of students and supports "additional resources targeted toward health and science education." Congress welcomes the direct testimony of Louis B. Campbell, chairman and CEO of Textron, that any patients bill of rights must include a provision to reduce lawsuits and "the damaging impact expanded liability will have on any employer-provided health-care."

High on the Roundtable's list of priorities is support for global trade, including the North America Free Trade Agreement and normalization of trade relations with China. The Roundtable is far less enthusiastic about environmental protection and insists in its "Blueprint 2000" that environmental protection be "linked to . . . economic vitality and growth . . . [through] free trade and technological innovation." The Roundtable does not hesitate to ask Congress for protection from hostile corporate raiders. H.B. Atwater, chairman and CEO of General Mills, once testified before Congress against "the abuse of capital markets . . . by the few manipulators who put companies into play for short-term financial gain."[13]

The Business Roundtable spends more than $10 million per year in *direct* lobbying activities. More important, the power of the Roundtable in Washington also derives from the funds member corporations pour into campaign chests of Congress members (see Table 8–1). Most of the money given by the Roundtable in recent elections has gone to Republicans. But when Democrats controlled Congress, most Democratic incumbents could count on major contributions from Roundtable corporations.

As an interest group, the Business Roundtable wins most but not all of its legislative battles in Washington. The Roundtable lost a lengthy battle over mandated family leaves in 1993 when a Democratic-controlled Congress sent the Family Leave Act to President Bill Clinton to sign as his first major legislative victory. Even more recently, in Republican-controlled Congresses, the Roundtable has been thwarted in its efforts to reform the nation's product liability laws. Its principal opponent in this struggle has been the American Association of Trial Lawyers, itself a major source of campaign financing together with individual law firms. (And, of course, lawyers are the largest single occupational group in Congress itself.) So even with all of its resources, the Business Roundtable does not win all its battles.

The chairman of the Business Roundtable, Robert N. Burt, CEO of the FMC Corporation, said in assuming his chairmanship: "My charge is to ensure that the Roundtable continues to play a major role in setting the course for America on key public policy issues, from trade to health care, education to the environment."[14]

---

[13] Testimony of H.B. Atwater, chairman of the Business Roundtable Task Force on Corporate Responsibility, before the House Committee on Telecommunications and Finance, June 11, 1987.

[14] Business Roundtable, press release, November 4, 1999.

TABLE 8–1   Business Roundtable Congressional Campaign Contributions

Organization Name	Total Amount Contributed	Percentage to Republicans	Percentage to Democrats
Philip Morris	$3,006,636	83	17
RJR Nabisco	1,352,931	85	15
AT&T	984,524	56	44
MCI Telecommunications	934,514	36	64
Federal Express	773,525	49	51
Anheuser-Busch	736,057	46	54
Time Warner	726,250	45	55
Chevron	702,306	75	25
NYNEX Corporation	651,602	63	37
Textron	648,000	58	42
Eli Lilly	627,825	70	30
Energy Corporation	580,975	49	51
WMX Technologies	551,200	66	34
Bank of America	546,798	65	35
Bristol-Myers Squibb	542,400	79	21
Coca-Cola	534,640	67	33
Travelers group	524,844	62	38
General Motors	501,775	85	15

Source: Center for Responsive Politics from Federal Election Commission data for 1998.

The Committee on Economic Development.   The Committee on Economic Development (CED) was founded by the nation's top corporate and financial elites during World War II with the goal of shaping the postwar world. The CED takes credit for the formation of the Marshall Plan that helped bring about the economic recovery of Western Europe after the war. It was instrumental in the formulation of the Full Employment Act of 1946 which, among other things, established the President's Council of Economic Advisers and the Joint Economic Committee of Congress. The CED took the early lead in encouraging economic globalization—shaping the Bretton Woods Agreement that led to the General Agreement on Tariff and Trade and later the World Bank and the International Monetary Fund. The CED worked closely with the Council on Foreign Relations in the creation of these international organizations.

CED does more than formulate policy. It also functions as a business interest group in Washington, D.C. It does so despite its own denial that it engages in lobbying activity: "CED trustees do not lobby, but they promote CED's stated positions through such activities as congressional testimony and one-on-one briefings with top government officials."[15]

The CED may have lost influence in recent years, both as a coordinating

[15] Council on Economic Development, *About the CED*, 1999, p. 2.

and consensus-building institution among elites, and as a defender of corporate interests in Washington, D.C. The CED does not appear to have been directly responsible for any significant new policy changes in recent years. Its efforts to reduce the regulatory authority of the Environmental Protection Agency, the Food and Drug administration, the Occupational Safety and Health Administration, and so forth, have largely failed. Its efforts at tort reform have been effectively checked by the nation's powerful legal community—the Washington law firms, the American Bar Association, the American Trial Lawyers Association, as well as the many lawyers who served in Congress themselves. But even more convincing evidence of CED's waning influence may be inferred from examining the membership of its Board of Trustees. No longer are the *heads* of top corporations and banks represented among the trustees, that is, the chairman and chief executive officers (CEOs). Instead, the trustees appear to be *vice*-presidents of larger corporations and CEOs of smaller firms.

THE BROOKINGS INSTITUTION

Dem- Domestic policy

The Brookings Institution remains the dominant policy-planning group for American domestic policy. This is true despite the growing influence of competing think tanks over the years. Brookings staffers dislike its reputation as a "liberal think tank," and they deny that Brookings tries to set national priorities. Yet the Brookings Institution has been very influential in planning the war on poverty, welfare and health-care reform, deficit reduction, and taxing and spending policies. The *New York Times* columnist and Harvard historian writing team, Leonard and Mark Silk, describe Brookings as the central locus of the Washington "policy network," where it does "its communicating over lunch, whether informally in the Brookings cafeteria or at the regular Friday lunch around a great oval table at which the staff and their guests keen over the events of the week like the chorus of an ancient Greek tragedy; through consulting, paid or unpaid, for government or business at conferences, in the advanced studies program; and, over time, by means of the revolving door of government employment."[16]

The Brookings Institution began as a modest component of the progressive movement of the early twentieth century. A wealthy St. Louis merchant, Robert Brookings,[17] established an Institute of Government Research in 1916 to promote "good government," fight "bossism," assist in municipal reform, and press for economy and efficiency in government. It worked closely with the National Civic Federation and other reformist, progressive

---

[16] Leonard Silk and Mark Silk, *The American Establishment* (New York: Basic Books, 1980), p. 160.

[17] Brookings also served as chairman of the board of trustees of Washington University in St. Louis for twenty years, building a small college into a major university.

organizations of that era. Brookings himself was appointed to the War Production Board by President Woodrow Wilson.

The original trustees of Brookings included Frederic H. Delano (wealthy banker and railroad executive, a member of the first Federal Reserve Board, and an uncle of President Franklin Delano Roosevelt), James F. Curtis (banker and assistant secretary of the treasury under President Taft), Arthur T. Hadley (president of Yale University), Herbert Hoover (then a self-made millionaire engineer and later secretary of commerce and President of the United States), and Felix Frankfurter (Harvard law professor, later to become Supreme Court Justice).

The first major policy decision of the Brookings Institution was the establishment of an annual federal budget. Before 1921, the Congress considered appropriation requests individually as they came from various departments and agencies. But the Brookings Institution proposed, and the Congress passed, the Budget and Accounting Act of 1921, which created for the first time an integrated federal budget prepared in the executive office of the President and presented to the Congress in a single budget message. This notable achievement was consistent with the early interests of the Brookings trustees in improving economy and efficiency in government.

The Brookings Institution assumed its present name in 1927, with another large gift from Robert Brookings, as well as donations from Carnegie, Rockefeller, and Eastman (Kodak). It also added Wall Street lawyer Dean Acheson to its trustees; he remained until his appointment as secretary of state in 1947. For many years, the full-time president and executive officer of Brookings was Robert D. Calkins, former dean of the School of Business at Columbia University.

Under the leadership of Robert Calkins, the Institution broke away from being "a sanctuary for conservatives" and recruited a staff of in-house liberal intellectuals. The funds for this effort came mainly from the Ford Foundation; later a Ford Foundation staff worker, Kermit Gordon, was named Brookings Institution president. (He served until his death in 1977.) First under Calkins and later under Gordon, Brookings fashioned itself as a policy-planning organization and rapidly gained prestige and prominence in elite circles. When Republicans captured the presidency in 1968, Brookings became a haven for unemployed liberal Democratic intellectuals and bureaucrats. Charles L. Schultze, former chairman of the Council of Economic Advisers, began the publication of an annual "counter-budget" as a critique of the Nixon budgets. These are now published regularly under the title "Setting National Priorities." President Kermit Gordon, drawing on his experience as budget director under President Johnson, pressed forward with the notion of an alternative to the presidential budget. Brookings staffers Charles Schultze and Alice Rivlin developed a proposal for a new congressional budget process and a Congressional Budget Office. In 1974, Congress obligingly established new budgetary procedures and created new and powerful House and Senate

Budget Committees, with a new joint Congressional Budget Office headed, of course, by Alice Rivlin. She returned to Brookings in 1983 after eight years of advising Congress on budget matters.

Brookings experienced a modest eclipse in power and influence during the 1980s. Brookings scholar Henry Aaron contends that social scientists generally were discredited by the failure of many of the Great Society programs to bring about their expected results.[18] This led to a breakdown in the liberal intellectual consensus on behalf of government intervention to solve social problems and contributed to the rising influence of "neoconservative" scholars. As the leading liberal think tank, Brookings suffered the popular disillusionment incurred by liberal reformers. Whatever the merits of Aaron's explanation, certainly we must add to it the disastrous economic performance of the 1970s—high inflation, low productivity, declining real incomes, and the general discredit this brought to Keynesian macroeconomics. As the Keynesians fell into disrepute, Brookings declined in influence. Finally, of course, Brookings's influence was weakened with the coming of the Reagan administration. If Brookings was the sole instrument of a truly consensual elite, it would have equal influence regardless of which administration was in office. But, in fact, Brookings's influence was minimal during the Reagan-Bush years.

The Clinton administration provided an opportunity for Brookings to reassert its dominant position in the policy-planning network. Alice Rivlin was appointed deputy director of the Office of Management and Budget (under director and former Congressman Leon Panetta) and helped craft the Clinton tax-increase and deficit-reduction legislation in 1993. Brookings staff were influential participants in developing Clinton's comprehensive health-care package, and Brookings economists long supported the North American Free Trade Agreement.

Louis W. Cabot, former chairman of the board of trustees of the Brookings Institution, declared that "The top challenge for Brookings is to anticipate the major policy issues of the future. . . . Thanks to Brookings' modest endowment, we are able to set our own agenda and focus on what we believe to be the most important public policy issues."[19] Do the trustees determine research directions at Brookings? Former President Bruce MacLaury has acknowledged that the trustees are deeply engaged in the activities of Brookings, to the point of vetoing proposed research projects, and that interventions by the trustees have caused controversy within the institution. Brookings scholars, with their university backgrounds, expect academic freedom. But MacLaury was quoted in the *New York Times* as saying: "There is always the question about the role of the trustees, particularly with regard to academic freedom. But we are a think tank. We are not a university."[20] Chairman

---

[18] Henry Aaron, Politics and the Professors (Washington, DC: Brookings Institution, 1976).
[19] The Brookings Institution, *Annual Report,* 1988, p. 3.
[20] Quoted in the *New York Times,* December 14, 1983, p. 8.

Louis W. Cabot states that "Our trustees enrich our research planning with pragmatic insights gained from experience in business and finance, government, the law, and academe. They provide the direction and commitment needed to keep Brookings and its work up to the standards we have set for ourselves."[21]

Brookings opposed George W. Bush's large, across-the-board tax cuts, supported more government spending for education and health care, and sought to curb elements of Bush's missile defense plans that contradicted the 1972 ABM Treaty. In foreign policy, Brookings strongly supports internationalism and globalism, and its recommendations parallel those of the Council on Foreign Relations.

COMPETITION AMONG ELITES: AEI AND HERITAGE

An oligarchic model does not preclude competition among elites. Not only do individuals strive for power and preeminence, organizations do so as well. Competition among policy-planning organizations has grown over the years. The Council on Foreign Relations and the Trilateral Commission remain preeminent in foreign affairs and international trade issues. But in domestic policy, the historic influence of the Brookings Institution has been challenged in recent decades by the development of competing organizations, notably the American Enterprise Institute and the Heritage Foundation.

Rep · Domestic Policy

The American Enterprise Institute. For many years, Republicans dreamed of a "Brookings Institution for Republicans" which would help offset the liberal bias of Brookings itself. In the late 1970s, that role was assumed by the American Enterprise Institute (AEI). The American Enterprise Association, as it was first called, was founded in 1943 by Lewis H. Brown, chairman of the Johns-Manville Corporation, to promote free enterprise. William J. Baroody, Sr., a staffer at the U.S. Chamber of Commerce, became executive director in 1962 and adopted the name American Enterprise Institute. William J. Baroody, Jr., assumed the presidency of AEI after his father. In 1976, the AEI provided a temporary haven for many Ford administration refugees, including Treasury Secretary William E. Simon, Transportation Secretary Carla Hills, CEA Chairman Herbert Stein, and AEI's "Distinguished Fellow," former President Gerald R. Ford. More important, however, the AEI began to attract distinguished neoconservative scholars, including sociologist Irving Kristol, commentator Michael Novak, economist Murray Weidenbaum (later chairman of the Council of Economic Advisers), and political scientists Seymour Martin Lipset, Ben Wattenberg, Austin Ranney, and Jeane Kirkpatrick (former U.N. ambassador). The AEI appealed to both Democrats and Republicans who were beginning to

[21] The Brookings Institution, *Annual Report,* 1988, p. 4.

have doubts about big government. President William Baroody, Jr., distinguished the AEI from Brookings:

> In confronting societal problems those who tend to gravitate to the AEI orbit would be inclined to look first for a market solution . . . while the other orbit people have a tendency to look for a government solution.[22]

But Robert V. Roosa, former chairman of the Brookings Institution, and senior partner in the Wall Street investment firm of Brown Brothers, Harriman & Co., resented the implications that Brookings is "liberal," while the AEI is "conservative":

> AEI is selling against Brookings. They don't have to do that—they have a role to fill. . . . We do some things on the conservative side—and more now. . . . We say to corporations "We're on your side too."[23]

AEI rose in influence in Washington during the Reagan Administration. It began to set the agenda for policy discussions—tax reductions, deregulation, crime fighting, welfare dependency, and increased defense spending. Even during the Reagan years, however, AEI never quite matched the power of the Brookings Institution in the 1960s and 1970s. Neither the Reagan nor Bush administrations relied directly on AEI to devise programs or write legislation. Instead, AEI's influence came to rest on the high quality of its policy research. Its flagship bimonthly, *The American Enterprise*, publishes some of the best articles on public policy in a lively and engaging style and format. Arguably, AEI's books and reports set the nation's standard for policy work.

AEI scholars laid the groundwork for the Welfare Reform Act of 1996. This work convinced many Democrats as well as Republicans in Congress that federal welfare entitlement programs, notably Aid to Families with Dependent Children, were contributing to family breakdown and welfare dependency. Welfare reform generally followed AEI-sponsored recommendations to eliminate the federal entitlement to cash aid, return welfare policymaking to the states, set limits on the length of time that people could be on welfare, and require teenage mothers to stay with their parents and in school as a condition of receiving cash aid.

Today, AEI involves itself in the full range of U.S. domestic and foreign policies, with special emphases on trade policy, government regulation, national security, and social welfare issues. Its top priorities include the following:

---

[22] Silk and Silk, *The American Establishment*, p. 179.
[23] Ibid.

- Tax reform: Exploring alternatives to the current federal income tax, including a flat tax and a national sales tax
- Social Security reform: Transforming Social Security from a government income-transfer program to a private retirement savings program
- Environmental protection: Using private market alternatives as opposed to government "command and control" methods
- Global environmentalism: Opposition to the surrender of U.S. sovereignty over environmental issues to international bodies
- Social welfare reform: Continuing welfare and Medicaid reforms under the Welfare Reform Act of 1996

Currently AEI boasts of a resident staff of fifty scholars and an annual budget approaching that of the Brookings Institution.

The Heritage Foundation.   Conservative ideologues have never been welcome in the Washington establishment. Yet influential conservative businessmen gradually came to understand that without an institutional base in Washington they could never establish a strong and continuing influence in the policy network. Their estrangement from the centers of power was captured in a statement from the Heritage Foundation:

> In those days (1975) we jokingly used to say a phone booth was just about big enough to hold a meeting of conservative intellectuals in Washington . . . we were considered irrelevant by the "opinion-makers" in the media and the power-brokers in the Congress ignored us . . . A conservative "think tank," they said, was a contradiction in terms; conservatives had no ideas. History, of course, has proven them wrong.[24]

So they set about the task of "building a solid institutional base" and "establishing a reputation for reliable scholarship and creative problem-solving." The result of their efforts was the Heritage Foundation.

The Heritage Foundation was the brainchild of several congressional staffers and conservative publicists, including Edwin Feulner and Paul Weyrich. The funding came from Colorado businessman-brewer Joseph Coors, who was later joined by two drugstore magnates, Jack Eckerd of Florida and Lewis I. Lehrman of New York. Heritage boasts that it accepts no government grants or contracts and that it has a larger number of individual contributors than any other think tank. Prominent among its contributors are the Richard Mellon Scaife and the John M. Olin foundations (see "The Vast Right-Wing Conspiracy" later in this chapter).

Unquestionably, competition among think tanks is affected by the outcome of national elections. The Heritage Foundation would have been

---

[24] Heritage Foundation, *Annual Report,* 1985, p. 1.

unlikely to win much influence in Washington had Ronald Reagan not been elected President. Heritage boasts that its 1980 book, *Mandate for Leadership*, set the policy agenda for the Reagan years. Heritage prides itself on being "on the top of the news" with quick *Backgrounders*—reports and memoranda ready at the drop of a press release. Scholarly books and monographs are not in style at Heritage. "Marketing is an integral part of Heritage's product," explains President Edwin Feulner. Rather, its emphasis is on current, topical, and brief analyses.

Heritage is "unabashedly conservative." Resident scholars at Heritage are not particularly distinguished. President Feulner explains, "AEI has the big names—the Herb Steins, the Arthur Burnses. We have young Ph.D.s just out of graduate school on their first or second job."[25] There is very little direct evidence of Heritage influence in public policy. The Reagan administration came to Washington with the most conservative agenda in fifty years. The Heritage Foundation helped publicize that agenda, but there are no specific policy initiatives that can be traced to Heritage. At its tenth anniversary banquet in 1984, Reagan hailed the Foundation as changing "the intellectual history of the West" and testified to its "enormous influence on Capitol Hill and—believe me, I know—at the White House." George Bush was even more extravagant, telling Heritage, "You have been real world movers." But these plaudits were designed more to polish the conservative images of the President and Vice-President than to describe the real influence of Heritage. Heritage inflates its own image by taking credit for policies that would have been enacted anyway. Liberals unintentionally cooperate in this image-making by attributing sinister power to this conservative think tank.

The Heritage Foundation "is committed to rolling back the liberal welfare state and building an America where freedom, opportunity, and civil society flourish."[26] Its principal publication, *Policy Review*, has gradually improved in content and quality, so that today it competes favorably with *The American Enterprise* in policy-relevant articles and essays.

Heritage has addressed many of the "hot-button" conservative issues: abortion, racial preferences in affirmative action programs, public vouchers for pupils to attend private religious schools, religion and morality in public life. Yet for the most part, politicians in Washington and in the states have given little more than rhetorical support for the positions advanced by the Heritage Foundation.

Perhaps Heritage's most important contribution to the policy formulation process will turn out to be its efforts to nourish the development of a network of conservative state and local think tanks throughout the nation. Among the more successful of these "mini think tanks" are the Manhattan Institute in New York City, the Reason Foundation in Los Angeles, the Heart-

[25] Charles Holden, "Heritage Foundation: Court Philosophers," *Science*, 211 (1981), 1019–20.
[26] Heritage Foundation, *Mission Statement*, 1999.

land Institute in Chicago, and the Texas Public Policy Foundation in San Antonio. If, indeed, federalism in the American system is ever revived—if there is a continuing "devolution" of policy responsibilities from the government in Washington to the states—then the strategy of Heritage to create a network of policy planning organizations throughout the states may prove farsighted.

LIBERAL AND CONSERVATIVE FACTIONS AMONG ELITES

We contend that there is, indeed, a broad consensus among America's leaders on fundamental values and future directions of the nation. Disagreement among various segments of the nation's elite occurs *within a framework of consensus* on underlying values. The range of disagreement is relatively narrow, and disagreement is generally confined to *means* rather than *ends*. It is doubtful that any elite, however hierarchical, is ever free of competing ambitions or contending ideas. Indeed, some conflict may be essential to the health of an elite system. Sociologist Suzanne Keller writes:

> The point need not be labored that doubt and conflicts are necessary: societies advance both as a result of achievements and as a result of disagreements and struggles over the ways to attain them. This is where power struggles play a major indispensable role. Loyalty to common goals does not preclude conflict over how they are to be realized.[27]

So we expect to find conventional "liberal" and "conservative" arguments occurring within a broad and unifying consensus.

The Liberal Establishment.   The traditional philosophy of America's elite has been liberal and public-regarding. By this we mean that institutional leaders have shown a willingness to take the welfare of others into account as an aspect of their own sense of well-being. They have been willing to use governmental power to correct perceived wrongs done to others. This is a familiar philosophy—elite responsibility for the welfare of the poor and downtrodden, particularly minority populations. The liberal establishment believes that it can change people's lives through the exercise of governmental power: end discrimination, abolish poverty, eliminate slums, ensure employment, uplift the poor, educate the masses, and instill dominant culture values in all citizens. The prevailing liberal impulse is to *do good*, to perform public services, and to assist the poorest in society.

Leadership for liberal reform has always come from America's upper social classes. This leadership is more likely to come from established "old

[27] Suzanne Keller, *Beyond the Ruling Class: Strategic Elites in Modern Society* (New York: Random House, 1968), p. 146.

families" rather than "new rich," self-made people. Before the Civil War, abolitionist leaders were "descended from old and socially dominant Northeastern families" and were clearly distinguished from the emerging "robber barons"—the new leaders of the Industrial Revolution. Later, when the children and grandchildren of the robber barons inherited positions of power, they turned away from the Darwinist philosophy of their parents and toward the social welfarism of the New Deal. Liberalism was championed not by the working class, but by men such as Franklin D. Roosevelt (Groton and Harvard), Adlai Stevenson (Choate School and Princeton), Averill Harriman (Groton and Yale), and John F. Kennedy (Choate School and Harvard).

The Neoconservatives. While American politics continues in the liberal tradition, that tradition is broad enough to encompass critics of "excessive" government interference in society. The war in Vietnam, the Great Society, urban rioting, campus unrest, Watergate, and inflation all combined in the 1960s and 1970s to raise doubts about the size and scope of governmental power. Elite interest in liberal reforms was tempered by the failures and costs of well-meaning yet ineffective (and sometimes harmful) public programs. Elites learned that society's problems cannot be solved simply by passing a law, creating a new bureaucracy, and spending a few billion dollars. War, poverty, ill-health, discrimination, joblessness, inflation, crime, ignorance, pollution, and unhappiness have afflicted society for a long time. Elites no longer assume that these problems can be erased from society by finding and implementing the "right" public policies.

In the 1980s "neoconservatism" tempered elite enthusiasm for large-scale government programs designed to cure society's ills. These new conservative elites continued to hold liberal, reformist values, but they no longer had the confidence and ambition (bordering on arrogance) of the liberals of the 1960s. They developed more respect for the free-market system, and became more respectful of traditional values and institutions, including religion, family, and the community. They believed in equality of opportunity where everyone is free to strive for whatever they wish, but they drew back from absolute equality, where the government ensures that everyone gets equal shares of everything. Finally, these conservatives came to believe that the United States must maintain a strong national defense if democracy is to survive in a world that is often hostile to American values.

Conservatives continued to disapprove of the unequal treatment suffered by racial minorities but generally opposed affirmative-action and busing programs that involved racial quotas. Conservatives were skeptical that laws, bureaucracies, regulations, and public spending could improve the nation's health or guarantee employment or protect the environment. They believed that government was being overloaded with tasks, many of which should be left to the individual, the family, the church, or the free-market system. Government had attempted to do too much for its citizens, and by failing to meet its promises, government had lost respect and legitimacy.[28]

The Reagan administration came to Washington in 1981 with a well-developed policy agenda. Government, Reagan argued, was the problem, not the solution. Government taxing, spending, and monetary policies promoted immediate consumption, instead of investment and economic growth. Government taxing and spending had to be lowered and inflation brought under control. And indeed double-digit inflation was cured with a stiff dose of high interest rates, and later both inflation and interest rates declined dramatically. In the Economic Recovery Tax Cut Act of 1981, personal income taxes were reduced on the average by 25 percent. More important, in this act and later in the Tax Reform Act of 1986, top marginal tax rates were reduced from 70 percent to 28 percent and many loopholes were closed. Unemployment fell and the numbers *and percentages* of Americans with jobs reached unprecedented high levels.

But the combination of lower taxes, increased defense spending, and continued high levels of social welfare spending produced unprecedented federal deficits. Indeed, the national debt *more than doubled* during the Reagan administration. Huge government deficits kept real interest rates high; the United States became the world's largest debtor nation; and future generations were burdened with heavy interest payments. Elites began to worry that America's prosperity was based on shaky debt foundations.

Clinton and the "New" Democrats. During the 1980s, Democratic leaders among governors and senators came together in the Democratic Leadership Council to create a "new" Democratic Party that would be closer to the center of the political spectrum. The chair of the Democratic Leadership Conference was the young, energetic, and successful governor of Arkansas, Bill Clinton. The concern of the council was that the Democratic Party's traditional support for social justice and social welfare programs was overshadowing its commitment to economic prosperity. Many council members argued that a healthy economy was a prerequisite to progress in social welfare. This view moved the Democratic Party in a more conservative direction. (Not all Democrats agreed with this agenda. African American leaders, including the Rev. Jesse Jackson, feared that the priorities of the council would result in the sacrifice of traditional Democratic Party commitments to minorities and the poor.) In the 1992 presidential election, Bill Clinton was in a strong position to take advantage of the faltering economy under George Bush, by stressing the "new" Democratic Party's commitment to the "middle class," and to avoid being labeled as a liberal defender of special interests.

A booming economy began to shrink annual federal deficits after the

---

[28] Peter Steinfels, *The Neoconservatives* (New York: Simon & Schuster, 1979).

1991–92 recession. And in 1993 Clinton succeeded in getting a Democratic-controlled Congress to pass a major tax increase, raising the top marginal income tax rate to 39.6 percent. (In 1991 President Bush had agreed to raise the top rate from Reagan's 28 percent to 31 percent, thus violating his pledge, "Read my lips! No new taxes!") Budget "caps" were enacted by the Republican Congress and worked surprisingly well in the 1990s to hold down government spending. Both Republicans and Democrats claimed credit for reducing annual deficits. Yet despite all the chest thumping in Washington, the decline in the size of the deficits and the surpluses beginning in 1999 were produced by the nation's dynamic economy. At the start of his second term Clinton acknowledged that he had no mandate for any new, large-scale government programs. But even if he had sought to return to a liberal agenda, it is not likely that the Republican Congress would have allowed him to get very far.

Divisions among Party Activists. The nation appeared more evenly divided politically in 2000 than perhaps any other time in the history of the Democratic and Republican parties. The presidential election was a virtual tie, and Congress was split almost equally between the parties. Although the "conservative" label continues to attract more adherents in public opinion polls than the "liberal" label, most Americans describe themselves as "moderates" or "middle-of-the-road."

It is true that Democratic and Republican party leaders are ideologically separated from each other. While exact percentages and specific questions vary from one election to the next, the general pattern is clear: Democratic Party activists are far more liberal, and Republican Party activists are far more conservative, than the general public (see Figure 8–2).

THE "VAST RIGHT-WING CONSPIRACY"

When Hillary Clinton complained that a "vast right-wing conspiracy" was behind the effort to impeach her husband, she no doubt had in mind the network of conservative foundations, think tanks, civic and cultural organizations, media outlets, and university-based programs that have arisen in recent years to advance conservative policy ideas.[29] The conservative policy network (see Figure 8–3) is far less moneyed and influential than the long-established liberal foundations and think tanks such as Ford, Rockefeller, Carnegie, MacArthur, and Brookings. Nevertheless, it has succeeded in creating new policy agendas in social welfare, federal entitlements, privatization of public functions, charter schools and vouchers, deregulation, market approaches to environmental protection, community policing and prison building, devolu-

---

[29] Portions of this discussion are taken from Thomas R. Dye, *Top Down Policymaking* (New York: Chatham House, 2001).

FIGURE 8–2   Ideological Divisions Between Democratic and Republican Party Activists*

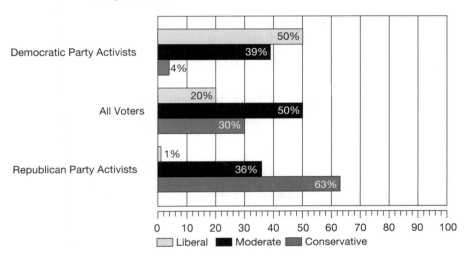

*Party national convention delegates in 1996.
Source: NBC News/*Wall Street Journal* Poll, as reported in *The Polling Report*, September 29, 1997.

tion of policy responsibilities to the states, and the content of television and motion picture productions.

The principal funding of the conservative policy network comes from five sources: the Scaife Foundations, headed by billionaire Richard Mellon Scaife; the Lynde and Harry Bradley Foundation in Milwaukee, Wisconsin; the John M. Olin Foundation; the Koch Family Foundations, headed by oil magnates David and Charles Koch; and the Adolph Coors Foundation, established by Colorado beer mogul Joseph Coors.

Scaife Family Foundations

Richard Mellon Scaife is the great-grandnephew and inheritor of the riches of one of the founders of America's steel industry, Andrew Mellon. The Mellon family fortunes remain tied to USX (formerly United States Steel), Mellon Bank and Trust, and Alcoa. According to former House Speaker Newt Gingrich, Scaife "really created modern conservatism." Scaife was an early and heavy contributor to GOPAC, the political fund that helped make Gingrich Speaker of the House in 1994. His foundations (Sarah Scaife Foundation, Scaife Family Foundation, Carthage Foundation, and Allegheny Foundation) have contributed large sums to a variety of organizations, including the Heritage foundation, the American Enterprise Institute, and the Hoover Institute

FIGURE 8–3 The "Vast Right-Wing Conspiracy"

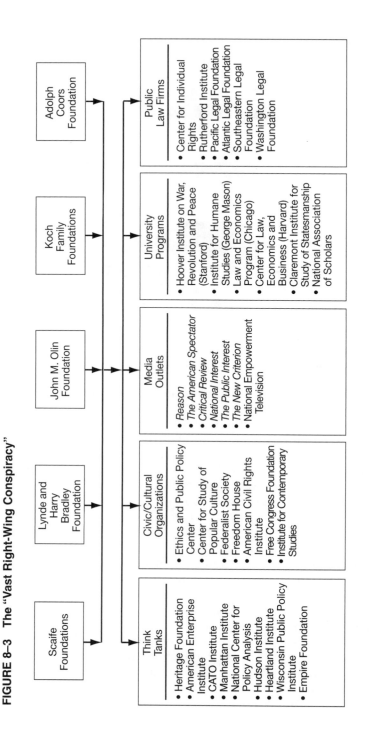

Source: Thomas R. Dye, *Top Down Policymaking* (New York: Chatham House, 2001).

on War, Revolution and Peace at Stanford University. His Allegheny Foundation has given millions to his hometown Pittsburgh's redevelopment.

But it was Scaife's bankrolling of several organizations involved in the movement to impeach President Bill Clinton that won him the enmity of Hillary Clinton. Scaife contributed heavily to the magazine *American Spectator* and its "Arkansas Project" that began the investigation into Clinton's early sexual indiscretions. Scaife is a major benefactor of the public policy school at Pepperdine University—the school that offered Independent Counsel Kenneth Starr a plush deanship that he intended to take after Clinton's impeachment but was forced by bad publicity to turn down. It was a reporter on the Scaife-owned Pittsburgh newspaper who published the book *The Strange Death of Vincent Foster*, suggesting that the White House counselor and close friend of Hillary may have been murdered. Scaife money also found its way to the once-little-known Rutherford Institute that provided the funding for Paula Jones to bring her suit for sexual harassment against Bill Clinton while he was governor of Arkansas. It is doubtful that Clinton would have been impeached by the U.S. House of Representatives without the resources supplied by Richard Mellon Scaife.

Bradley Foundation

The Lynde and Harry Bradley Foundation has skillfully directed its limited resources to advance conservative policy initiatives. (Brothers Lynde and Harry made their fortune in electronic and radio components and then sold their successful corporation to Rockwell International, the aerospace and defense industry conglomerate.) The foundation was instrumental in creating the first public educational school voucher program in its hometown, Milwaukee. The Milwaukee program has now become the model for the school voucher movement throughout the nation. Bradley was also an early major sponsor of National Empowerment Television (NET), the conservative movement's cable television outlet.

The Bradley Foundation publicly laments the flow of authority in the nation "toward centralized, bureaucratic, service-providing institutions" that treat citizens as "clients." It seeks to "reinvigorate and reempower the traditional, local institutions—families, school, churches, and neighborhoods." In addition to heavy support of the American Enterprise Institute and the Heritage Foundation in Washington, Bradley has attempted to fund a variety of state-level conservative think tanks, including the Hudson Institute (Indiana), the Manhattan Institute (New York), the Heartland Institute (Illinois), and the Wisconsin Policy Research Institute. Bradley also funds conservative scholars through fellowship grants that it offers to both think tanks and universities: Bradley Fellows are funded at the Ethics and Public Policy Center in Washington, George Mason University, Georgetown University, Harvard University, the Heritage Foundation, Michigan State University, New York University, Stanford University, the University of Chicago, and the University of Wisconsin–Milwaukee, among others. The Bradley Foundation also helps support the National Association of Scholars in its nationwide effort to organize college and university faculty to fight "political correctness" on campus.

Bradley has also funded individual scholars who have produced influential books on public policy. It funded Charles Murray's book *Losing Ground,* which helped to inspire the welfare reform movement, and his coauthored controversial book *The Bell Curve,* which argues among other things that efforts to train and educate the least intelligent people in society are bound to fail.

John M. Olin Foundation

The John M. Olin Foundation has attempted to sponsor a conservative presence at some of the nation's leading universities. Olin's president, William Simon, the former Secretary of the Treasury in the Reagan administration, has urged his elite colleagues in business and finance to stop "financing left-wing intellectuals and institutions which espouse the exact opposite of what they believe in."

The Olin Foundation has been instrumental in the development of "Law and Economics" programs in universities throughout the nation. These programs emphasize free-market economics as it applies to law. Olin-supported programs exist at the University of Chicago, Harvard University, George Mason University, and Yale University, among others. The foundation also helps to sponsor the Federalist Society, an association of conservative law school students.

Olin, like Bradley, also funds the work of selected conservative scholars. Olin Fellowships supported Allan Bloom's influential *The Closing of the American Mind,* a devastating critique of America's declining cultural and intellectual standards; Dinesh D'Souza's *The End of Racism,* arguing that affirmative action programs are no longer necessary; and the work of the conservative movement's unsuccessful nominee for the U.S. Supreme Court, Robert Bork, including *The Tempting of America,* an argument that the Constitution has been undermined by political forces that create new "rights' for their own advantage.

Koch Family Foundations

Koch Industries, an oil, natural gas, and land management company, is one of the largest privately owned companies in America. Three family foundations are operated by the Kochs (the Charles G. Koch, David H. Koch, and Claude R. Lambe Foundations). These foundations constitute the principal financial backing for the libertarian movement in America.

The major beneficiary of the Koch foundations has been the CATO

Institute, a small think tank committed to libertarian ideas. It came to Washington in 1981 as an offspring of the Libertarian Party but gradually entered mainstream policy debates with free-market, limited-government, and anti-regulatory studies and recommendations. (It is named for *Cato's Letters,* libertarian pamphlets that were distributed in the American colonies in the early 1700s and played a major role in laying the philosophical foundation for the American Revolution.) According to the CATO Institute, "A pervasive intolerance for individual rights is shown by government's arbitrary intrusion into private economic transactions and its disregard for civil liberties." True to its own beliefs, the institute accepts no government funding.

Mainstream conservatives generally applaud CATO's efforts to free the economy from government intervention and reduce taxes and the size of government. But they cringe at CATO's positions on social policy, for example, its call to legalize drugs. CATO also opposes spending for national defense and foreign aid, and it urges a general withdrawal of the United States from world politics. It publishes the *CATO Policy Review* as well as the more scholarly *CATO Journal.*

The Koch Foundations also support *Reason* magazine, a media outlet for libertarian ideas, as well as the Institute for Justice, a libertarian public interest law firm in Washington. It also channels funds into grants and fellowships for conservative university programs, notably the Institute for Humane Studies at George Mason University.

Adolph Coors Foundation

The Adolph Coors brewing company of Colorado was founded in 1983 by Adolph Coors, Sr., and it has remained a family-owned company since then. The Adolph Coors Foundation, headed by descendants Joseph and William Coors, emerged in the 1970s as a major source of funding for the conservative policy agenda.

The initial funding for the establishment of the Heritage Foundation came in 1973 from Joseph Coors; he was assisted in this effort by two drugstore magnets, Jack Eckerd of Florida and Lewis I. Lehrman of New York. They were not satisfied with the more moderate neoconservatism of the American Enterprise Institute. They deliberately recruited younger and more passionate writers to Heritage. They wanted a think tank that would be "on top of the news" and always ready to provide a quick "backgrounder" for reporters.

Heritage boasts that its *Mandate for Leadership* report in 1980 was the blueprint for the Reagan administration, that Reagan's early policy successes were "primarily due to the fact that his script had already been written for him by the Heritage Foundation before he won the election."

It was Coors Foundation money that helped to underwrite the successful effort to thwart the Equal Rights Amendment (ERA). The foundation was a major supporter of Phyllis Schlafly's Eagle Forum, which led the opposition in the states to the ratification of the ERA. The foundation has also provided major funding for Accuracy in Media, an organization formed to combat liberal bias in the media, and for the Free Congress Foundation, an active ideological interest group in Washington, D.C.

THE "PROXIMATE POLICY-MAKERS"

The activities of the "proximate policy-makers"—the President, Congress, federal agencies, congressional committees, White House staff, and interest groups—in the policy-making process are described in countless textbooks. The term *proximate policy-maker* is derived from political scientist Charles E. Lindblom, who uses it merely to distinguish between citizens and elected officials: "Except in small political systems that can be run by something like a New England town meeting, not all citizens can be the immediate, or *proximate*, makers of policy. They yield the immediate (or proximate) task of decision to a small minority."[30] In typically pluralist fashion, Lindblom views the activities of the proximate policy-makers as the *whole* of the policy-making process. But our oligarchic model of public policy-making views the activities of the proximate policy-makers as only the *final phase* of a much more complex process. This is the open, public stage of policy-making, and it attracts the attention of the mass media and most political scientists. This public phase of policy-making is much easier to study than the private actions of corporations, foundations, universities, policy-planning groups, and mass media executives. Most pluralists concentrate their attention on this phase of public policy-making and conclude that it is simply a process of bargaining, competition, and compromise among governmental officials.

Undoubtedly, bargaining, competition, persuasion, and compromise over policy issues continue throughout this final law-making phase of policy-making. This is particularly true in the formulation of domestic policy; by contrast, the President is much freer to pursue elite recommendations in foreign and military policy areas without extensive accommodation of congressional and interest-group pressures. Of course, many elite recommendations fail to win the approval of Congress or even of the President in the first year or two they are proposed. Conflict between the President and Congress, or between Democrats and Republicans, or liberals and conservatives, and so forth, may delay or alter the final actions of the proximate policy-makers.

But the agenda for policy consideration has been set by other elites *before* the "proximate policy-makers" become actively involved in the policy-

[30] Charles E. Lindblom, *The Policy-Making Process* (Englewood Cliffs, N.J.: Prentice Hall, 1968), p. 30.

making process. The major directions of policy change have been determined, and the mass media have prepared the public for new policies and programs.

Members of Congress and the president and White House staff must be mindful of the policy concerns of the heavy campaign contributors who put them in office and keep them there The same institutional elites that provide the funds for the policy-making process also provide the funds for the electoral process. There can be little surprise that the enactments of the proximate policy-makers do not vary much from the preferences of the elites.

The formal law-making process concerns itself with details of public policy: Who gets the "political" credit, what agencies get control of the program, and exactly how much money will be spent? These are not unimportant questions, but they are raised and decided within the context of policy goals and directions that have already been determined. These decisions of the "proximate policy-makers" tend to center about the *means* rather than the *ends* of public policy.

SUMMARY

Pluralist scholars focus their attention on the activities of "the proximate policy-makers"—the President, Congress, the courts, and bureaucracy. They observe competition, bargaining, and compromise among and within these public bodies over specific policies and programs. They observe the role of parties, interest groups, and constituents in shaping the decision-making behavior of these proximate policy-makers. But it is quite possible that the activities of the proximate policy-makers are merely the final phase of a much more complex structure of national policy formation.

Our oligarchical model of national policy-making attempts to trace elite interaction in determining the major directions of national policy It portrays the role of the proximate policy-makers as one of implementing through law the policies that have been formulated by a network of elite-financed and elite-directed policy-planning groups, foundations, and universities. The proximate policy-makers act only after the agenda for policy-making has already been set, the major directions of policy changes have been decided, and all that remains is the determination of programmatic specifics.

The initial resources for research, study, planning, and formulation of policy come from donations of corporate and personal wealth. These resources are channeled into foundations, universities, and policy-planning groups. Moreover, top corporate elites also sit on the governing boards of these institutions to help determine how their money will be spent The policy-planning groups—such as the Council on Foreign Relations, the

Trilateral Commission, the Business Roundtable, the Committee on Economic Development, the Brookings Institution, the American Enterprise Institute, and the Heritage Foundation—play a central role in bringing together individuals at the top of the corporate and governmental worlds, the foundations, the law firms, and the mass media, in order to reach a consensus about policy direction.

9

Institutional Elites in America

INSTITUTIONAL POWER IN AMERICA

Power in America is organized into large institutions, private as well as public—corporations, banks, investment firms, governmental bureaucracies, media empires, law firms, universities, foundations, cultural and civic organizations. The nation's resources are concentrated in a relatively few large institutions, and control over these institutional resources is the major source of power in society. The people at the top of these institutions—those who are in a position to direct, manage, and guide institutional programs, policies, and activities—compose the nation's elite.

The *systematic* study of the nation's institutional elite is still in an exploratory stage. Although a great deal has been written about "the power elite," much of it has been speculative, impressionistic, and polemical. Serious difficulties confront the social scientist who wishes to move away from anecdote and ideology to serious scientific research on national elites—research that "names names," attempts operational definitions, develops testable hypotheses, and produces some reliable information about national leadership.

The first task confronting social science is to develop an operational definition of national elite. Such a definition must be consistent with the notion that great power resides in the institutional structure of society; it must also enable us to identify by name and position those individuals who possess great power in America. Our own definition of a *national institutional elite* produced

7,314 elite positions. Taken collectively, individuals in these positions controlled almost three-quarters of the nation's industrial (nonfinancial) assets, almost two-thirds of all banking assets, and more than three-quarters of all insurance assets, and they directed the nation's largest investment firms. They commanded over half of all assets of private foundations and universities and controlled the television networks, the national press, and the major newspaper chains. They dominated the nation's top law firms and the most prestigious civic and cultural associations, and they occupied key federal government posts in the executive, legislative, and judicial branches and the top military commands.

Our selection of positions of institutional power involved many subjective judgments, but it provided a starting place for a systematic inquiry into the character of America's elite structure. It allowed us to begin investigation into a number of important questions: Who are the people at the top of the institutional structure of America? How did they get there? What are their backgrounds, attitudes, and values? How concentrated or dispersed is their power? Do they agree or disagree on the fundamental goals of society? How much cohesion or competition characterizes their interrelationships? How do they go about making important policy decisions or undertaking new policy directions?

HIERARCHY AND POLYARCHY AMONG INSTITUTIONAL ELITES

Before summarizing our data on institutional elites, it might be helpful to gain some theoretical perspectives on our findings by suggesting *why* we might expect to find evidence of either hierarchy or polyarchy in our results.

European social theorists—notably Weber and Durkheim—provide theoretical explanations of why social structures become specialized in advanced societies, and why coordination mechanisms are required. These theorists suggest that increasing functional *differentiation* of elites occurs with increasing socioeconomic development. In a primitive society, it is difficult to speak of separate economic, political, military, or administrative power roles; in primitive life, these power roles are merged together with other roles, including kinship, religion, and magical roles. But as separate economic, political, bureaucratic, and military institutions develop, and as specialized power roles are created within these institutions, separate elite groups emerge at the top of separate institutional structures. The increased division of labor, the scale and complexity of modern social organizations, and the specialization in knowledge, all combine to create functional differentiation among institutional elites. This suggests polyarchy among elites in an advanced society such as the United States.

Yet even though specialized elite groups are required to direct relatively autonomous institutional sectors, there must also be some social mechanisms to coordinate the exercise of power by various elites in society. This requirement of *coordination* limits the autonomy of various institutional elites. Thus, specialization acts to bring elites together, as well as to force them apart. Social theory does not necessarily specify *how* coordination of power is to be achieved in modern society. Nor does it specify *how much* unity is required to maintain a relatively stable social system or, conversely, how much competition can be permitted. Certainly there must be *some* coordination if society is to function as a whole. The amount of coordination can vary a great deal, however, and the mechanisms for coordination among elites differ from one society to another.

One means of coordination is to keep the relative size of elite groups small. This smallness itself facilitates communication. If there are relatively few people who actually direct institutional activity, then these people can have extraordinary influence on national policy. What's more, the small size of these groups means that institutional leaders are known and accessible to each other. Of course, policy-planning groups, governmental commissions, and advisory councils, or informal meetings and conferences, are instrumental in bringing "specialists" together. But how small *is* America's elite? C. Wright Mills, wisely perhaps, avoids any estimate of the size of "the power elite"; he says only that it is "a handful of men."[1] Floyd Hunter estimates the size of "top leadership" to be "between one hundred and two hundred men."[2] We have already indicated that our definition of the elite produces an estimated size of 7,314 positions occupied by 5,778 individuals—considerably more than implied in the power elite literature, but still few enough to permit a great deal of personal interaction.

Another coordinating mechanism is to be found in the methods by which elites are recruited. The fact that elites who are recruited to different institutional roles share the same social class and educational backgrounds should provide a basis for understanding and communication. Social homogeneity, kinship links, similarity of educational experience, common membership in clubs, common religious and ethnic affiliations, all help to promote unity of outlook. Yet at the same time we know that a certain amount of "circulation of elites" (upward mobility) is essential for the stability of a social system. This means that some heterogeneity in social background must be tolerated. But again social theory fails to quantify the amount of heterogeneity that can be expected.

Still another form of coordination is a general consensus among elites on the rules to resolve conflicts and to preserve the stability of the social system itself. Common values serve to unify the elites of various institutional systems. Moreover, agreement among elites to abide by the rule of law and to

---

[1] C. Wright Mills, *The Power Elite* (New York: Oxford University Press, 1956), p. 7.

[2] Floyd Hunter, *Top Leadership, U.S.A.* (Chapel Hill, University of North Carolina Press, 1959), p. 176.

minimize violence has a strong utilitarian motive, namely to preserve stable working arrangements among elite groups. Finally, unifying values also legitimize the exercise of power by elites over masses. So the preservation of the value system performs the dual function of providing the basis of elite unity, while at the same time rationalizing and justifying for the masses the exercise of elite power. Unfortunately, social theory does not tell us *how much* consensus is required among elites to facilitate coordination and preserve a stable social system. Social theory tells us that elites must agree on more matters than they disagree, but it fails to specify how broad or narrow the range of issues can be.

Because social theory suggests *both* convergence and differentiation among institutional elites, it is possible to develop competing theoretical models of the social system—models which emphasize either hierarchy or polyarchy. For example, the notion of the "power elite" developed by C. Wright Mills implies *hierarchy* among economic, political, and military power-holders. The idea suggests unity and coordination among leaders of functionally differentiated social institutions. Mills speculates that a large-scale, centralized, complex, industrial society *necessitates* coordination:

> At the pinnacle of each of the three enlarged and centralized domains, there have arisen those higher circles which make up the economic, the political, and the military elites. At the top of the economy, among the corporate rich, there are the chief executives; at the top of the political order, the members of the political directorate; at the top of the military establishment, the elite of soldier-statesmen clustered in and around the Joint Chiefs of Staff in the upper echelon. . . . Each of these domains of power—the warlords, the corporation chieftains, the political directorate—tend to come together, to form the power elite of America.[3]

Thus, the hierarchical or elitist model rests upon the theoretical proposition that increasing complexity requires a high degree of coordination and consequently a great concentration of power.

In contrast, the polyarchical or pluralist model emphasizes differentiation in institutional structures and leadership positions—with different sets of leaders and different institutional sectors of society and with little or no overlap, except perhaps by elected officials responsible to the general public. According to this view, elites are largely specialists, and leadership roles are confined to a narrow range of institutional decisions. These specialists are recruited through separate institutional channels—they are not drawn exclusively from business or finance. Further, the functional specialization of institutional elites results in competition for power, a struggle in which competing elites represent and draw their strength from functionally separate systems of

---

[3] Mills, *The Power Elite*, pp. 8–9.

society. How do pluralists assume coordination is achieved among elites? The argument is that functionally differentiated power structures produce an equilibrium of competing elites. Resulting checks and balances of competition are considered desirable to prevent the concentration of power and assure the responsibility of elites.

In short, social theory postulates both hierarchy *and* polyarchy among elites in the social system. It is the task of systematic social science research to determine just *how much* convergence or differentiation exists among elites in the national system.

SUMMARY OF FINDINGS

Our findings do not all fit neatly into either a hierarchical, elitist model of power, or a polyarchical, pluralist model of power. We find evidence of *both* hierarchy and polyarchy in the nation's institutional elite structure. Let us try to summarize our principle findings regarding the questions posed at the beginning of this volume.

Concentration of Institutional Resources.   The nation's resources are concentrated in a relatively small number of large institutions. Almost half of the nation's industrial assets are concentrated in 100 industrial corporations; almost two-thirds of U.S. banking assets are concentrated in the fifty largest banks. More than three-quarters of the nation's insurance assets are concentrated in just fifty companies; thirty-eight foundations control nearly half of all foundation assets; thirty-four universities control two-thirds of all private endowment funds in higher education; and seven media empires dominate television, the press, film, music, and the Internet. It is highly probable that thirty Wall Street and Washington law firms exercise comparable dominance in the legal field; that ten Wall Street investment firms dominate decision-making in securities; and that a dozen cultural and civic organizations dominate music, drama, the arts, and civic affairs. The federal government alone now accounts for 20 percent of the gross national product and two-thirds of all government spending. More important, concentration of resources in the nation's largest institutions is increasing over time.

The Size of the Nation's Elite.   Approximately 6,000 individuals in 7,000 positions exercise formal authority over institutions that control roughly half of the nation's resources in industry, finance, insurance, mass media, foundations, education, law, and civic and cultural affairs. This definition of the elite is fairly large numerically, yet these individuals constitute an extremely small percentage of the nation's total population of 281 million people—less than three-thousandths of 1 percent! However, this figure is considerably larger than that implied in the "power elite" literature.

Perhaps the question of hierarchy or polyarchy depends on whether one wants to emphasize numbers or percentages. To emphasize hierarchy, one can comment on the tiny *percentage* of the population that possesses such great authority. To emphasize polyarchy, one can comment on the fairly large *number* of individuals at the top of the nation's institutional structure; certainly there is room for competition within so large a group.

Interlocking versus Specialization. Despite concentration of institutional resources, there is clear evidence of specialization among institutional leaders. Eighty-five percent of the institutional elites identified in our study were specialists, holding only one post of the 7,314 "top" posts. Of course, many of these individuals held other institutional positions in a wide variety of corporate, civic, and cultural organizations, but these were not "top" positions as we defined them. Only 15 percent of our institutional elites were interlockers—individuals holding more than one top post at the same time.

There are, however, important concentrations of combined corporate, governmental, and social power in America. Large corporations such as Exxon-Mobil have many interlocking director relationships with industrial corporations, banks, insurance companies, and investment firms. In addition, there is concentration of power among the great wealthy, entrepreneurial families. One of the most important of these concentrations over the years has been the Rockefeller family group, which has had an extensive network in industrial, financial, political, civic, educational, and cultural institutions.

Inheritors versus Climbers. There is a great deal of upward mobility in American society, as well as "circulation of elites." We estimate that less than 10 percent of top corporate elites inherited their position and power; the vast majority climbed the rungs of the corporate ladder. Most governmental elites—whether in the executive bureaucracy, Congress, or the courts—rose from fairly obscure positions. Elected political leaders frequently come from parochial backgrounds and continue to maintain ties with local clubs and groups.

Separate Channels of Recruitment. There are multiple paths to the top. Our top elites were recruited through a variety of channels. Governmental leaders were recruited mainly from law and government. Corporate leaders emerged from the managerial ranks of industrial corporations, banks, insurance companies, and investment firms. Military leaders were recruited exclusively through the military ranks. Most top lawyers rose through the ranks of the large, well-known law firms, and mass media executives were recruited primarily from newspaper and television. Only in the foundations, universities, and cultural and civic associations was the formal leadership drawn from other sectors of society.

Social Class and Elite Recruitment. Individuals at the top are overwhelmingly upper and upper-middle class in social origin. Even those who climbed the institutional ladder to high position generally started with the advantages of a middle-class upbringing. Nearly all top institutional elites are college-educated, and half hold advanced degrees. Elites are notably "Ivy League": over 50 percent of top corporate leaders and over 40 percent of top governmental leaders are alumni of just twelve well-known private universities. Moreover, a substantial proportion of corporate and government leaders attended one of just thirty-three private "name" prep schools.

Although women have made notable progress in recent decades in acquiring top institutional positions, they still hold only about 10 percent of corporate directorships, and only two serve as chairman and chief executive officer of a top 100 corporation. Women have been more successful in gaining top government posts.

Very few African Americans occupy top positions in the institutional structure of the nation. While blacks have served in Cabinet posts in recent presidential administrations, only a very small number of blacks have been admitted to the boardrooms of corporate America. None serve as a chief executive officer of a top 100 corporation.

Corporate elites are somewhat more "upper class" in origin than are governmental elites. Governmental elites had slightly lower proportions of private prep school types and Ivy Leaguers than corporate elites, and governmental elites were less Eastern and urban in their origins than corporate elites. Governmental leaders in our study had more advanced professional degrees (generally law degrees) than did corporate elites.

Conflict and Consensus among Elites. Elites in all sectors of American society share a consensus about the fundamental values of private enterprise, limited government, and due process of law. Moreover, since the Roosevelt era, elites have generally supported liberal, public-regarding, social welfare programs—including Social Security, fair labor standards, unemployment compensation, a federally aided welfare system, government regulation of public utilities, and countercyclical fiscal and monetary policies. Elite consensus also includes a desire to end racial discrimination—and to bring more minority Americans into the mainstream of the political and economic system.

In the 1980s neoconservative ideas dampened elite enthusiasm for large, costly government programs aimed at curing the nation's social ills. In the 1990s neoliberal reforms give priority to stimulating economic growth over older liberal efforts to redistribute income.

Elite disagreement occurs *within* a consensus over fundamental values. The range of disagreement is relatively narrow and tends to be confined to means rather than ends.

Factionalism among Elites. Traditional pluralist theory emphasizes competition between Democrats and Republicans, liberals and conservatives, labor and management, and other conventional struggles among interest groups. Elitist theory, on the other hand, emphasizes underlying cohesion among elite groups, but still admits of some factionalism.

A recognized source of factionalism is the emergence of new sources of wealth and new "self-made" individuals who do not fully share the prevailing values of established elites. New wealth and old wealth have traditionally created fault lines within elites.

We have described one source of elite factionalism in recent decades as a split between Sunbelt "cowboys" and Eastern established "yankees." The cowboys accumulated their wealth and power in the years following World War II, in such enterprises as independent oil, the aerospace industry, computer and communications technology, discount drugs and merchandising, fast food chains, and real estate development in the Sunbelt (from southern California to Texas and Florida). The self-made cowboys are not as liberal or public-regarding or as social welfare–oriented as the yankees. The yankees inhabited older established institutions of power, most of which are headquartered in New York and Washington. The yankees were educated in the tradition of noblesse oblige—elite responsibility for the welfare of the masses. Despite the prominence of many new persons of wealth, established Eastern institutional wealth and power continue to dominate national life.

We have also noted that media elites—television network moguls, newspaper executives, Hollywood producers, reporters, and writers—are more liberal in their social and political views than most corporate elites. Jews are heavily represented in this sector of America's leadership. Nonetheless, virtually all media elites endorse a free enterprise system, oppose limits on top incomes, and wish to see talent, merit, and achievement well rewarded.

Finally, elite factionalism within the policy-making process occurs along conventional liberal and conservative lines. It is important to remember that the liberal-conservative arguments in America are about the *means* of achieving agreed-upon *ends*, rather than conflict over the legitimacy of American political and economic institutions. Liberal reform and public-regardingness have a long history of support from the nation's oldest and most revered families—from the Roosevelts to the Kennedys. Modern liberal policy prescriptions are regularly offered by America's most respected and longest established foundations and think tanks—the Brookings Institution, the Ford Foundation, the Rockefeller Foundation, and the Carnegie Corporation. Conservatives rebounded in the Reagan years, strengthening their own policy-planning organizations—notably the American Enterprise Institute and the

Heritage Foundation. A smaller network of even more conservative foundations and think tanks is more nettlesome to the liberal establishment than it is challenging.

An Oligarchic Model of National Policy-Making. Traditional pluralist theory focuses attention on the activities of the proximate policy-makers in the policy-making process, and the interaction of parties, interest groups, the President and Congress, and other public actors in the determination of national policy. In contrast, our oligarchic model of national policy-making views the role of the proximate policy-makers as one of deciding specific means of implementing major policy goals and directions which have *already been determined* by elite interaction.

Our oligarchic model assumes that the initial resources for research, study, planning, organization, and implementation of national policies are derived from corporate and personal wealth. This wealth is channeled into foundations, universities, and policy-planning institutions, where corporate representatives and top wealth-holders exercise ultimate power on the governing boards. Universities and intellectuals respond to the research emphases determined by the foundations.

Influential policy-planning groups—notably the Council on Foreign Relations, the Trilateral Commission, the Business Roundtable, the Committee on Economic Development, the Brookings Institution, the American Enterprise Institute, and the Heritage Foundation—may employ university research teams to analyze national problems. But their more important function is consensus-building among elites—bringing together individuals at the top of corporate and financial institutions, the universities, the foundations, and the top law firms, as well as the leading intellectuals, the mass media, and influential figures in government. Their goal is to develop policy recommendations having general elite support. These are then communicated to the proximate policy-makers directly and through the mass media. At this point government agencies begin their research into the policy alternatives suggested by the foundations and policy-planning groups. The role of the various public agencies is thus primarily to fill in the details of the policy directions determined earlier. Eventually, government agencies, in conjunction with the intellectuals, foundation executives, and policy-planning-group representatives, prepare specific legislative proposals, which then begin to circulate among the proximate policy-makers, notably White House and congressional committee staffs.

The federal law-making process involves bargaining, competition, persuasion, and compromise, as generally set forth in pluralist political theory. But this interaction occurs *after* the agenda for policy-making has been established and the major directions of policy changes have been determined. The decisions of proximate policy-makers are not unimportant, but they tend to center about the *means* rather than the *ends* of national policy.

POWER: INSIDER AND OUTSIDER VIEWS

Powerful people seldom publicly acknowledge their own power. They do not intend to mislead. Rather, they see their environment as pluralistic, competitive, and constantly changing. They do not see themselves as "elites"; they are acutely aware of their defeats, frustrations, and limitations. They view "ruling-class" theorists as hopelessly naïve, unschooled, and inexperienced.

From an insider's perspective, the policy "process" appears highly competitive, constantly changing, and occasionally chaotic, in the way that pluralists describe it.[4] Winning in the power "game" is the goal. Players in the game strive to influence policy in order to win prestige, celebrity, and a reputation for power. The competition is fierce. No one wins every battle; defeats, frustrations, and standoffs are experienced by even the most powerful players. Winners today are losers tomorrow. Insiders describe the Washington policy process from this individualistic viewpoint. There is no central direction to the process. Issues change almost daily; no one regularly controls the agenda.

To outsiders, however, the policy network appears highly structured. If there are hundreds who have acquired the status of Washington insiders, there are tens of thousands who have not. Students of the policy network who are themselves outside of that network tend to see a highly structured set of relationships among corporations, foundations, think tanks, and government. They attribute little importance to the petty jostling for prestige, status, and influence among individuals—politicians, bureaucrats, businessmen, or intellectuals. They perceive this competition to be narrow in scope and bounded by institutional constraints. They perceive a consensus on behalf of economic growth, a stable business cycle, incentives for investment, economy and efficiency in government, a stable two-party system, and maintaining popular support for political institutions. Disagreement occurs over the means to achieve these ends, not over the ends themselves. Outsiders describe the policy network from an organizational and societal perspective, rather than from an individual perspective.

WHO'S RUNNING AMERICA?

Systematic research on national leadership is no easy task. We do not yet have sufficient evidence to confirm or deny the major tenets of elitist or pluralist models of national power. Our research on institutional elites produces evidence of both hierarchy and polyarchy in the nation's elite structure.

Our purpose has been to present what we believe to be interesting data on national institutional elites. We will leave it to our readers to relate this

[4] See Nelson Polsby, "Tanks but No Tanks," *Public Opinion* (April–May 1983), pp. 14–16.

data to their own theory or theories of power in society. We do believe, however, that a systematic understanding of power and elites must begin with operational definitions, testable hypotheses, and reliable data if we ever expect to rise above the level of speculation, anecdote, or polemics in this field of study.

Index

A

Aaron, Henry J., 186
Abraham, Henry J., 89
Abraham, Spencer, 79
African Americans, 152–54
Agenda-setting, 97–99
Akers, John F., 31–32
Alba, Richard D., 147
Albright, Madeleine, 75, 157
Allen, Michael Patrick, 137, 140, 142, 146
Allen, Paul, 167
Allaire, Paul A., 128
American Enterprise Institute (AEI), 187–91
Anderson, Robert B., 75
AOL-Time Warner, 101–2
Armey, Dick, 83
Ashcroft, John, 78
Aspin, Les, 77
AT&T, 23

B

Bachrach, Peter, 5
Baker, James A., III, 75, 76, 122
Ballmer, Steve, 167
Baltzell, E. Digby, 149
Banking "reform," 43–45
Banks, 39–49
Baird, Zoe, 130
Baran, Paul A., 24
Baratz, Morton S., 5
Baroody, William, Jr., 188
Bass brothers, 162
Bechtel, Steven D., 160
Berle, Adolf, 24, 49–50
Birnbach, Lisa, 148
Blumenthal, Warner Michael, 76
Bohemian Grove, 149
Bradley Foundation, 196, 197–98
Bradley, Lynde and Harry, 199
Brady, Nicholas, 76
Brimmer, Andrew F., 152

Brokaw, Tom, 106–7
Brookings Institution, 129–31, 184–87
Brown, Harold, 77
Brown, Ron, 153–54
Bryan, John H., 129
Bundy, McGeorge, 29
Burch, Charles G., 26
Burch, Phillip H., Jr., 81
Burt, Robert N., 129
Bush administration, 77–82
Bush, George H. W., 67–73
Bush, George W., 67–73, 78
Bush v. Gore, 73
Business Roundtable, 129, 180–84

C

Cabinet, 73–82
Cabot, Louis W., 130, 185, 187
Calkins, Robert, 185
Campaigns finance, 57–60
Califano, Joseph A., 122
Card, Andrew, 79
Carlucci, Frank, 122
Carlyle Group, 122
Chao, Elaine, 79, 157
Chase Manhatten, 143
Cheney, Richard B., 77, 78
Chappaquiddiak, 85
Christopher, Warren, 75
Citigroup, 41–42
Civic establishment, 115–35
Class, 150–52, 209
Clausen, Alden W., 130
Clinton, Bill, 62–67, 193–94
Clinton, Hillary, 86–88, 194
CNN, 103–4
Clubs, 149–50
Cohen, William S., 77
Colman, William T., 152
Committee on Economic Develop-
    ment, 128–29, 180–84
Condit, Philip M., 129

Congress, 82–84
Congressional "Establishment," 82–84
Connally, John B., 75
Conservatives, 187–91, 191–200
Coors, Adolph, 196, 199–200
Corporate "counter-revolutions," 30–31
Corporate "raiders," 33–35
Corporations, 13–24, 30–37
Council on Foreign Relations, 126–28,
    175–180
"Cowboys," 158–65
Cutler, Lloyd N., 131

D

Dahl, Robert A., 6, 7, 137
Daniels, Mitchell, 79
Daschle, Thomas, 83
Dillon, Douglass, 75
Dole, Elizabeth, 156
Dole, Robert, 65–66
Doyle, Frank P., 129
Domhoff, G. William, 138, 139, 148,
    149, 151
Dukakis, Michael, 64
Dulles, John Foster, 74
Dye, Thomas R., 139, 194, 196

E

Ehrenhalt, Alan, 58
Elites
    characteristics, 146–51
    civic, 115–34
    congressional, 82–84
    corporate, 13–38
    dimensions, 10–11
    executive (federal), 73–82
    factionalism, 210–11
    government, 56–96
    hierarchy, 204–7
    institutional, 3–5, 203–12

judicial, 88–93
media, 97–103
money, 39–55
military, 93–95
polyarchy, 204–7
policy-making, 171–202
recruitment, 146–51
structure, 135–70
"Establishment," 115–17
Evans, Donald L., 78
Executives (federal), 73–82
Exxon-Mobil, 141

F

FTAA, 20
"Fat cats" contributors, 57–58, 59–60
Federal Reserve Board, 45–48
Financial Services Modernization Act,
    43–45
Fiorina, Carleton "Carly" S., 154–55
Ford, family, 27–30
Ford Foundation, 28–29
Ford, Gerald R., 41
Ford, Henry, II, 27–29
Ford, William Clay, Jr., 29–30
Fortune 500, 17–18
Foundations, 123–26
Fraker, Susan, 158
Fulbright, William J., 62
Fussell, Paul, 150

G

Galbraith, John Kenneth, 25
Gates, Bill, 167–68
General Electric, 101
Gephardt, Dick, 83
Gerstner, Louis V., 32–33, 128
Gilmartin, Raymond V., 129
Glass-Steagall Act, 43

Globalization, 16–21
Gordon, Kermit, 185
Gore, Al, 71–73
Gorman, Joseph T., 129
Goulden, Joseph G., 118
Government, 56–96
Graber, Doris A., 109
Graham, Katherine, 104–6
Greenspan, Alan, 47–48
Guliani, Rudolph, 88

H

Haig, Alexander M., 74
Halberstrom, David, 73
Hamilton, Alexander, 2
Harris, Patricia Roberts, 153
Hass, Robert D., 130
Hasseltine, William A., 130
Hastert, Dennis, 83
Henry, William A., 97
Heritage Foundation, 187–91
Herman, Edward S., 18, 22
Hewitt, Don, 65
Hills, Carla A., 128, 156
Hofstadter, Richard, 139
Holden, Charles, 190
Hostile takeovers, 33–35
Humpreys, George M., 75
Hunt family, 160–61
Hunter, Floyd, 205
Hutchins, Robert, 29

I

IBM, 23, 31–33
Inheritors, 26–30, 67–73, 208
Insurance companies, 39–41
"Interlockers," 139–42, 208
International Monetary Fund (IMF),
    20

J

Jackson, Jesse, 64
Janowitz, Morris, 94
Jennings, Peter, 106–7
Johnson, James A., 130
Jordan, Vernon E., Jr., 125, 130, 152
Judges, 88–93

K

Kaplan, Helene, 154
Keller, Suzane, 147, 191
Kennedy, David, 75
Kennedy, John F., 84
Kennedy, Joseph P., Sr., 84
Kennedy, Robert F., 84
Kennedy, "Ted," 84–86
Kirkpatrick, Jeanne, 156
Kissenger, Henry, 74
Koch family, 196, 198–99
Koenig, Thomas, 138
Kolko, Gabriel, 137

L

Lawyers, 117–23
Lasswell, Harold, 3
Lee, Charles E., 129
Lerner, Daniel, 3
Liberals, 108–10, 184–87, 191–94
Lichter, S. Robert, 109, 110, 111
Lindberg, Ferdinand, 149
Lindblom, Charles E., 200
Lobbyists, 121–23
Lott, Trent, 83
Lynd, Robert, 3

M

Managers, 24–26
Martinez, Mel, 79

Matthews, Donald R., 146
Means, Gardiner, 24
Media, 97–103
Mergers and acquisitions, 13–16
Michels, Robert, 3
Milbraith, Lester, 175
Military, 93–95
Miller, G. William, 76
Mills, C. Wright, 3, 4, 51, 93, 117–18,
     137, 205, 206
Mineta, Norman Y., 79
Moore, Gwen, 138, 147, 158
Morgans, Howard, 25
Mosca, Gaetano, 2
Mulcahy, Anne, 155

N

NAFTA, 20
"Neoconservatives," 192–93
Newsmakers, 106–12
Newsweek, 99–102, 104–5
NewsCorp, 101–2
New York Times, 99–102
Norton, Gale, 79, 157

O

O'Conner, Sandra Day, 91–92
O'Leary, Hazel R., 156
O'Neill, Paul H., 78
Oligarchy, 172–75, 211
Olin Foundation, 196, 198
Olin, John M., 198
Olsen, Kenneth, 35
Ostrander, Susan A., 150

P

Paige, Roderick, 79
Pareto, Vilfredo, 2

Perot, H. Ross, 65, 162–65
Perry, William J., 77
Peterson, Peter J., 127
Phillips, Kevin, 105
Pierce, Samuel R., 153
Planned Parenthood v Casey, 92
Pluralism, 5–7, 135–42, 204–7
Policy
    elite preference, 171–72
    oligarchic model, 172–75, 211–21
    process, 172–75
    planning, 174–80
Policy-planning, 126–31, 171–202
Politicians, 58, 61–73
Polsby, Nelson, 6, 212
Power
    civic, 115–17
    economic, 13–21
    financial, 39–47
    governmental, 56–62
    hierarchy, 204–7
    institutional, 3–5, 203–4
    media, 97–103
    polyarchy, 204–7
    positions of, 7–10
    wealth and, 49–54
Powell, Colin, 78, 81, 94–95
Prep school, 148–49
Principi, Anthony, 79
"Proximate policy-makers," 200–201

R

Rand, Ayn, 47
Rather, Dan, 106–7
Reagan, Ronald, 68–70, 190
Redstone, Sumner M., 102
Regan, Donald T., 76
Reno, Janet, 156
Rice, Condoleeza, 79, 157
"Right-wing conspiracy," 194–200
Robinson, Michael J., 108
Rockefeller, David, 142–46, 177–78,
    179–80

Rockefeller family, 142–46
Rockman, Bert A., 67
Rogers, William P., 74
Roosa, Robert V., 188
Rothman, Stanley, 109, 110, 111
Rubin, Robert E., 41, 43, 76
Rudmond, Warren, 130
Rumsfeld, Donald, 78
Rusk, Dean, 74

S

Scaife family, 195–97
Scaife, Richard Mellon, 195
Schlesinger, James R., 77
Schmidhauser, John R., 89
Schultz, George P., 75
Schultze, Robert O., 4
Seagram, 101–2
Securities and Exchange Commission,
    98–99
Shalala, Donna E., 156
Shaw v Reno, 92
Sherill, Robert, 85
Silk, Leonard, 115–17, 184
Silk, Mark, 115–17, 184
Simon, William E., 76
Snow, John W., 129
Sony, 101–2
"Specialists," 139–42, 208
Starr Report, 66
Steinfels, Peter, 193
Steward, James B., 118
"Superlawyers," 117–21
"Superrich," 49–54
Supreme Court, 80–93
Sweezy, Paul M., 24

T

Television networks, 99–102
Thomas, Clarence, 89–91

Thomas, Franklin A., 153
Thompson, Tommy G., 79
Time, 99–102
Trade, 16–20
Trilateral Commission, 128, 175–80
Trump, Donald, 165–67
Tuccille, Jerome, 166
Turner, Ted, 103–4

U

Useem, Michael, 139, 140
USA Today, 99–102
U.S. News & World Report, 99–102
U.S. v Standard Oil, 143
Universities, 131–33

V

Vance, Cyrus, 74, 127
Veneman, Ann M., 79, 157
Viacom, 101–2
Volcker, Paul A., 47, 128

W

Walker, Jack L., 7
Wall Street Journal, 99–102

Walt Disney, 101–2
Walt, Stephen M., 130
Wattenberg, Ben J., 108
Wharton, Clifton R., Jr., 153
Washington Post, 99–102, 104–5, 106
Weber, Max, 3
Weill, Stanford I., 41
Weinburger, Casper W., 77
White, Theodore, 97
Wolff, Edward N., 130
Women, 154–58
World Bank, 20
World Trade Organization (WTO), 20

Y

"Yankees," 158–65

Z

Zetlin, Maurice, 140